For:

....

From:

....

THE
STORY

DEVOTIONAL

ZONDERVAN

The Story Devotional
Copyright © 2014 by Zondervan

Requests for information should be addressed to:

Zondervan, 3900 Sparks Dr., SE, Grand Rapids, MI 49546

ISBN 978-0-310-08475-4

Cover design: Greg Jackson, Thinkpen
Crown of thorns photograph: Oksana Bratanova, Shutterstock.com
Interior design: Walter Petrie

Printed in the United States

16 17 18 19 20 21 22 23 /RRD/ 25 24 23 22 21 20 19 18 17 16 15 14 13 12 11 10 9 8 7 6 5 4 3 2

Give thanks to the LORD, for he is good;
　　his love endures forever.
Let the redeemed of the LORD tell their story—
　　those he redeemed from the hand of the foe,
those he gathered from the lands,
　　from east and west, from north and south.

PSALM 107:1–3

THE OLD
TESTAMENT

OUT OF NOTHING, SOMETHING

In the beginning God created the heavens and the earth. Now the earth was formless and empty, darkness was over the surface of the deep. . . . And God said, "Let there be light," and there was light.

GENESIS 1:1–3

We all know the power of words. You may remember what the bully said to you on the kindergarten playground, or what one of your parents said to you in a moment of utter frustration.

On the other hand, maybe you remember as if it were yesterday what the coach said to let you know he believed in you. Or when your sixth-grade teacher helped you recognize in yourself an area of giftedness.

Human words are powerful—powerful to tear down and powerful to build up. And God's words are infinitely more powerful. "God said"—and things happened! Where nothing had been, there was now something!

Consider what words God has spoken over you: you are his chosen (Colossians 3:12), loved (Ephesians 5:25), provided for (Matthew 6:32–33), protected (Psalm 18:2), and his child (1 John 3:1). What God speaks, happens; so live in the reality of what he says about you!

LET THE CREATIVE POWER OF GOD'S WORDS
RE-CREATE YOU IN CHRIST'S IMAGE.

God said, "Let the land produce vegetation: seed-bearing plants and trees on the land that bear fruit with seed in it, according to their various kinds." And it was so.

GENESIS 1:11

The simple statement "Let the land produce vegetation" belies the almost unimaginable complexity needed for the task.

Plants need water and the God-designed water cycle—evaporation, condensation, precipitation. Plants need sunlight, and God had placed the earth the perfect distance from the sun so that this planet could sustain life. God created different plants for warm and wet and cool and dry climates. Plants need a constant source of carbon dioxide—and the animals God was planning needed a constant source of oxygen. The perfect symbiotic relationship—per God's design.

God also saw that each plant had the right nutrients, the ideal temperature, and the necessary protection from the elements. "Let the land produce vegetation"—those simple words hardly suggest the intricacy, the complexity, of God's creation, and they don't begin to explain the mystery of the spark of life existing in every seed.

WHAT KIND OF POWER ARE YOU SPEAKING
INTO PEOPLE'S LIVES WITH YOUR WORDS—
CREATIVE POWER OR DESTRUCTIVE?

A GLIMPSE OF GOD'S GLORY

God made two great lights—the greater light to govern the day
and the lesser light to govern the night. He also made the stars. .
. . And God saw that it was good.

GENESIS 1:16, 18

As Psalm 19:1 says, the heavens truly do declare the glory of God, and those glorious heavens are mind-bogglingly vast.

If Earth were the size of a grape, Jupiter would be a large grapefruit; Saturn, an orange; Uranus and Neptune, lemons; and the sun's diameter, five feet.

Now imagine the grape-sized Earth on the corner of a city block. The moon would be about a foot from the grape-Earth. The sun would be about a city block away—and Jupiter, five blocks away from the sun. Saturn, ten blocks; Uranus, twenty blocks; and Neptune, thirty. And you'd be the size of an atom.[1] And there's the massive star Betelguese, the red supergiant Mu Cephei, and VY Canis Majoris with its 1.7-billion-mile diameter.[2]

God's heavens declare his glory—his size, his magnificence, his grandeur, his majesty, his power, his order, his wonder. When you look at the stars, let them prompt you to worship their maker—and yours!

YOUR GOD HOLDS THE PLANETS
IN THEIR ORBITS *AND* NUMBERS
THE HAIRS ON YOUR HEAD.

AN INTELLIGENT DESIGN

God created the great creatures of the sea and every living thing
with which the water teems and that moves about in it, according
to their kinds, and every winged bird according to its kind. And
God saw that it was good.

GENESIS 1:21

If a pocket watch washed up on shore and was discovered by people who had never seen one before, what might their reactions be after they inspected the moving second hand and its inner workings? Would anyone consider it an amazing result of pure chance? Would anyone suggest that all the materials coincidentally came together in the perfect size, shape, and organization and, once all was in place, the watch started to work? Doubtful, isn't it? The very existence of the pocket watch suggests the existence of a Creator.

Individuals today look around at God's amazing creation and don't see (or don't *let* themselves see) that there must be a Creator behind it all. Each one of the variety of creatures living in the skies and in the oceans eats, breathes, and reproduces . . . by chance?

We human beings are without excuse: every aspect of creation points to our Creator-God!

MAY GOD'S AMAZING CREATION
PROMPT US TO PRAISE HIM!

God said, "Let the land produce living creatures according to their kinds: the livestock, the creatures that move along the ground, and the wild animals, each according to its kind." And it was so.

GENESIS 1:24

What critters come to mind when you hear the word *livestock*? Cows and horses and pigs? What about Brahman bulls and water buffalo and donkeys and llamas? And did you know over eight hundred breeds of cattle are recognized around the world?

What do you think of when you hear the words *wild animals*? Don't limit yourself to lions and tigers and bears. What about manatees, platypi, and anteaters?

Then there are those members of the animal world you've probably never met: the blobfish, the aye-aye, the star-nosed mole, the three-foot, coconut-eating coconut crab, and the list goes on. The creativity God used in designing the animal kingdom is only a fraction of the energy he used in making you.

THE CARE GOD EXERCISED IN CRAFTING YOU IS THE PINNACLE OF GOD'S CREATIVE CRAFTSMANSHIP, CARE, AND JOY!

GOD'S HANDIWORK

So God created mankind in his own image,
in the image of God he created them;
male and female he created them.

GENESIS 1:27

You are created in God's own image. You are not a biological accident. You are not some beating-the-infinite-odds chance arrangement of cells into organs into systems into a body.

No, you are created and crafted. You are "God's handiwork" (Ephesians 2:10). And he created not only your body, but he "created [your] inmost being" (Psalm 139:13). And the model for this work of art? Himself. You are created in God's image.

This image is not physical. God's image is reflected in our "inmost being," in our abilities to think and reason, understand good and evil, create and invent, make choices, appreciate beauty, be in relationship, have a sense of justice, and love.

And this image of God is reflected in every human being, in our enemies as well as our neighbors. May we see everyone around us as God sees them: as his precious handiwork.

CREATED IN GOD'S IMAGE, MAY
WE LIVE—MAY WE SPEAK, ACT,
INTERACT—IN A WAY THAT HONORS
HIM AND REFLECTS HIS IMAGE.

THE BEST FOR LAST

*God blessed [the man and the woman] and said to them, "Be
fruitful and increase in number; fill the earth and subdue it." . . .
God saw all that he had made, and it was very good. And
there was evening, and there was morning—the sixth day.*

GENESIS 1:28, 31

Maybe you've noticed the chorus in Genesis 1—"And God saw
that it was good." Of course our perfect and infinitely wise,
powerful, and good God would make his creation "good."

But did you notice the variation on that chorus? After the Lord
completed his creative efforts, he made human beings in his image,
he blessed us with the responsibility of caring for his creation, and
he pronounced his work "very good."

Yes, God definitely saved his best creation for last. Human
beings have been called the crown of his creation. As such, we are
blessed with the opportunity to be in relationship with the Holy
and Eternal One, our Savior and Redeemer. And that privilege to
be in relationship with God—to be welcomed by God as his friend
and his child—is also "very good."

YOU ARE GOD'S HANDCRAFTED
CREATION, ONE OF HIS MASTERPIECES.

COUNTERINTUITIVE

*The LORD God commanded the man, "You are free to eat
from any tree in the garden; but you must not eat from the tree
of the knowledge of good and evil, for when you eat from it you
will certainly die."*

The study was simple. Case #1: Let the elementary school students play on a playground without a fence: they were free to go wherever they wanted—the basketball courts, hopscotch grids, four-squares, tetherballs, jungle gyms. Case #2: Let the elementary school students play on that same playground, but now with a fence around the perimeter.

In the first case, the researchers were surprised to see the students cluster in the middle of the play area. In the second case—when a fence set the boundaries—the students took full advantage of the entire area and all the fun it offered.

Boundaries mean freedom, and the one boundary in Eden was simple: "You must not eat from the tree of the knowledge of good and evil." God established this boundary—and this is true for every law he established—for the good of the people he loves. Life goes well when we live within the fence God has provided us.

GOD'S BOUNDARIES MEAN YOUR FREEDOM!

KNOWING OUR NEEDS— AND MEETING THEM

The LORD God said, "It is not good for the man to be alone. I will make a helper suitable for him." . . .

So the LORD God caused the man to fall into a deep sleep; and . . . he took one of the man's ribs. . . . Then the LORD God made a woman from the rib.

GENESIS 2:18, 21–22

Do you have a friend who knows what you need without your having to say a word? What a blessing to be known and loved like that! And God loved Adam that way.

At God's instruction, Adam had just done a basic inventory of every animal the Lord had created and given each a name. The last of the menagerie passed by, "but for Adam no suitable helper was found" (Genesis 2:20). Without Adam even voicing the need or desire, and perhaps without Adam even recognizing it on his own, God knew exactly what Adam needed. Our Creator-God was not finished yet!

God outdid himself in crafting a "helper suitable" for Adam: she took his breath away.

God knew Adam's need for companionship and gave him a gift beyond his imagining. Likewise, God knows your needs, and he will meet them—often with a blessing beyond your imagining!

THE LORD KNOWS OUR NEEDS AND GENEROUSLY MEETS THEM.

[The serpent] said to the woman, "Did God really say, 'You must not eat from any tree in the garden'?"

GENESIS 3:1

Picture a snake-oil peddler from the Old West. That special tonic of his could cure anything and everything that folks in the crowd were suffering from—guaranteed! Really!

And that word, *really*, on the serpant's tongue in the garden. "Did God *really* say . . .?" Can't you hear the word pronounced, drawn out, dripping with disbelief? "*Reaaaally?*"

The crafty serpent's expression of disbelief continued, underlining God's "unreasonable" rule: "You mean you can't eat from *any* of these beautiful trees? You can't eat *any* of this delicious-looking fruit?"

Taking the bait, Eve agreed that God had been awfully strict with Adam and her. She clarified that they could eat from any and all trees except that tree in the middle—and that one they couldn't even touch!

Of course the serpent didn't correct Eve's overstatement, for she was playing right into his hand. He even sweetened the deal: "Eat the fruit from that tree, and the effects will be amazing! You will be like God!" The snake's snake-oil pitch was complete.

IF YOU'RE DOUBTING GOD'S GUIDELINES
FOR LIFE, THAT MAY BE SATAN SPEAKING.

When the woman saw that the fruit of the tree was good for food and pleasing to the eye, and also desirable for gaining wisdom, she took some and ate it. She also gave some to her husband, who was with her, and he ate it.

GENESIS 3:6

Maybe you've noticed that we're not especially interested in something—until someone says, "No!" We don't especially want to do something—until someone says, "Don't!" *No* and *Don't* can sometimes prompt action more quickly than encouragement would!

So, Eve wondered, *what could be so bad about that fruit?* Clearly, it was "good for food." Could anything so "pleasing to the eye" be bad? Wouldn't it be good to gain wisdom? And wouldn't God want them to enjoy all he had created? In a word, *no*—and he had clearly said so.

One wonders what Eve was thinking as she "gave some to her husband," why Adam, "who was with her," was silent, and why he ate. Moot points, all. Their eyes were opened. They realized they were naked.

We human beings are attracted to forbidden fruit. And being like God sounds great—doing what we want, when we want, the way we want—whatever the warnings and despite the fact that God said *no*.

DON'T LET "DON'T" TEMPT YOU TO DO!

BEFORE THEY ATE—AND AFTER

The man and his wife heard the sound of the LORD God as he was walking in the garden in the cool of the day, and they hid from the LORD God among the trees of the garden. But the LORD God called to the man, "Where are you?"

GENESIS 3:8–9

B *efore* Adam and Eve ate the fruit, fellowship with each other was easy, comfortable, free of any type of barrier because they were free of sin. Their privileged fellowship with the Lord was open, relaxed, life-giving, satisfying. He had given them this beautiful garden home, and he was meeting all their needs. Why would they want anything else?

But *after* Adam and Eve acted in order to be like God—to be independent, on their own, instead of dependent on him—the hiding and the blame began.

The two hid from each other behind coverings made of fig leaves. And the two hid from God.

The man blamed not only the woman but also God himself who had put her with him. The woman blamed the serpent's deception.

The sweet fellowship of God, man, and woman had been shattered when they embraced sin rather than their Creator. Yet God did not turn his back on them.

WHATEVER YOUR FELLOWSHIP-SHATTERING SIN, GOD WILL NOT TURN HIS BACK ON YOU.

"BECAUSE YOU HAVE DONE THIS"

> To the woman [the LORD God] said,
> "I will make your pains in childbearing very severe." . . .
> To Adam he said . . .
> "By the sweat of your brow
> you will eat your food
> until you return to the ground."

GENESIS 3:16–17, 19

They had boldly disobeyed, but afterward neither was willing to take responsibility, to ask forgiveness, to repent. So the Holy God responded with a curse, but within God's curses are reasons for hope.

The serpent was cursed, the woman would experience pain in childbirth, and the man would have to work hard to wrest food from the ground. Yet hear the promises and the hope. God made work harder for man, yet he limited the days of that hard work. Also, God's holy wrath did not mean the end of the human race: the woman would know the joy of being a mother—and the woman's offspring would one day crush the serpent's.

Consequences and promises are intertwined in a pronouncement of judgment and mercy. God's justice and his love for humanity intersect here in Eden.

DON'T DOUBT GOD'S LOVE WHEN
YOU ARE EXPERIENCING THE
CONSEQUENCES OF YOUR ACTIONS.

OUR COMPASSIONATE
AND GRACIOUS GOD

The LORD *God made garments of skin for Adam and his wife and clothed them. And the* LORD *God said, "The man . . . must not be allowed to . . . take also from the tree of life and eat, and live forever." So the* LORD *God banished him from the Garden of Eden.*

GENESIS 3:21–23

When he placed the man in the garden, God established a rule. Adam and Eve broke that rule. The consequences would come—and with them, God's compassion and grace.

First, God clothed Adam and Eve. He killed an animal he had created—its blood was shed—to cover the nakedness of the man and woman. Then, showing more grace, God sent Adam and Eve out of the garden, lest they eat from the tree of life and "live forever." A fallen world, populated by sinners, is no place anyone would want to live forever!

Our disobedience, our sin has continued. But two thousand years ago more blood was shed. This time the blood of Jesus was spilled in order to cover—to pay the price for—our sins and to enable us to be in relationship with God now and forever.

Life outside the garden can make us long for the intimate fellowship with God that Adam and Eve knew in the garden.

GOD'S GRACE TOWARD US SINNERS
COST HIM HIS HOLY SON.

CROUCHING SIN

The LORD looked with favor on Abel and his offering, but on Cain and his offering he did not look with favor. So Cain was very angry, and his face was downcast. . . .

Now Cain said to his brother Abel, "Let's go out to the field." While they were in the field, Cain attacked his brother Abel and killed him.

GENESIS 4:4–5, 8

Why did God reject Cain's offering? Maybe Cain had not offered his best. Perhaps his heart's attitude had not been right, and his offering was more an act of duty than a gift of gratitude. "The LORD looks at the heart," so God knew (1 Samuel 16:7). We can only guess about Cain's heart, but we can be confident that God is always just, always good, always righteous. The fault could only be Cain's.

God had cautioned the angry Cain: "Sin is crouching at your door" (v. 7)—and sin pounced. Angry, perhaps at God, and possibly jealous (God *had* accepted Abel's sacrifice), Cain slew his brother.

In this tragedy, we see the ongoing ripple effect of sin. Adam and Eve were estranged from God and from one another. Now two blood brothers were estranged, one the murderer, the other the victim. All were far removed from garden living.

SIN IS CROUCHING AT THE DOOR.
WHAT IS YOUR DEFENSE?

HEARTBROKEN YET FAITHFUL

The Lord saw how great the wickedness of the human race had become on the earth, and that every inclination of the thoughts of the human heart was only evil all the time. The Lord regretted that he had made human beings on the earth, and his heart was deeply troubled.

GENESIS 6:5–6

Regret is a heavy burden. We can never rewind the clock. Often we can do absolutely nothing to make right what is wrong, to unsay or undo those things that hurt someone we love.

But when God experienced regret "that he had made human beings," he announced a plan of action. Radical action. As in "wipe from the face of the earth the human race I have created" as well as the animals, birds, and other creatures he had delighted in.

But more significant than his action—an act he promised to never again do—is his heart.

Sinful human beings did not choose to love him and live according to his ways, and he was "deeply troubled." God's heart will always break when people—when you—turn away from him.

Yet God responded to the faithfulness he did find: he spared Noah and his family from the destruction to come. God will always notice, acknowledge, and honor your faithfulness to him.

THE FAITHFULNESS OF ONE SHINES BRIGHTLY IN THE WORLD'S DARKNESS.

LORD, DID I HEAR YOU RIGHT?

God said to Noah, "I am going to put an end to all people. . . . So
make yourself an ark. . . . You will enter the ark—you and your
sons and your wife and your sons' wives with you. You are to bring
into the ark two of all living creatures, male and female, to keep
them alive with you."

GENESIS 6:13–14, 18–19

Three hundred cubits long, fifty cubits wide, and thirty cubits
high. Think football fields. One and a half football fields long
and three-quarters of a football field wide, to be precise. And think,
regarding its height, at least a four-story building. Yes, the ark God
commanded Noah to build for the coming rainstorm was huge.

And what would the neighbors have thought about Noah's
project? "Rain? Water falling from the sky? Next you'll be trying to
convince us that some band of red, orange, yellow, green, blue, and
purple will be arcing across the sky!"

There was nothing easy about Noah's assignment. And there
may have been nothing appealing about having "two of all living
creatures" as shipmates. But—looking for a positive in this—jelly-
fish, sharks, piranhas, alligators, and anacondas did not need a place
on the boat! They'd do just fine with the precipitation! We may not
feel equipped for the task, but God provides.

WHEN GOD CALLS, HE ENABLES.

LIFE IN THE ARK—AND YOU ARE THERE!

For forty days the flood kept coming on the earth. . . . The waters flooded the earth for a hundred and fifty days.

GENESIS 7:17, 24

I t lasted a little longer than a year, that multisensory experience on steroids. Yes, we're talking about Noah's extraordinary time aboard the ark.

Sights: Parrots, peacocks, pandas, polar bears.

Sounds: Caws, growls, roars, trumpetings.

Touch: Puppies, porcupines, kittens, snakes.

Smells: Unhappy skunks. And the stable floors . . .

Tastes: With smells that intense, who could really taste food?

God calls. We obey, and it's not always a luxury cruise.

God had told Noah to bring onboard the ark "two of all living creatures, male and female" (Genesis 6:19). The future of the animal world was, literally, riding with Noah! Noah could at least know the satisfaction of obeying God. The rest was up to the Almighty.

And maybe that solid sense of contentment that comes with obeying God made the sounds and smells very, very unimportant.

WHATEVER THE SURROUNDINGS, BEING RIGHT WHERE GOD WANTS US TO BE IS BETTER THAN BEING ANYWHERE ELSE.

WHEW! I MEAN, THANK YOU!

God remembered Noah . . . and he sent a wind over the earth. . . .
The water receded steadily. . . . The ark came to rest. . . .

Then God said to Noah, "Come out of the ark, you and your
wife and your sons and their wives." So Noah came out. . . . All
the animals . . . came out of the ark. Then Noah built an altar to
the LORD.

GENESIS 8:1, 3–4, 15–16, 18–20

Noah and his family spent a week on the ark before the rain began (Genesis 7:4). Then came forty days and forty nights of rain (v. 12), and the resulting flood lasted for a hundred and fifty days (v. 24). For another one hundred and fifty days the water steadily receded (8:3). After forty days, Noah sent a raven and then a dove for any sign that the earth was dry. Seven days later the dove went out again and this time returned with an olive leaf. Then God spoke: "Come out of the ark."

What would your reaction have been? "Whew!" "Glad that's over!" "I never want to visit a zoo as long as I live!" Noah's reaction was none of those. He built an altar, worshiped the Lord, and thanked him for his faithfulness. A good example for all of us.

MAY WE REACT TO GOD'S FAITHFULNESS
NOT JUST WITH RELIEF BUT WITH REJOICING!

"NEVER AGAIN!"

God said to Noah . . . "I now establish my covenant with you and with your descendants after you. . . . Never again will all life be destroyed by the waters of a flood. . . ."

And God said . . . "I have set my rainbow in the clouds, and it will be the sign of the covenant."

GENESIS 9:8–9,11–13

Pinky promise!" "Cross my heart!" Somehow just saying, "I promise" doesn't seem sufficient. As if there were a gray area when it comes to keeping a promise. But there is no gray area: a promise is kept, or it's not. And God always keeps his promises. Always.

Consider the promise God made in Genesis 9. The once angry, heartbroken God had exercised his judgment and sent a flood that covered the earth. After the waters receded, God made this promise: "Never again will all life be destroyed by the waters of a flood."

The Almighty didn't need to do anything to reinforce the validity of his eternal promise—but he chose to: "I have set my rainbow in the clouds, and it will be the sign of the covenant between me and the earth."

The physical beauty of a rainbow spanning the sky is just part of the story. The more important part is the spiritual beauty of God's faithfulness to us, his unfaithful people.

GOD PROMISES UNFAITHFUL PEOPLE
HIS UNENDING FAITHFULNESS.

COULD YOU PLEASE BE MORE SPECIFIC?

The LORD had said to Abram, "Go from your country, your people and your father's household to the land I will show you." . . .
So Abram went.

GENESIS 12:1, 4

One cup of flour, 3.9 quarts of oil every 7,500 miles, 20 minutes of exercise a day. We like specific instructions in our daily life.

We also have some experience planning trips. We'll arrive at point A by a certain time, travel 250 miles the next day, get to point B, and then start driving again at 6:30 a.m.

Maybe we need the details because we are finite human beings. Maybe we like those specifics because of the illusion of control they give us. Clearly, our infinite God plans trips a little differently.

"Go from your country . . ." The *from* is implied in the *go*, so that instruction is not terribly helpful. "To . . ."—okay, this is what we need. I'll program it into the GPS—"the land I will show you." My GPS doesn't like that destination! *I* don't like that destination!

What a picture—what a definition—of faith. "Go where I will show you," God essentially instructs. Notice the implicit promise: his showing you will mean his presence with you. And he wants to go with you because he loves you.

GO! IS NOT AS DAUNTING WHEN YOU'RE JOURNEYING WITH GOD.

BY DEFINITION

By faith Abraham, when called to go to a place he would later receive as his inheritance, obeyed and went, even though he did not know where he was going.

HEBREWS 11:8

By definition, faith involves a gap in total understanding. At least a slight fissure exists in the otherwise solid foundation of confidence. And some fissures are wider than others.

Will the chair hold you? You won't know for sure until you sit on it. Is the burger at your favorite fast-food restaurant safe to eat? You can't be positive until after you eat it. Is that pilot experienced enough to be flying this plane? He looks so young—only upon a safe landing will you be able to vouch for his competence.

Responding to God's call on our lives requires faith, because often a fissure is immediately apparent. God called Abram—later Abraham—to leave his homeland, and Abraham "obeyed and went, even though he did not know where he was going." That fissure would seem bigger to some of us than it would to others.

We honor our God whenever we choose to trust him and step across whatever fissure we encounter.

GROW YOUR CONFIDENCE IN
GOD BY STEPPING OUT IN FAITH
DESPITE THE FISSURE.

THE BEST ANSWER TO PRAYER

The word of the LORD came to [Abraham] . . . "A son who is your own flesh and blood will be your heir." He took him outside and said, "Look up at the sky and count the stars—if indeed you can count them." Then he said to him, "So shall your offspring be."

Abram believed the LORD, and he credited it to him as righteousness.

GENESIS 15:4–6

Abraham had a very specific question for God—the God who had at one point promised to make him a great nation (Genesis 12:2). Abraham and Sarah were still childless, so how exactly was God planning to keep his promise? Abraham raised this issue, respectfully addressing the Promise-Maker as "Sovereign LORD" (15:2).

God didn't answer with a specific time; he didn't give Abraham a due date to plan around. Instead, God reiterated his promise and offered an object lesson. Of course Abraham couldn't count the stars in the sky. Neither would he be able to count his descendants. But in the meantime, God gave him no real specifics.

Sometimes when you have a question for the Lord, he may answer with only his presence. And his presence will sustain you more than any details you thought you wanted.

WHEN GOD ANSWERS YOUR PRAYERS WITH HIS PRESENCE, THAT WILL TRULY BE ALL YOU NEED.

AN UNLIKELY CAST OF CHARACTERS

Against all hope, Abraham in hope believed and so became the father of many nations. . . . He did not waver through unbelief regarding the promise of God . . . being fully persuaded that God had power to do what he had promised.

ROMANS 4:18, 20–21

Abraham had all the wrong qualifications for being a founder of God's nation.

- Abraham's relatives worshiped other gods. He had not grown up in the church.
- Abraham's family lived in a country far away from what would become the promised land.
- Abraham and Sarah were way beyond childbearing years, and no children meant no people to populate God's nation.

God would not let any of these realities thwart his plan for Abraham and Sarah—his plan for the entire human race to be blessed through these two who somehow made it through all the casting calls.

NOTHING WILL KEEP GOD'S GOOD PLANS FOR YOU FROM UNFOLDING.

HELPING GOD

Hagar bore Abram a son, and Abram gave the name Ishmael to the son she had borne.

GENESIS 16:15

Sarah was only trying to help. But the fact is, God doesn't need our help. Sarah was simply doing what the culture prescribed for childlessness. But God's ways and the world's ways are rarely in sync.

Sarah suggested that Abraham sleep with her maid Hagar. Abraham agreed. Hagar conceived. Jealous Sarah sent Hagar away. Then God sent an angel after Hagar with a command ("Go back to your mistress," v. 9), a promise ("I will increase your descendants," v. 10), and a prophecy regarding her son ("He will live in hostility toward all his brothers," v. 12).

Life would now be much more complicated—and not just for Abraham as he dealt with Hagar, their son, and still childless Sarah. The complications extend into the twenty-first century: Arab-Israeli and Muslim-Jew/Christian conflicts trace their roots back to Ishmael and Isaac.

God doesn't need our help to fulfill his plans. Our cooperation, yes, and our submission, but not our help.

WE HONOR GOD WHEN WE SUBMIT AND OBEY; HE DOESN'T NEED OUR HELP.

A SIGN OF THE COVENANT

God said to Abraham . . . "This is my covenant with you and your descendants after you. . . . Every male among you shall be circumcised. . . . And it will be the sign of the covenant between me and you."

GENESIS 17:9–11, 13

Couldn't it have been a certain article of clothing? A distinctive haircut? Maybe even a piercing or tattoo? But God chose something else as a sign that the Jewish people belonged to him.

Back when Abram was living in Ur, God promised to make him "a great nation" (Genesis 12:2). On another occasion, God told Abraham that he would have as many descendants as there are stars in the sky. And then God instituted a sign of that covenant of blessings: every male in Israel was to be circumcised on the eighth day of his life. Why did God choose this sign?

Thoughts are that circumcision is an extremely personal and intimate sign, reflecting the kind of relationship God wants with his people. Also, circumcision involves the organ of reproduction, appropriate for a promise of countless descendants. Yet this sign of belonging to God was hidden, private. Still, God—for his own reasons—insisted on it.

Again, whatever he commands, we just have to obey. He doesn't have to explain himself.

OBEY EVEN WHEN YOU DON'T UNDERSTAND!

GRACE THAT'S WORTH THE WAIT

*Now the LORD was gracious to Sarah as he had said, and
the LORD did for Sarah what he had promised. Sarah became
pregnant and bore a son to Abraham in his old age. . . .*

*Abraham was a hundred years old when his son Isaac was
born to him.*

GENESIS 21:1–2, 5

When has God called you to blind obedience? To act according to a pretty bare-bones call or command? Maybe you're in such a season right now, putting one foot in front of the other and watching for evidence of God's reassuring presence.

God had told Abraham, "Go!" God didn't specify the where. God had promised Abraham both a son of his own as heir and descendants as countless "as the sand on the seashore" (Genesis 22:17). God didn't specify the when.

Whenever we step out with unanswered questions, that space where we wish there were answers is actually room for faith, room for trust. And God will never disappoint. Great is his faithfulness. Great is his grace.

STEP OUT IN FAITH, EXPECTING YOUR
GRACIOUS FATHER TO DO THE GOOD
HE LOVES TO DO FOR HIS CHILDREN.

LAUGHTER IN HER OLD AGE

Abraham gave the name Isaac to the son Sarah bore him. . . .
Sarah said, "God has brought me laughter, and everyone who
hears about this will laugh with me."

GENESIS 21:3, 6

Think about laughter you've heard in the past few days. Maybe unbridled laughter of joy, or a bitter laughter of heartache. Maybe warm laughter with a dear friend, a mocking laugh, or the you-either-laugh-or-cry kind of laugh. Laughter can communicate a lot.

Abraham laughed at the thought of his having a child after a century on this planet (Genesis 17:17). Sarah also laughed; her childbearing years were ancient history (18:12)!

Of course God wouldn't appreciate their laughter of disbelief, but he undoubtedly joined in the laughter of rejoicing, of delight, and of awe as Abraham and Sarah celebrated the birth of their long-awaited son. Their joy at this precious baby, their gratitude for God's faithfulness, and their amazement at his timing all bubbled over in laughter that couldn't and shouldn't have been contained.

Their mouths were filled with laughter because the Lord had done great things for them. And did you know that *Isaac* means "laughter; he laughs"?

THANK GOD FOR THOSE OCCASIONS
WHEN HIS BLESSINGS HAVE CAUSED
YOUR JOY TO OVERFLOW IN LAUGHTER!

OUR UNPREDICTABLE GOD

Then God said, "Take your son, your only son, whom you love—Isaac—and go to the region of Moriah. Sacrifice him there as a burnt offering on a mountain I will show you."

GENESIS 22:2

Who is the most unpredictable person you know? Maybe it's the person you see in the mirror.

If you are unpredictable, you have yet another trait in common with the Almighty. This God of wonders had—at long last—blessed Abraham with the son he had promised. God had undoubtedly relished the rejoicing: he loves to give! But now he commanded the unpredictable, the unexpected, the unimaginable: "Take your son, your only son, whom you love—Isaac—and . . . sacrifice him there as a burnt offering."

We aren't privy to Abraham's thoughts, his immediate reaction, or any conversation he and the Lord had. Any parent can easily imagine the reaction and the thoughts running through Abraham's mind.

We simply read that "early the next morning Abraham got up and loaded his donkey" (v. 3). We don't hear any of that conversation either. But we see actions that speak more loudly than a recorded dialogue would: Abraham did all he needed to do to prepare to obey God even though the command was incomprehensible.

A GOD WE COULD FULLY UNDERSTAND WOULDN'T BE A VERY BIG GOD!

GIVING OUR BEST

Abraham took the wood for the burnt offering and placed it on his son Isaac, and he himself carried the fire and the knife. . . .

"The fire and wood are here," Isaac said, "but where is the lamb for the burnt offering?"

Abraham answered, "God himself will provide the lamb for the burnt offering, my son." And the two of them went on together.

GENESIS 22:6–8

Delayed gratification. We don't like it, but we can vouch for the fact that it often, if not always, helps us appreciate even more whatever we are waiting for.

Abraham had waited twenty-five years between the promise of an heir and the birth of Isaac. Yet now God was asking Abraham to sacrifice the precious blessing of his son—who was also the key to the fulfillment of God's covenant of innumerable descendants. Each step of obedience Abraham took toward Moriah was a step closer to doing the unthinkable. We read this account knowing the end, but Abraham had to live this series of events without knowing the end!

God called Abraham to give him the best he had: his only son. And Abraham set out on the path of obedience.

WOULD YOU BE WILLING TO GIVE GOD YOUR BEST?

ACTIONS SPEAK LOUDLY

Abraham built an altar there and arranged the wood on it. He
bound his son Isaac and laid him on the altar, on top of the wood.
Then he reached out his hand and took the knife to slay his son.

GENESIS 22:9–10

Numbness can be a touch of grace. In an emergency, the tears may not come right away. Instead, you may feel nothing but numb, enabling you to do what needs to be done.

We don't know what Abraham was thinking or feeling, or if he was feeling anything. Was Abraham robotically preparing for the sacrifice God had commanded? Or was Abraham praying with a kind of passion he had never before prayed with? This was Abraham's Gethsemane experience: he wrestled with God over whether the Lord's will or his own will would be done.

Imagine the moment Abraham picked up the knife. His heart was racing—as was Isaac's. Reasoning "that God could even raise the dead" (Hebrews 11:19), Abraham lifted the knife above his son. At that exact moment, "the angel of the LORD called out . . . 'Do not lay a hand on the boy. . . . Now I know that you fear God'" (Genesis 22:11–12).

Abraham's actions spoke of his bold, willing-to-take-risks, "I'll go even though I don't know where I'm going" faith. And God was pleased.

WHAT DO YOUR ACTIONS SAY ABOUT HOW MUCH YOU TRUST GOD?

PERFECT TIMING!

*"Do not lay a hand on the boy," he said. "Do not do anything
to him. Now I know that you fear God, because you have not
withheld from me your son, your only son."*

*Abraham looked up and there in a thicket he saw a
ram caught by its horns. He went over and took the ram and
sacrificed it as a burnt offering instead of his son.*

GENESIS 22:12–13

What situation comes to mind when you think of the phrase
"just in the nick of time"? In other words, what did God do
to make his presence known exactly when you needed him to act?

If we asked Abraham and Isaac what "just in the nick of time"
reminded them of, they would certainly say, "The almost-sacrifice!"

God can have a dramatic sense of timing. Yet when his timing seems geared to the last possible split second, he's not toying
with you. He's growing you. In those pressured moments of waiting,
wondering, even panicking, we review what we know about God.
We cry out to our great God, acknowledging our great need for him.
However the situation plays out, we learn something about trust and
submission and faith and dying to self. We grow.

Anything worthwhile comes at a cost. And a closer relationship with God is worth any cost.

GOD PROVIDES WHAT IS NEEDED
EXACTLY WHEN IT IS NEEDED.

DARK DECEIT

"Now I am sending this message to my lord, that I may find favor in your eyes."

GENESIS 32:5

Most families—if not all—have some darker moments in their history. Sometimes those moments come when we decide to act—and not always in God-honoring ways—rather than wait for God's guidance. God's chosen people were no different.

Consider Esau and Jacob, Isaac and Rebekah's twins. Even in Rebekah's womb, the boys jostled each other. As they grew up, their differences became even more apparent. Esau loved the outdoors, became a skilled hunter, and was his father's favorite. Jacob was quiet; he stayed at home and was his mother's favorite. The stage was set for the perfect storm—and it came.

One day a hungry Esau asked Jacob for some stew. Jacob seized the moment and sold him a bowl in exchange for the birthright, the older brother's double share of the inheritance.

Later, a dying Isaac asked for wild meat before he spoke his blessing over Esau. When Rebekah overheard Isaac's request, she and Jacob schemed. Jacob fooled Isaac, and thinking he was blessing Esau, Isaac blessed deceitful Jacob.

GOD-HONORING RESULTS COME WHEN YOU WAIT ON HIM RATHER THAN TAKING MATTERS INTO YOUR OWN HANDS.

YOUR PART, GOD'S PART

Then Jacob prayed, "O God . . . save me, I pray, from the hand of my brother Esau, for I am afraid he will come and attack me."

GENESIS 32:9, 11

Few people like confrontation, especially after a long estrangement: *What will I say? What will that person say? What would be a good response? What if I just make matters worse?*

And, as he anticipated seeing his brother Esau, Jacob might have wondered all that and more: it had been twenty years since Jacob and their mother Rebekah had schemed to steal first-born Esau's blessing from their father. *During those twenty years, did the coals of anger die out, or were they kept as red-hot as ever?*

After sending carefully planned gifts ahead, Jacob set out. When he saw Esau and four hundred men coming his direction, he organized his female servants, his two wives Leah and Rachel, and his children—and Jacob himself bowed to Esau seven times as the two approached each other. Then God's blessing on Jacob's efforts to make peace was clear: "Esau ran to meet Jacob and embraced him; he threw his arms around his neck and kissed him. And they wept" (Genesis 33:4).

Jacob humbled himself, Esau forgave, and God blessed.

WHERE WOULD GOD HAVE YOU HUMBLE YOURSELF OR EXTEND FORGIVENESS?

WRESTLING WITH GOD

Jacob was left alone, and a man wrestled with him till daybreak. . . . Then the man said, "Let me go, for it is daybreak. . . . Your name will no longer be Jacob, but Israel, because you have struggled with God and with humans and have overcome."

GENESIS 32:24, 26, 28

We use the term *wrestle* figuratively: we wrestle with God when what we know—or at least what we think we know—about God's goodness and love and power and mercy and grace doesn't seem to fit with what we experienced and what we are feeling. These wrestling matches can be excruciating and exhausting.

Jacob—whose name means "deceiver; grabber"—literally and physically wrestled with God. We don't have details about techniques, holds, or pins. We have something far more interesting: a humbled heart. Jacob had persevered in the match and saw that he would not, could not prevail against the Holy One.

Israel probably means "he struggles with God," certainly an appropriate name for God's nation. Centuries of struggling to be faithful to God, to honor him, and to obey him lay ahead for God's chosen yet fickle people, Israel.

PERSEVERE! BLESSINGS FOLLOW STRUGGLES LIKE MORNING FOLLOWS NIGHT.

A 180-DEGREE TURN

Jacob said to his household . . . "Get rid of the foreign gods you have with you, and purify yourselves. . . . Then come, let us go up to Bethel, where I will build an altar to God. . . . So they gave Jacob all the foreign gods . . . and Jacob buried them under the oak at Shechem.

GENESIS 35:2–4

Maybe you've had a "Come to Jesus" moment, a point in your life when you finally realized you were headed in the wrong direction, that you were going nowhere fast, that you were not making Mom proud, that you could hardly look at yourself in the mirror.

Jacob had chronic hip pain to remind him of his "Come to Jesus" moment—and clearly the moment affected more than his hip. His heart was changed too: he called the people to abandon their false gods and turn to the one true God, the One who answered Jacob's prayers and "has been with me wherever I have gone" (Genesis 35:3).

Then the Lord blessed Jacob by reiterating the promises spoken to his grandfather and his father: "A nation and a community of nations will come from you. . . . The land I gave to Abraham and Isaac I also give to you, and I will give this land to your descendants after you" (Genesis 35:11–12).

Great is God's faithfulness to all generations!

WRITE DOWN FOR FUTURE GENERATIONS
STORIES OF GOD'S FAITHFULNESS TO
GENERATIONS OF YOUR FAMILY.

GOING, GOING, GONE!

Joseph went after his brothers. . . . But they saw him in the distance, and . . . they plotted to kill him. . . .

Judah said to his brothers, "What will we gain if we kill our brother and cover up his blood? Come, let's sell him . . ."

GENESIS 37:17–18, 26–27

Some people put more stock in birth order than others. What about you and your siblings? What about your own children? Is the firstborn responsible, careful, high-achieving? Is the middle child a pleaser and a peacemaker? And what about the baby? Maybe spoiled and self-centered? Maybe fun-loving and attention-seeking?

Jacob had twelve sons, and at least for the youngest, birth order was key. But so was parenting. Jacob made it no secret that baby Joseph was his favorite (yes, coat-of-many-colors Joseph), and Joseph made it no secret that he'd had dreams about ruling over his brothers. Not a great setup for happy meals around the family table!

From the oldest to the second youngest (so much for peacemaking middle children!), Joseph's brothers plotted to kill him. That plan changed: they merely sold him. But the goat blood on the robe convinced Jacob that his Joseph was dead.

Once again, human free will had made a mess of God's design.

PRAY ABOUT WHAT, IF ANY,
SIBLING RELATIONSHIP GOD
WOULD HAVE YOU NURTURE.

STANDING OUT FROM THE CROWD

The L ord gave [Joseph] success in everything he did. . . .
Potiphar put him in charge of his household, and he entrusted to
his care everything he owned.

GENESIS 39:3–4

Have you noticed? Common courtesy isn't as common as it used to be, which means it doesn't take much to stand out from the crowd. A simple "Hello," "Thank you," or "May I help?" makes you one of a small minority these days, and people notice.

Potiphar, Pharaoh's right-hand man, couldn't help but notice this new slave named Joseph. This young man from Israel—only seventeen years old—was remarkable in his work ethic, his manners, his kindness, and his resourcefulness. The Lord was as aware as Potiphar was, and he blessed Joseph's efforts.

Perhaps Joseph worked so hard and well because he was working for the one true God. Doing whatever you do in service of the Lord and to honor him makes any work satisfying, and greatly pleases your Audience of One. You will stand out in the crowd as God's light in a world of busyness, darkness, isolation, and grumbling.

WHAT ABOUT THE WAY YOU DO
YOUR JOB—AT HOME AND/OR IN
THE WORKPLACE—MAKES YOU
STAND OUT FOR THE LORD?

STANDING STRONG

His master's wife took notice of Joseph and said, "Come to bed with me!"

But he refused. . . . "How then could I do such a wicked thing and sin against God?" And though she spoke to Joseph day after day, he refused to go to bed with her or even be with her.

GENESIS 39:7–10

I f you went on trial for being a God-follower, would there be enough evidence to convict you? Let's learn from Joseph.

Like Potiphar, his unnamed wife also couldn't help but notice Joseph, for he "was well-built and handsome" (Genesis 39:6). So she issued the invitation—or command—"Come to bed with me!"

Joseph called the adultery "wicked" and refused to betray his master and "sin against God." Joseph knew that he would be answering to the Holy One for any unholy act he chose to be involved in, and Joseph would have none of it. His code of ethics was different from the Egyptian world's—and the twenty-first-century world's as well.

As one of God's chosen people, Joseph stood strong in what he knew was right.

WHEN YOU'RE SWIMMING UPSTREAM
AGAINST THE CULTURE, WHAT
HELPS YOU STAND STRONG IN
WHAT YOU KNOW IS RIGHT?

THE HIGH COST OF INTEGRITY

While Joseph was there in the prison, the LORD *was with*
him; he showed him kindness and granted him favor in the eyes
of the prison warden. . . . The LORD *was with Joseph and gave*
him success in whatever he did.

GENESIS 39:20–21, 23

njustice, unfairness, betrayal, cruelty, sabotage, blackmail—acts
like these sow seeds of bitterness. What starts as anger and doesn't
give way to forgiveness results in a bitter, hardened heart.

Joseph certainly had reason to be angry and bitter. He had been
framed by Potiphar's wife for something he hadn't done (details in
Genesis 39). Then he had been thrown into prison by Potiphar, who
believed his wife's account instead of his servant's. But while Joseph
was in prison, it was déjà vu all over again: God blessed him.

Jesus explained what Joseph experienced: "In this world you
will have trouble" (John 16:33). Doing what is right doesn't often
earn us a standing ovation from the world around us. In fact, doing
what God calls us to do can result in trouble. But even when right
action leads to hard times, you can know the reward of God using
those hard times to further capture your heart and shape your life.

WHAT IS THE BIGGEST PRICE YOU HAVE
PAID FOR LIVING GOD'S WAY INSTEAD OF
THE WORLD'S? WHAT RESULTING GOOD
MADE THE ACT WORTH THE COST?

ACKNOWLEDGE THE SOURCE

Pharaoh said to Joseph, "I had a dream, and no one can interpret it. But I have heard it said of you that when you hear a dream you can interpret it."

"I cannot do it," Joseph replied to Pharaoh, "but God will give Pharaoh the answer he desires."

GENESIS 41:15–16

D o you remember your dreams? Or are you not even sure you *do* dream because you never remember any?

Joseph knew about dreams. Two dreams he'd had back home had been key to alienating his brothers—all eleven of them (Genesis 37). Now, in prison, he helped two prisoners understand their disturbing dreams (Genesis 40). One of them was freed from prison, and he remembered Joseph when, two years later, Pharaoh had some troubling dreams that the wise men of Egypt did not understand.

Yes, Joseph knew about dreams, and he knew that the source of his ability to understand dreams was Almighty God. Joseph gave credit where credit was due, yielded himself to God's power, and made himself available to serve Pharoah, leader of all Egypt.

SAY, "HERE AM I, LORD" AS YOU ASK HIS GUIDANCE FOR WHERE TO USE THE ABILITIES HE HAS GIVEN YOU.

A CIRCUITOUS PATH

Pharaoh said to Joseph, "Since God has made all this known to you, there is no one so discerning and wise as you. You shall be in charge of my palace, and all my people are to submit to your orders."

GENESIS 41:39–40

Often in the job market, it's not what you know but who you know that seems to matter. Maybe because of someone you know, you were in the right place at the right time to meet your spouse, land a job, or learn the house was for sale.

Being in jail hardly seemed like the right place for Joseph. Getting to know the royal cupbearer and baker probably didn't seem significant. But Joseph knew Someone who would make all these things matter for Joseph, for Egypt, and for people in Israel.

Joseph knew God, so when Pharaoh went on about cows and grain, God told Joseph what those dreams meant: "Seven years of great abundance are coming throughout the land of Egypt, but seven years of famine will follow them" (Genesis 41:29–30).

Who better to put in charge of saving grain during the seven good years and rationing out the grain during the seven bad years than Joseph himself? The path had been circuitous, but Joseph knew that God had gotten him to exactly where he needed to be.

NO EXPERIENCE, PAIN, OR HARDSHIP IS WASTED IN GOD'S ECONOMY.

IT'S STARTING TO MAKE SENSE

Then ten of Joseph's brothers went down to buy grain from Egypt. But Jacob did not send Benjamin, Joseph's brother, with the others, because he was afraid that harm might come to him.

GENESIS 42:3–4

Weather forecasters have a pretty sweet job: they can be 100 percent wrong more often than not and still get paid. The same is hardly true for doctors, surgeons, teachers, engineers, nurses, or attorneys, to name a few.

Turns out that if the ruling-Egypt gig didn't work out, the dreaming Pharoah might have been a very successful weather forecaster. He nailed not only the weather but also the timing: seven years of a bountiful harvest were followed by seven years of famine.

The famine was severe through all of Egypt and into other lands, including in Canaan, the promised land that Joseph's family called home. Jacob was not going to watch his family perish due to lack of food.

Guess who would soon come calling in the court of Pharaoh? What a small world!

EVERY EXPERIENCE, TURN OF EVENTS, WEATHER PATTERN, APPARENT MISHAP, AND EVEN GREAT DISASTER FIT INTO GOD'S BIGGER AND ALWAYS-GOOD PLAN.

THE DECEIVER'S SON DECEIVES

*Joseph was the governor of the land, the person who sold grain
to all its people. So when Joseph's brothers arrived, they bowed
down to him with their faces to the ground. . . . Although Joseph
recognized his brothers, they did not recognize him.*

That person just said hello to me—by name! What part of my life is
she from? Present? Past? Church? Neighborhood? Work? The gym?
It's hard to be recognized but not recognize.

And Joseph made it even harder on his ten brothers when
he recognized them, but they didn't recognize him. Joseph spoke
harshly: "Where do you come from?" He accused them of being
spies. He required one brother to stay as collateral while the others
took food to Canaan in an act of extortion—"You'll get food if I
get to see your youngest brother" (v. 15, paraphrased). Joseph compelled Jacob to do exactly what he didn't want to do: let Benjamin
go to Egypt.

But the famine was real, and Joseph had food. He also had defi-
nite, if not deceitful, ideas about how to deal with his siblings.

THE END DOESN'T JUSTIFY THE MEANS,
YET CONSIDER WHY JOSEPH DID
WHAT HE DID—AND WHY YOU TOO
SOMETIMES CHOOSE TO DECEIVE.

HUNGER PANGS

Now the famine was still severe in the land. So when they had eaten all the grain they had brought from Egypt, their father said to them, "Go back and buy us a little more food."

GENESIS 43:1–2

We first-world, twenty-first-century types don't understand hunger. We have way too many options and way too easy access to many of those options: fast food and fine dining; eat-in, take-out, and eat-out; call, fax, e-mail, or text your order in; grocery stores, warehouse stores, convenience stores, and farmers' markets. And some grocery stores will even deliver.

No wonder the idea of a famine is hard to imagine. If weather impacts a crop, we pay more for that item at the store—but we aren't at risk of starving! Jacob's family faced the risk of starving once again. They were hungry, and the only place to get food was Egypt.

This trip would cost the family more than silver. The potential cost was Jacob's beloved Benjamin: if Benjamin didn't accompany his brothers, the man in charge would not give them food. Physical hunger compels people to do exactly what they don't want to do.

MAY WE HUNGER FOR SPIRITUAL
FOOD THE WAY PEOPLE DURING A
FAMINE LONG FOR PHYSICAL FOOD—
AS IF OUR LIFE DEPENDS ON IT!

A FAMILY REUNION

Joseph said to his brothers . . . "I am your brother Joseph, the one you sold into Egypt! And now, do not be distressed and do not be angry with yourselves for selling me here, because . . . God sent me ahead of you to preserve for you a remnant on earth and to save your lives by a great deliverance."

GENESIS 45:4–5, 7

Family reunions can be emotionally dicey. As the gathering unfolds, so can old hurts, buried feelings, and unresolved issues. And afterward, attendees may have a lot to process across the emotional spectrum.

Genesis 45 shows a different sort of family reunion. Initially, only Joseph was aware that all the brothers were dining together. After the meal was over and the brothers were preparing to return home, Joseph had a servant put his cup in Benjamin's bag of grain, setting him up to look like a thief. The ploy worked, and Benjamin was sentenced to become Joseph's slave. The brothers explained to Joseph that their father would die of a broken heart if they returned without Benjamin. After all, Jacob had already lost the other of Rachel's two sons when Joseph was (supposedly) torn to pieces by wild animals.

The time had come for the big announcement: "I am Joseph!"

GOD IS FULL OF SURPRISES! HE RARELY DOES THINGS THE WAY WE WOULD EXPECT. WHEN HAS GOD SURPRISED YOU?

Joseph said to his brothers . . . "It was not you who sent me here, but God. . . . You shall live in the region of Goshen and be near me. . . . I will provide for you there, because five years of famine are still to come. Otherwise you and your household . . . will become destitute."

GENESIS 45:4, 8, 10–11

It started in the garden: we too readily blame others for our poor decisions or difficult circumstances. And while our sin does indeed impact one another, the bottom line is God's sovereignty. He is either sovereign, or he's not. There is no middle ground.

Rather than blaming his brothers, Joseph chose to rest in God's sovereignty and to celebrate the ultimate goodness that he clearly was bringing from the painful, lonely, dark twenty-two years Joseph had experienced since his brothers had sold him into slavery.

Looking back on his life and seeing God's redemptive actions, Joseph was able to extend remarkable grace to his brothers. Suddenly his life made sense. Yes, his story had been difficult, but he could rejoice in God's story: in anticipation of this famine, God had placed Joseph in the unique position of being able to give food to Jacob and thus preserve the line of God's chosen people, Israel. Indeed, God had sent Joseph for a purpose!

IT'S BLACK AND WHITE: GOD IS EITHER SOVEREIGN OR HE'S NOT.

*Joseph said to [his brothers], "Don't be afraid. . . . You intended
to harm me, but God intended it for good to accomplish what
is now being done, the saving of many lives. So then, don't be
afraid." . . . And he reassured them and spoke kindly.*

GENESIS 50:19–21

Hindsight really is twenty-twenty. When we look back on our
lives, and perhaps especially when we look back from a spiritual
perspective, the events that made no sense as we lived through them
suddenly make total sense. We see painful and seemingly pointless
circumstances as extremely significant. That paradigm shift doesn't
discount the pain, but it definitely redeems it.

And Joseph would be the first to tell you so. God's good came
out of his brothers' jealous, evil motives. Selling Joseph into slavery
was the sinful act that God redeemed as he placed Joseph in a position of life-saving power and authority. Yes, their father, Jacob, had
died after living in Egypt for seventeen years, but Joseph was not
about to exact revenge now that Jacob had breathed his last.

Resting in God's sovereignty enables us to be kind to those
who have hurt us and gives us hope for current situations that seem
purposeless.

YOUR REDEEMER GOD IS ABLE TO
MAKE BEAUTY OUT OF ASHES,
INCLUDING ASHES IN YOUR LIFE.

CIVIL DISOBEDIENCE

The Israelites were exceedingly fruitful; they multiplied greatly . . . and became so numerous that the land was filled with them. . . .

Then Pharaoh gave this order to all his people: "Every Hebrew boy that is born you must throw into the Nile."

EXODUS 1:7, 22

One remarkable aspect of America's experiment in democracy is the peaceful transition between governments. Current events as well as history show that a change of leadership is not always smooth, the new leader is not always respected, and the change of regime can be disastrous for the ruled.

Such was the case when Egypt got a new king. Unaware of the key role Joseph had played in preserving the people of Egypt during the seven-year famine, this pharaoh was instead all too aware of the vast number of Israelites who could, if the opportunity arose, join Egypt's enemies. The solution was brutal slavery for God's chosen people—and then the ruthless slaughter of Hebrew baby boys.

One woman ignored this cold-blooded law, and when she gave birth to a son, "she hid him for three months" (Exodus 2:2). The stage was set for God to work—and he would work mightily.

CHOOSE GOD'S LIFE-GIVING LAW
OVER THE WORLD'S RULES WHENEVER
THE TWO ARE IN CONFLICT.

DIVINE CHOREOGRAPHY

Pharaoh's daughter went down to the Nile to bathe. . . . She saw the basket among the reeds. . . . She opened it and saw the baby. He was crying, and she felt sorry for him. "This is one of the Hebrew babies," she said.

Then his sister asked Pharaoh's daughter, "Shall I go and get one of the Hebrew women to nurse the baby for you?"

"Yes, go," she answered. So the girl went and got the baby's mother.

EXODUS 2:5–8

What was the easiest class you took in school? Often, simple classes are referred to as "Basket Weaving 101"—but there's really nothing all that simple about weaving a basket. Especially a basket big enough to hold a three-month-old baby and waterproof enough to withstand the waters of the Nile. But that is exactly what this one resourceful mom did.

And God sent Pharaoh's daughter to bathe just as the baby in the basket floated by. The baby cried and attracted her attention. God then had the baby's older sister step forward and offer to find a Hebrew woman to nurse the baby. Pharaoh's daughter agreed, so the baby's older sister went to get the baby's actual mother to nurse this hungry young boy. God moves people to exactly where he wants and needs them to be!

THANK GOD FOR HIS DIVINE CHOREOGRAPHY.

THE BEST OF BOTH WORLDS

The girl went and got the baby's mother. . . . The woman
took the baby and nursed him. When the child grew older, she
took him to Pharaoh's daughter and he became her son. She
named him Moses, saying, "I drew him out of the water."

EXODUS 2:8–10

The mind of a little one is like a sponge—and that means lullabies matter! Maybe Moses' mother sang classic Hebrew songs to her little boy when she nursed him and rocked him to sleep. And maybe during his waking hours, they pretended to be traveling Abraham in a Simon Says game, played Noah's ark, wrestled just as Jacob had wrestled God, and talked about the Lord's amazing faithfulness, goodness, and love. Baby Moses was raised in the home of godly Hebrew parents; his identity as one of God's chosen people was firmly established.

Then came the time for Moses to move into Pharaoh's palace, where he got a different kind of education. Now he enjoyed a front-row seat to the inner workings of the Egyptian government, and he learned lessons about leadership. The palace environment was his home, the Egyptian language was his adopted tongue, and he had first-hand experience in the Egyptian culture. God was preparing Moses.

RETRACE THE PATH GOD HAS LED YOU
ON, THANKING HIM FOR PREPARING YOU
FOR WHAT HAS COME—AND WILL COME.

ONE-ON-ONE TIME

[Moses went] out to where his own people were and watched
them at their hard labor. He saw an Egyptian beating a
Hebrew. . . . Looking this way and that and seeing no one, he
killed the Egyptian and hid him in the sand. . . .

When Pharaoh heard of this, he tried to kill Moses, but Moses
fled and went to live in Midian.

EXODUS 2:11–12, 15

Of all the things we do, those impulsive acts are the ones that tend to get us into the most trouble. It's not that it seemed like such a good idea at the time. It's more like we didn't even consider its goodness or badness or any possible consequences. We just acted! The legal term for such unpremeditated actions is "crime of passion."

And Moses may have indeed been guilty of such a crime when he killed the Egyptian who had been beating a fellow Hebrew. Moses had not forgotten his roots; he couldn't stand idly by. When he realized that his deed was no secret, Moses needed to leave Egypt. He had a price on his head, and he knew it.

And that's how God moved Moses to the desert where, for forty years, God further prepared Moses for a task he never would have volunteered for.

GOD SOMETIMES MOVES US FROM
WHAT WE KNOW SO WE CAN
GET TO KNOW HIM BETTER.

GOD'S UNMISTAKABLE PRESENCE

Moses was tending the flock. . . . The angel of the LORD
appeared to him in flames of fire from within a bush. . . .

God called to him from within the bush, "Moses! Moses!"
And Moses said, "Here I am."

"Do not come any closer," God said. "Take off your sandals,
for the place where you are standing is holy ground." Then he
said, "I am the God of your father, the God of Abraham, the
God of Isaac and the God of Jacob." At this, Moses hid his face,
because he was afraid to look at God.

EXODUS 3:1–2, 4–6

Sometimes God subtly makes his presence known. At other
times there is no mistaking his presence and power.

God certainly chose a unique way to make his presence known
to the now-shepherd Moses. As if a bush on fire in the middle of a
sandy desert wouldn't be odd enough! Then came a voice from the
fiery bush. And not just any voice, but the voice of the Lord. And
the first word the voice spoke was Moses' name.

Moses found himself on holy ground as God identified himself.
And the voice was unmistakably God's.

LOOK FOR GOD'S PRESENCE IN THE BIG,
IN THE LITTLE, IN THE MYSTERY OF LIFE!

*The LORD said, "I have indeed seen the misery of my people
in Egypt. I have heard them crying out because of their slave
drivers, and I am concerned about their suffering. . . . So now,
go. I am sending you to Pharaoh to bring my people the Israelites
out of Egypt." . . .*

And God said, "I will be with you."

EXODUS 3:7, 10, 12

It's hard to ignore the suffering of someone you love. Ask any parent if you haven't experienced it yourself. You would trade places with the one you love during the one-month shots, the interaction with the kindergarten bully, the first broken heart, the pink slip at the job. Instead, you pray, you comfort, you listen, you hurt.

Of course God, the perfect Parent, was very aware of the suffering of his chosen people in Egypt. Of course he heard their cries. Of course he knew that they were being treated unfairly and cruelly. And now was the time to act.

God called Moses to help and made him the promise, "I will be with you."

COULD GOD WANT YOU TO BE
INVOLVED IN HELPING TO RELIEVE THE
SUFFERING YOU'RE AWARE OF?

Moses said to the LORD, "Pardon your servant, Lord. I have never been eloquent . . . I am slow of speech and tongue."

The LORD said to him . . . "I will help you speak and will teach you what to say."

But Moses said, "Pardon your servant, Lord. Please send someone else."

Then the LORD's anger burned against Moses.

EXODUS 4:10–15

Tongue-tied. The cute classmate in seventh grade could do it to you. So could the basketball coach when you first went out for the team. And then there's the CEO when you have to do those quarterly presentations. It can happen to the best of us.

Moses insisted that he was chronically tongue-tied. Yet, ironically, Moses seemed to be doing just fine as he spoke with the Almighty, the Holy One, the Eternal God, his Creator, the King of kings. The excuse of "I'm not very good" can be a cover for "I'm afraid," "I don't want to step out of my comfort zone," "What if I don't do well?" and countless other so-called reasons.

God got angry, yet God provided Aaron. Two *are* better than one, but when you are called, you are equipped.

MAYBE SOMETIMES GOD WANTS TO BE
THE SECOND OF YOUR TWOSOME.

PROMISES VERSUS HARSH REALITY

"I am the LORD, and I will bring you out from under the yoke
of the Egyptians. I will free you from being slaves. . . . I will be
your God. . . . I will bring you to the land I swore . . . to give to
Abraham, to Isaac and to Jacob. . . . I am the LORD."

EXODUS 6:6–8

When have God's promises seemed far removed from your everyday reality? He promises his presence, but you feel so alone. He promises to provide, yet you don't know how you'll pay rent this month. He promises strength to arise from joy in him, but your lack of joy makes it hard to get out of bed.

Moses' first visit to Pharaoh didn't go well, and the Hebrews suffered because of it. Now they had to gather their own straw for their brick making, but their daily quota of bricks was not reduced.

Of course this harsh new demand set the Hebrew people to grumbling: "Now that you've gone to Pharaoh, Moses, our work is even harder." "If the Egyptians took a sword to us, our death would be faster!"

Moses went to God for answers, and he responded by reiterating his promises. Choosing to believe God's promises means peace and hope—for you as well as for the Hebrew slaves.

IN THE DARKNESS OF A HARSH REALITY,
LET GOD'S PROMISES FILL YOU WITH THE
LIGHT OF PEACE AND HOPE IN HIM.

ACTIONS SPEAK LOUDEST

The Egyptian magicians did the same things by their secret arts, and Pharaoh's heart became hard; he would not listen to Moses and Aaron, just as the LORD had said.

EXODUS 7:22

Conflict, rivalry, competition—human beings throughout time have experienced these. Sometimes the coming together in order to go against each other is just for sport, but on other occasions the stakes are life or death. That was the situation in the battle of Moses versus Pharaoh.

Moses and Aaron went before Pharaoh. Aaron's staff became a snake; he held his staff over the Nile, turning it to blood; he commanded frogs to fill Egypt; Pharaoh's magicians could do the same.

Then God started flexing his muscles—the Lord sent gnats, flies, a disease that killed the livestock, boils that covered people and animals alike, destructive hail, hungry locusts, and frightening darkness. Each time Pharaoh said Moses and the Hebrew people could leave—and each time Pharaoh changed his mind. What would it take to compel Pharaoh to let God's people go?

By the way, God's chosen people were not touched by the plagues. Even when darkness fell, there was light in the land of Goshen where the Israelites lived.

GOD CAN OVERCOME A STUBBORN HEART
AND FILL A SOFTENED ONE WITH HOPE.

FOR YOUR GOOD

At midnight the Lord struck down all the firstborn in Egypt, from the firstborn of Pharaoh . . . to the firstborn of the prisoner . . . and the firstborn of all the livestock as well. . . . There was loud wailing in Egypt, for there was not a house without someone dead.

EXODUS 12:29–30

How do you do with instructions? Are you a do-it-yourselfer who doesn't even look at them until you're stuck? Sometimes we can follow instructions pretty loosely, and everything turns out fine. But sometimes a lot is at stake, and following every detail of the instructions is essential.

Such was the case for the children of Israel when God explained what they needed to do to escape the "destroyer" that he would send to decimate the Egyptian population. Every Hebrew family was to kill a lamb and use a branch of hyssop to put some of its blood on the top and both sides of the door frame. "When the LORD goes through the land to strike down the Egyptians, he will see the blood . . . and will pass over that doorway" (Exodus 12:23).

At midnight, the angel of death passed over Egypt, and God's chosen people were spared the agony the Egyptians experienced.

GOD'S COMMANDS AND
INSTRUCTIONS ARE FOR YOUR GOOD.
ARE YOU FOLLOWING THEM?

"LEAVE!"

During the night Pharaoh summoned Moses and Aaron and said, "Up! Leave my people, you and the Israelites! . . . Take your flocks and herds, as you have said, and go." . . .

The Egyptians urged the people to hurry and leave the country. "For otherwise," they said, "we will all die!"

EXODUS 12:31–33

Road trips can be great fun—and a ton of work before, during, and after. Before—Make the lists, gather all the items, pack 'em up. During—"Are we there yet?" "I'm hungry!" After—Unpack the car and start way too many loads of laundry. The Hebrew people's journey out of Egypt was a ton of work too.

After being in Egypt for 430 years, 600,000 men were leaving the land (Exodus 12:40, 37). Add women and children, and easily a million people, if not closer to two million, were on the move.[3] Sounds like a logistical nightmare!

What would be involved in providing food and water for so many? One estimate said 1,500 tons of food to feed the people, 4,000 tons of wood to use as fuel, and 11,000,000 gallons of water to sustain the men, women, and children—*each day*![4]

Only God could handle logistics like these—and he did! Remember that no problem in your life is too complex for God to handle.

GOD IS IN THE DETAILS!

BETTER THAN A GPS

By day the LORD went ahead of them in a pillar of cloud to guide them on their way and by night in a pillar of fire to give them light. . . . Neither the pillar of cloud by day nor the pillar of fire by night left its place in front of the people.

EXODUS 13:21–22

It's a classic stereotype. Men will never ask for directions, women will never hesitate to ask for directions. Tension can build: if only he had looked at a map! If only she had downloaded directions!

The people of Israel were a mixed group of never-asking-for-directions men and never-hesitating-to-ask women. Yet there were no arguments about the right way to go.

The Lord led the people with a pillar of cloud during the day and a pillar of fire at night. They could travel when the temperature was tolerable and the weather allowed. They could travel with total confidence that they were going where God wanted them to go.

The Lord still leads his people today, with the guiding light of his Word and the sanctifying fire of its truth. Opening the Book is not terribly strenuous. Even if it were, the directions inside would be worth the effort.

GOD, TEACH ME TO FOLLOW THE GUIDING LIGHT OF YOUR WORD AND THE SANCTIFYING FIRE OF ITS TRUTH.

Moses stretched out his hand over the sea, and all that night the LORD drove the sea back with a strong east wind and turned it into dry land. The waters were divided, and the Israelites went through the sea on dry ground, with a wall of water on their right and on their left.

EXODUS 14:21–22

Before the fire-breathing dragon could attack, the dashing knight in shining armor saved the fair maiden. Before the fire consumed the house, the firefighter courageously entered the blaze and rescued the frightened child. Before the Egyptian army cornered the terrified Israelites on the bank of the Red Sea, God acted! Even in our scariest moments, God is with us.

Despite the Israelites complaining—"Was it because there were no graves in Egypt that you brought us to the desert to die? . . . It would have been better for us to serve the Egyptians than to die in the desert!" (Exodus 14:11–12)—rather than praying, God acted.

Having reassured the people, "The LORD will fight for you; you need only to be still" (v. 14), Moses did what God had instructed by stretching out his hand over the water, and God parted the Red Sea so his chosen people could cross.

WHAT LOOKS LIKE A BARRIER TO YOU IS A CHANCE FOR GOD TO ACT AND GET FULL CREDIT.

GOD'S GOT THIS

The LORD said to Moses, "Stretch out your hand over the sea so that the waters may flow back over the Egyptians." . . . Moses stretched out his hand over the sea, and at daybreak the sea went back to its place. . . . The water covered the chariots and horsemen—the entire army of Pharaoh. . . . Not one of them survived.

EXODUS 14:26–28

W*hat have I done? It seemed like such a good idea at the time.* Thoughts like that may have been going through Pharaoh's mind as the dust settled, the dust from the horrifyingly apocalyptic night and Israel's departure. Every family was grieving the heart-wrenching loss of their firstborn, but life must go on. But how could it now that Egypt's workforce had left? The nation's economy would collapse. Those Hebrew slaves must be brought back!

So Pharaoh and his army pursued them. Thanks to God's intervention, the people of Israel had crossed the Red Sea on dry ground. When the Egyptians followed, God "jammed the wheels of their chariots" (Exodus 14:25). Suddenly the Egyptians were keenly aware that the Sender of the plagues was continuing to act on behalf of his people, but their realization came too late. "Not one of them survived."

If you find yourself questioning a decision, look to the Lord for guidance and remember that he is in control.

GOD DOESN'T DO THINGS HALFWAY.

DAY 63
"WHAT IS IT?"

In the morning there was a layer of dew around the camp. When the dew was gone, thin flakes like frost on the ground appeared on the desert floor. When the Israelites saw it, they said to each other, "What is it?" For they did not know what it was.

Moses said to them, "It is the bread the LORD has given you to eat."

EXODUS 16:13–15

It had been awhile since the Hebrew children had eaten "pots of meat and . . . all the food we wanted" (Exodus 16:3), and they were hungry, cranky, and grumbling. Their compassionate God—acting more graciously than human parents might respond to whining—heard and acted.

The menu was simple: bread that was immediately dubbed *manna* (meaning "What is it?") in the morning and evening. Every morning and every evening, the children of Israel were to look to God for his provision. And every day, he provided. Let this be a reminder that God provides what you need, not always what you want.

TRUST GOD TO PROVIDE FOR YOU EVERY MORNING, EVERY EVENING, AND EVERY MOMENT IN BETWEEN.

GOD'S PATIENCE AND PROVISION

There was no water for the people to drink. . . . They grumbled against Moses. They said, "Why did you bring us up out of Egypt to make us and our children and livestock die of thirst?"

Then Moses cried out to the LORD, "What am I to do with these people? . . ."

The LORD answered Moses, "Go out in front of the people. . . . Take in your hand the staff with which you struck the Nile, and go. Strike the rock, and water will come out of it for the people to drink."

EXODUS 17:1, 3–6

Have you noticed what's on sale the first two weeks of January? Exercise clothes, gym memberships, and fitness equipment. It's time to get healthy, but strong muscles and lower blood pressure don't happen overnight. Neither do strong faith muscles.

Wouldn't God's provision of manna every single morning encourage trust? Wouldn't the double amount he gave for the Sabbath—and leftovers that "did not stink or get maggots in it" the way they did on other days (Exodus 16:24)—fuel confidence that he would always be faithful? Apparently they had a very short memory when it came to God's miracles (the plagues, Passover, the Red Sea, the destruction of the Egyptian army, to name a few) and, at the moment, they were very thirsty. Once again, God provided.

LIFE IS FULL OF FAITH-BUILDING MOMENTS.

TIME OUT!

The LORD called to [Moses] from the mountain and said, "Tell the people of Israel: 'You yourselves have seen what I did to Egypt, and how I carried you on eagles' wings and brought you to myself. Now if you obey me fully . . . then out of all nations you will be my treasured possession.'"

EXODUS 19:3–5

Time-outs are good for out-of-control kids, overworked adults, and out-of-balance priorities. The Hebrews needed a time-out to remember how God had provided for them.

It had been two months since the Hebrew slaves had fled Egypt where they had seen God decimate crops, destroy livestock, and make the Egyptians miserable. Then God had released the waters of the Red Sea and annihilated the entire Egyptian army.

Now, as the million-plus people camped in front of Mount Sinai, God spoke through Moses. First came the reminder of all he had done to Egypt, "how I carried you on eagles' wings and brought you to myself." God's purpose was more about his relationship with his people than another nation's defeat. So he encouraged the people to obey him and, as a result, know the privileged position as "my treasured possession." It would be Israel's choice.

REMEMBERING GOD'S PAST FAITHFULNESS CAN HELP YOU CHOOSE OBEDIENCE TODAY AND KNOW BLESSINGS TOMORROW.

IT MUST BE IMPORTANT!

*The LORD said to Moses, "Go to the people and consecrate them
today and tomorrow. Have them wash their clothes and be
ready by the third day, because on that day the LORD will come
down on Mount Sinai in the sight of all the people."*

EXODUS 19:10–11

B e prepared is a good motto for the Boy Scouts—or anyone! But
preparation can mean a lot of different things depending on the
person and the occasion. The bride-to-be has many details to attend
to in preparation for her wedding. Athletes spend countless hours
training to be ready to compete.

In this scene from Exodus, God clearly needed his people prepared for something important. They were to be consecrated, dressed
in clean clothes, and ready to approach Mount Sinai when the ram's
horn sounded because "the LORD will come down on Mount Sinai."

When we go before this same God, washed in the blood of Jesus
and forgiven for our sins, we don't go through these external exercises.
We should, however, prepare our hearts and enter into the Almighty's
presence with the same degree of awe and respect. Make time today
and every day to be quiet with your God.

MAY WE ENTER GOD'S PRESENCE
WITH AWE AND RESPECT!

OUR AWESOME GOD

On the morning of the third day there was thunder and lightning, with a thick cloud over the mountain, and a very loud trumpet blast. Everyone in the camp trembled. Then Moses led the people out of the camp to meet with God, and they stood at the foot of the mountain. Mount Sinai was covered with smoke, because the LORD descended on it in fire. The smoke billowed up from it like smoke from a furnace, and the whole mountain trembled violently.

EXODUS 19:16–18

When have you been most awed by God? Maybe you marveled at his handiwork apparent in the countless stars in the desert sky, or gasped at cresting waves with their ten-foot faces, or wondered at the miracle of a newborn.

Consider now the different kind of awe-inspiring scene in Exodus 19. Thunder and lightning—right in front of you! You felt the crash of the thunder. The trumpet blast must have overwhelmed. Then the mountain trembled as "smoke billowed up from it." When God called Moses, that command was not to be ignored.

WHETHER HE SPEAKS SILENTLY IN A WHISPER, OR WITH THUNDER AND LIGHTNING, GOD IS NOT TO BE IGNORED.

LOVING GOD

"You shall have no other gods before me.

"You shall not make for yourself an image in the form of anything in heaven above or on the earth beneath or in the waters below. . . .

"You shall not misuse the name of the LORD your God. . . .

"Remember the Sabbath day by keeping it holy."

EXODUS 20:3–4, 7–8

When has the buildup to something proven to be utterly anticlimactic? The surprise birthday party that was not a surprise. The much-anticipated football game that was a blowout. The critically acclaimed movie that made you yawn. Sometimes a greatly anticipated event can be a bust.

But that was not the case at Sinai. The scene was loud as thunder rumbled, lightning crackled, and smoke billowed out of the mountaintop. The thick cloud covering the mountain added an almost tangible eeriness. Such was the scene for God's delivery of the ten best-known rules humankind has ever heard.

There at Mount Sinai, God spoke through Moses and blessed his people with clear instructions about how they were to live, visibly different from the world and completely dedicated to him. There would be no guesswork involved. But just how well would they do?

TAKE A LOOK IN THE MIRROR OF GOD'S LAWS
AND LISTEN FOR HIM TO GIVE YOU GUIDANCE.

FREEDOM-GIVING LAW

> "Honor your father and your mother . . .
> "You shall not murder.
> "You shall not commit adultery.
> "You shall not steal.
> "You shall not give false testimony against your neighbor.
> "You shall not covet . . . anything that belongs to your
>   neighbor."

EXODUS 20:12–17

Think about it. Without being limited to going only where the iron railroad tracks had been nailed into the ground, a train would go absolutely nowhere.

Similarly, God's straightforward, no-nonsense rules—his *limiting* instructions—for how the Israelites were to relate to him (commands 1 to 4) and to one another (commands 5 to 10) are actually our means to freedom. Laws give us freedom just as the railroad tracks give the train freedom to move.

Now consider the heavy burdens that come with breaking the six laws listed above. There is no freedom in living with guilt, shame, or regret. Following God's law means freedom from all of that—and more.

EMBRACE THE GOD-GIVEN COMMANDMENTS
TO DISCOVER TRUTH IN YOUR LIFE.

PUTTING IT IN STONE

The LORD said to Moses, "Come up to me on the mountain and stay here, and I will give you the tablets of stone with the law and commandments I have written for their instruction."

EXODUS 24:12

Maybe you've played Telephone. People sit in a line, and one person whispers something to the next person. Then that person whispers it to the next person and so on until the end of the line. The end result is never an accurate retelling of the original message.

The people who had heard the Ten Commandments couldn't afford to get these fundamental laws wrong. So Moses read them the Book of the Covenant and, by sprinkling blood on the people, established the covenant with the Lord.

Then, lest his people forget his law, God called Moses to come get "tablets of stone with the law and commandments I have written for their instruction."

CHALLENGE YOURSELF TO MEMORIZE
A VERSE OR TWO OF SCRIPTURE THIS
WEEK—LEST YOU FORGET GOD'S TRUTH.

ALL THAT GLITTERS

*When the people saw that Moses was so long in coming down
from the mountain, they gathered around Aaron and said,
"Come, make us gods who will go before us." . . .*

*So all the people took off their earrings and brought them to
Aaron. He . . . made . . . an idol cast in the shape of a calf. . . .
They said, "These are your gods, Israel, who brought you up out
of Egypt."*

EXODUS 32:1, 3–4

Some things people do can make us wonder. Why was the driver
going thirty-five miles per hour on the freeway? Why is she
going to bungee jump off the bridge?

And, yes, Moses had been meeting with God for forty days and
forty nights, but why did these chosen people think it was a good
idea to melt their gold, form it into a god, and credit it with delivering them from slavery in Egypt? Why?

For the same reasons that we—many centuries later—find ourselves worshiping status, income, education, material possessions,
self. We are easily distracted from what matters most, and then the
what-matters-most fades in importance.

FOCUS ON THE HEAVENLY FATHER TO LIVE
YOUR LIFE ACCORDING TO HIS WILL.

FOOLISH BEHAVIOR, RIGHTEOUS ANGER

*The LORD said to Moses, "Go down, because your people,
whom you brought up out of Egypt, have become corrupt. They
have been quick to turn away from what I commanded them and
have made themselves an idol cast in the shape of a calf. They
have bowed down to it and sacrificed to it. . . .*

*"I have seen these people . . . and they are a stiff-necked people.
Now leave me alone so that my anger may burn against them and
that I may destroy them."*

EXODUS 32:7–10

Your people have become corrupt," God said to Moses. After
all he had done to deliver, protect, lead, and provide for them,
these "stiff-necked people" made an idol of gold and credited that
idol for what their holy God had done for them! The Lord's anger
burned, and he planned to destroy those he had created, those he
had chosen, those he loved.

Moses reasoned with God ("Don't let Egypt mock you for bringing your people out to die in the desert" and "Don't forget your
promises to Abraham" [see Exodus 32:12–13]), and God relented.
Then it was Moses' turn to feel enraged: he threw down the tablets,
and they broke into pieces at the foot of the mountain.

IT'S FAR EASIER TO RECOGNIZE OTHER
PEOPLE'S FOOLISHNESS THAN OUR OWN.

SERIOUS BUSINESS

*Moses saw that the people were running wild. . . . So he . . . said,
"Whoever is for the LORD, come to me." And all the Levites
rallied to him.*

*Then he said to them, "This is what the LORD, the God of Israel,
says: 'Go back and forth through the camp from one end to the other,
each killing his brother and friend and neighbor.'" . . . That day
about three thousand of the people died.*

EXODUS 32:25–28

We can be passionate about a variety of things and invest a lot of time and energy in our workouts, Yorkies, or cars. While none of these are bad in and of themselves, we can take them too seriously—and not take seriously enough the things we should. Our sin, for instance.

God takes sin very seriously—and he always has. Aaron protested, "They gave me the gold, and I threw it into the fire, and out came this calf!" (Exodus 32:24). Right, Aaron! When the Hebrew children worshiped a golden calf, God called for action. Three thousand people lost their lives, and Moses knew he still needed atonement for their abominable act.

Moses approached the Lord and offered his life (v. 32). God struck his chosen people with a plague because of their calf-glorifying escapade (v. 35). Sin is serious business.

WHEN I REGARD MY SIN TOO LIGHTLY,
HOLY GOD, TURN MY EYES TO THE CROSS.

GOODNESS AND GLORY UNIMAGINABLE

The LORD said, "There is a place near me where you may stand on a rock. When my glory passes by, I will put you in a cleft in the rock and cover you with my hand until I have passed by. Then I will remove my hand and you will see my back; but my face must not be seen."

EXODUS 33:21–23

What is the boldest request you've ever made? Maybe you fought against a public school policy that didn't let your child talk about Christmas. Maybe you boldly asked someone to marry you! Probably no request tops Moses' request of God: "Show me your glory" (Exodus 33:18).

Our response to a bold request can be irritation ("What nerve!") or annoyance. God's response to Moses' request was very different but totally in character. Compassionate and gracious, God passed by Moses. After that, God regularly spoke with him. Every time, Moses' "radiant" face would reflect God's glory and frighten the people, so Moses would put on a veil (34:35).

MAY WE LONG TO KNOW GOD IN ALL
HIS GLORY—AND MAY WE REFLECT
HIS GLORY IN THE WAY WE LIVE!

DON'T MAKE HIM ANGRY—AGAIN!

The cloud of the LORD was . . . in the sight of all the Israelites during all their travels.

Now the people complained about their hardships . . . and when he heard them his anger was aroused. Then fire from the LORD burned among them and consumed some of the outskirts of the camp.

EXODUS 40:38; NUMBERS 11:1

We all know that sense of exasperation. The solution, the wise approach, the safest path—it seems so obvious. Oh, can't we have great insight and wisdom regarding other people's life situations! But we can lose all objectivity when we look at our own circumstances. And the children of Israel definitely had that problem.

Let's review. The Lord had rescued them from slavery and had been leading them with the cloud and with fire. He traveled with his people, feeding them and providing them with water. He also kept their clothes from wearing out and their feet from swelling (Deuteronomy 8:4). God provided the essentials, and his people complained. And God doesn't appreciate our complaining.

GIVE ME EYES TO SEE THE BLESSINGS
YOU FILL MY LIFE WITH—AND THE
HUMILITY TO SAY "THANK YOU."

The rabble with them began to crave other food, and again the Israelites started wailing and said, "If only we had meat to eat! We remember the fish we ate in Egypt at no cost—also the cucumbers, melons, leeks, onions and garlic. But now . . . we never see anything but this manna!"

NUMBERS 11:4–6

Variety or familiarity? Do you order something different every time you go to your favorite restaurant? Do you have oatmeal for breakfast 365 days a year?

During their yearlong campout at the base of Mount Sinai, the Hebrew children were blessed by God's teaching them who he was and what he required of them: "I am holy, so you are to be holy"—and compassionate, merciful, and just. God set guidelines for marriage and punishments for crimes. He instructed about offerings, he anointed priests, and he established animal sacrifices so people could atone for their sin. And he faithfully fed the people manna. In the morning and in the evening. Only manna.

And the people complained—and "the LORD became exceedingly angry, and Moses was troubled" (Numbers 11:10).

And about that "fish at no cost": at no cost except backbreaking labor under harsh taskmasters? That's selective memory!

MAY I CHOOSE GRATITUDE OVER
COMPLAINING, TODAY AND EVERY DAY.

SEEING WITH EYES OF FAITH

*The LORD said to Moses, "Send some men to explore the land
of Canaan, which I am giving to the Israelites." . . .*

*At the end of forty days they returned. . . . "We went into the
land, and it does flow with milk and honey! Here is its fruit. But
the people who live there are powerful, and the cities are fortified
and very large." . . .*

*Caleb . . . said, "We should go up and take possession of the
land, for we can certainly do it."*

NUMBERS 13:1–2, 25, 27–28, 30

Two people can witness the same event yet offer two very different accounts of what happened. Sometimes it's hard to believe
that two people are describing, for instance, the same car accident.

The men who explored Canaan came back with different per-
spectives. The consensus was, "It does flow with milk and honey,"
and who could argue about its fruitfulness? The men had "cut off a
branch bearing a single cluster of grapes. Two of them carried it on
a pole between them" (Numbers 13:23).

The Lord had said he was "giving" this rich land to the Israelites,
yet in that land were powerful people and large, fortified cities. Pros
and cons—and which perspective was God's perspective?

TEACH ME TO SEE LIFE'S CHALLENGES
FROM YOUR PERSPECTIVE, ALMIGHTY GOD!

TO GO OR NOT TO GO?

*[Joshua and Caleb] who were among those who had explored
the land . . . [said], "The land is . . . exceedingly good. If
the LORD is pleased with us, he will lead us into that land, a land
flowing with milk and honey, and will give it to us. Only do not
rebel against the LORD. And do not be afraid of the people of the
land. . . . Their protection is gone, but the LORD is with us."*

NUMBERS 14:6–9

Have you ever searched the Internet for the results of the Olympic fifty-meter freestyle swim to see who won—and then watched the race? Maybe you only watched a movie once you were reassured it had a happy ending. Unfortunately, life doesn't work that way: the people standing at the border of Canaan couldn't know what would happen next any more than we can know what the next chapter of our life will contain.

On the "don't go" side were those saying that the land "devours those living in it" and that "we seemed like grasshoppers" (Numbers 13:32–33). On the minority "let's go" side were Joshua and Caleb. Confident that the Lord was with them, they were absolutely certain they should enter the land.

And that's what faith is: not looking into a crystal ball to see what will happen, but looking to the Lord.

SINCE THE LORD IS WITH YOU, YOU
NEVER NEED TO BE AFRAID.

PRAYING BOLDLY

The LORD said to Moses, "How long will these people treat me with contempt . . . in spite of all the signs I have performed among them? I will strike them down with a plague and destroy them."

NUMBERS 14:11–12

When has someone been able to talk you down, to keep you from acting irrationally, from taking a step out of anger rather than wisdom? That was a blessing! And when have you had the opportunity to try to talk someone down, a longsuffering someone who, understandably, had finally had enough? Not an easy task, yet that's the position Moses found himself in as he faced an angry God.

Initially Moses reminded God of his reputation: "What would it look like if all the people died? Nations would dishonor you if you didn't do what you had vowed to do for your people!" (see Numbers 14:13–16).

Then Moses reminded the Lord of what he had proclaimed about himself and the promises implicit in those traits: "The LORD is slow to anger, abounding in love and forgiving sin and rebellion" (Numbers 14:18).

When Moses then asked God to forgive the people's sin, he did.

LIKE MOSES, WHEN YOU PLEAD BEFORE GOD, REMEMBER HIS PROMISES.

CONSEQUENCES

The LORD replied, "I have forgiven them, as you asked.
Nevertheless . . . [tell them], 'In this wilderness your bodies will
fall—every one of you twenty years old or more . . . who has
grumbled against me.'"

NUMBERS 14:20–21, 29

Consequences are good parenting tools. Rather than running to school with a forgotten lunch, Mom can teach responsibility by letting Johnny be a little hungrier than usual at the end of the school day. Instead of immediately replacing the lost smartphone, Dad can set up a payment plan for Susie. Johnny will probably do a better job remembering his lunch and Susie a better job taking care of her phone. To a greater degree, our perfect Parent also allows consequences for our sin to help teach us what we need to learn.

For forty days, the twelve God-appointed spies had explored the land of Canaan, but only Caleb and Joshua came back ready to conquer the land. Disagreeing, the others stirred up grumbling and rebellion among the people. God struck them down with the plague (Numbers 14:37) and then pronounced the logical consequence: "I won't let you enter the land."

GOD'S FORGIVENESS OF OUR SIN
DOESN'T MEAN THE REMOVAL
OF ALL CONSEQUENCES.

STIFF CONSEQUENCES

The LORD said to Moses . . . "Speak to that rock before their eyes and it will pour out its water. . . ."

So Moses took the staff from the LORD's presence. . . . He and Aaron gathered the assembly together in front of the rock. . . . Then Moses raised his arm and struck the rock twice with his staff. Water gushed out, and the community and their livestock drank.

NUMBERS 20:7–11

Grumbling and complaining can kill any joy in life. And we human beings can always and easily find something—or several somethings—to complain about, but the choice is always ours.

The children of Israel didn't have an easy time choosing joy over complaining—and can you imagine listening to all of their whining for forty years? Moses had reached his breaking point.

Again, the people needed water. Again, the people complained. And again, God graciously provided.

But God had instructed Moses to speak to the rock, and Moses struck the rock instead. However frustrated he was with the people, he demonstrated a lack of both trust in God and respect for his presence. As a result, neither Moses nor Aaron would enter the promised land.

OBEY GOD. ALWAYS.

PARTING WORDS

"The LORD your God has blessed you in all the work of your hands. He has watched over your journey through this vast wilderness. These forty years the LORD your God has been with you, and you have not lacked anything.

"Understand, then, that it is not because of your righteousness that the LORD your God is giving you this good land to possess, for you are a stiff-necked people."

DEUTERONOMY 2:7; 9:6

You're being promoted! Before you leave your old job, you'll likely have a number of details to sort out.

Moses was about to be promoted—to heaven—and he had to address details such as driving the nations out of Canaan, offering guidelines about worship, and encouraging people to follow God. No small task!

"Hear, O Israel: The LORD our God, the LORD is one. Love the LORD your God with all your heart and with all your soul and with all your strength. These commandments that I give you today are to be on your hearts. Impress them on your children" (Deuteronomy 6:4–7).

So Moses passed the mantle to Joshua, and he left the people with this charge—which is just as relevant for us today:

REMEMBER WHO YOU ARE AND TO WHOM YOU BELONG!

TRUE TO HIS WORD

The LORD told Moses, "Go . . . and view Canaan. . . .
Because both of you broke faith with me . . . at the waters
of Meribah Kadesh. . . . You will see the land only from a
distance." . . .

Moses climbed Mount Nebo. . . . The LORD showed him the
whole land. . . . And Moses the servant of the LORD died.

DEUTERONOMY 32:48–49, 51–52; 34:1, 5

Did you have all the answers about raising kids—until you had a child of your own? Would you see mothers and fathers in action and not understand what they were doing—and then you had kids? Parenting is hard work. One example is carrying out consequences of wrong actions. That is what our perfect Parent does here.

Near the end of Moses' forty years of leading the Israelites, he dealt with the Edomites, Aaron's death, the Canaanites, God-ordained snakes, the Amorites, and more. His leadership through all of this—not to mention the forty years—did not serve as penance or absolve him of his sinful act. Moses still faced the sad consequences.

And maybe this was a heavenly Father moment that hurt the Parent as much, if not more, than it hurt the child. And this pain was nothing compared to what would happen at Calvary.

WE MAY NOT UNDERSTAND ALL OF GOD'S
DECISIONS, BUT WE MUST ALWAYS HAVE
FAITH THAT THEY ARE THE RIGHT DECISIONS.

"BE STRONG!"

After the death of Moses, the LORD said to Joshua. . . . "I will
give you every place where you set your foot. . . .

"As I was with Moses, so I will be with you; I will never leave
you nor forsake you. Be strong and courageous.

"Be strong and very courageous. Be careful to obey all the
law my servant Moses gave you. . . . Be strong and courageous.
Do not be afraid; do not be discouraged, for the LORD your God
will be with you wherever you go."

JOSHUA 1:1, 3, 5–7, 9

I 'm okay, Mommy! Don't worry!" insists the toddler climbing the
tree. "I'll be okay, Mom! Don't worry!" says the newly-licensed
teenage driver. "I'll be okay, Mom! Don't worry!" says the heading-
to-the-wilderness backpacker. There's nothing like a chorus of
"Don't worry!" to fuel worry. Or at least some healthy concern.

Interestingly, someone has noticed that "Fear not!" appears 365
times in the Bible—one for every day of the year. If these refrains
don't foster fear, they at least prompt some healthy concern. After
all, why would God tell us—again and again—"Fear not" if we had
nothing to fear? He knows our hearts; he knows our limitations
more clearly than we do; and he knows the battles we'll encounter
living for him in this fallen world. So let's heed his words.

BE STRONG AND VERY
COURAGEOUS IN YOUR FAITH.

PEOPLE ARE WATCHING

*Before the spies lay down for the night, [Rahab] . . . said to
them, "I know that the LORD has given you this land . . . We
have heard how the LORD dried up the water of the Red Sea for
you when you came out of Egypt. . . . The LORD your God is
God in heaven above and on the earth below."*

heard it in passing. I just have this sense. I kinda put two and two
together. They sat down and spelled it out to me. I read it somewhere.
I knew from watching how he lived.

You've undoubtedly learned in all these ways and maybe others. They range from intentional to accidental, from focused effort
to peripheral osmosis. In what ways have you learned about Jesus?

Rahab knew a lot about God. She'd heard about the wonders
God had done. Somehow she'd learned that "the LORD has given
you this land." The spies she hid may have been the first believers
she'd actually met, and maybe they helped nurture her faith by their
actions as well as their words. God had worked in his mysterious
ways, and now Rahab staked her life on the God of the spies she
protected.

THE ONLY BIBLE SOME PEOPLE
WILL EVER READ IS YOUR LIFE.

YOU WANT ME TO DO WHAT?

*The LORD said to Joshua . . . "March around the city once
with all the armed men. Do this for six days. Have seven priests
carry trumpets of rams' horns in front of the ark. On the seventh
day, march around the city seven times, with the priests blowing
the trumpets. When you hear them sound a long blast on the
trumpets, have the whole army give a loud shout; then the wall of
the city will collapse and the army will go up, everyone straight in."*

JOSHUA 6:2–5

"Y ou want me to do what?" In some ways that question is understandable. The task seems out of your comfort zone, beyond
your reach, or utterly ridiculous.

"You want me to do what?" was not, however, Joshua's response
to God's unique strategy for his army's conquest of the walled city
of Jericho.

God's surefire plan for conquering the city involved walking
and trumpets blowing and shouting. But rather than questioning
God and scratching his head, Joshua called the priests and began to
arrange the procession that would circle Jericho once a day for six
days and seven times on the seventh day.

FOLLOW JOSHUA'S EXAMPLE:
OBEY HOWEVER MUCH GOD'S
COMMAND STRETCHES YOU.

When the trumpets sounded, the army shouted, and at the sound of the trumpet, when the men gave a loud shout, the wall collapsed; so everyone charged straight in, and they took the city. They . . . destroyed with the sword every living thing in it— men and women, young and old, cattle, sheep and donkeys.

JOSHUA 6:20–21

When have you seen the seemingly impossible actually happen? She dug down deep and won that race. He not only graduated—but graduated with honors. The daredevil completed the stunt, the figure skater landed the triple axel, and the last person you ever would have expected accepted Jesus as Savior and Lord. The impossible is not so impossible when the Lord is involved.

Nothing is impossible with God, but it can be difficult to walk through to the moment when God shows up and makes the impossible happen. Do you think these soldiers felt maybe just a little foolish as they took a walking field trip around the mighty city of Jericho? Do you think there might have been taunting by the residents of Jericho? Joshua's fighting men literally stepped out in faith—and the impossible happened. So never say never when you're stepping toward the impossible per God's command.

NEVER SAY NEVER—BUT ALWAYS SAY "THANK YOU" TO THE DOER OF THE IMPOSSIBLE.

A PROMISE KEPT

*Joshua said to the two men who had spied out the land, "Go into
[Rahab's] house and bring her out and all who belong to her, in
accordance with your oath to her." . . .*

*[The army of Israel] burned the whole city [of Jericho] and
everything in it. . . . But Joshua spared Rahab . . . with her
family and all who belonged to her, because she hid the men
Joshua had sent as spies to Jericho—and she lives among the
Israelites to this day.*

JOSHUA 6:22, 24–25

F ew things hurt like a broken promise can. Maybe you know
that from experience.

But Joshua made good on his spies' promise to Rahab. Before he
and his men destroyed the city of Jericho, they rescued her and her
entire family. Then the city burned.

But that's not the last mention of Rahab in Scripture. She
earned a place in the Hebrews 11 Hall of Faith (v. 31). Perhaps even
more remarkable is the place she has in the genealogy of the Lord:
Rahab and Salmon were the parents of Boaz; Boaz and Ruth were
the parents of Obed; Obed was the father of Jesse; and Jesse, the
father of King David (Matthew 1:5–6). And the rest is history.

PROMISES KEPT CAN HAVE
UNEXPECTED, FAR-REACHING, AND
WONDERFUL CONSEQUENCES.

AMBUSHED!

The LORD said to Joshua, "Do not be afraid; do not be discouraged. . . . For I have delivered into your hands the king of Ai, his people, his city and his land. You shall do to Ai and its king as you did to Jericho and its king, except that you may carry off their plunder and livestock for yourselves. Set an ambush behind the city." . . .

Twelve thousand men and women fell that day—all the people of Ai.

JOSHUA 8:1–2, 25

A congressman's wife once said, "You go to Washington, DC, a tourist, you come back a patriot." Walking where founding fathers walked, seeing Lincoln's hat in the Smithsonian, visiting Jefferson's Monticello, standing in the Capitol rotunda—suddenly history is much more real.

A visit to the Holy Land offers that same kind of experience. To walk where Jesus walked, to stand at the Jordan River, to sail in the Sea of Galilee—suddenly history and your Lord are much more real.

Sometimes the site of an event cannot be visited—and the site of Ai cannot be visited. Joshua and his army made sure of that. Ai is "a permanent heap of ruins, a desolate place to this day" (Joshua 8:28).

DON'T BE AMBUSHED BY THOSE WHO DON'T TRUST THE ACCURACY OF GOD'S WORD.

FIGHTING FOR HIS PEOPLE

On the day the LORD gave the Amorites over to Israel, Joshua
said to the LORD in the presence of Israel:
"Sun, stand still over Gibeon. . . ."
So the sun stood still . . .
till the nation avenged itself on its enemies. . . .
The sun stopped in the middle of the sky and delayed going
down about a full day.

JOSHUA 10:12–13

Sometimes there's just no satisfying explanation. "You have to take a nap because I'm the mom." "It's a school tradition." "The sun delayed going down about a full day."

Is there a satisfying explanation for that last statement? People who don't want to believe will read it, not be able to explain it, and simply dismiss every verse of Scripture.

That there is no scientific evidence or explanation for this Joshua 10 passage doesn't mean the event didn't happen. We know that God could have refracted the light, or slowed the earth's rotation, or stopped the entire universe—all with equal ease! The sun, moon, and stars obey the Creator who placed them in the sky by the power of his word.[5]

GOD FIGHTS FOR HIS PEOPLE
IN ALL KINDS OF WAYS.

LAST-RESORT JUSTICE

> *Joshua took all these royal cities and their kings and put them to the sword. He totally destroyed them. . . . The Israelites carried off all the plunder and livestock of these cities, but all the people they put to the sword until they completely destroyed them, not sparing anyone that breathed. . . . [Joshua] left nothing undone of all that the LORD commanded Moses.*

JOSHUA 11:12, 14–15

The question "Why would God allow this?" may be very personal and quite painful for you. Sometimes he doesn't reveal much about why, but he is pleased and glorified as we walk the journey of faith without complete understanding of him and his ways.

Sometimes, though, a little information can bring great insight into the Lord's mysterious ways. Consider the Canaanites and the issue of our just God allowing—even commanding—Joshua to wipe certain peoples and cities off the map.

Canaan was a nation of evil and sin, of incest, prostitution, homosexuality, bestiality, and child sacrifice.[6] Our Holy God chose to destroy this contaminated nation lest their contamination spread to his chosen people (Deuteronomy 7:1–6). But wipe out everyone? As the Bible's accounts of Noah and Rahab show, God will spare the righteous individuals he finds in this dark and sin-filled world.

GOD NOTICES, BLESSES, AND PROTECTS THE RIGHTEOUS.

JOSHUA'S PARTING WORDS

"Choose for yourselves this day whom you will serve. . . . But as for me and my household, we will serve the LORD."

JOSHUA 24:15–16

We make routine choices every day of our lives: what to eat, what to wear. Some choices we make less often: where to live, where to work. Other choices are permanent: getting married, and having children. At least one choice we make has eternal significance, and that's the issue Joshua addressed before he died: whom will you serve?

Joshua reminded the people of Israel what we need to be reminded of: "Not one of all the good promises the LORD your God gave you has failed" (Joshua 23:14). Joshua also reminded the people that God had not hesitated and would not hesitate to punish disobedience (v. 16).

Following God and obeying his commands is no easier today than it was in Joshua's day. The choice to be one of God's people is the choice to swim upstream, to encounter spiritual warfare, to feel like—to *be*—a stranger on this planet (Philippians 3:20). Choosing to serve God means being people of the Word, people of prayer, people who love and obey him—and that choice will mean eternal blessings.

WHOM ARE YOU SERVING? THIS CHOICE HAS
ETERNAL SIGNIFICANCE, SO CHOOSE WISELY.

THE PATTERN

Whenever the LORD raised up a judge for [his people], he was with the judge and saved them out of the hands of their enemies as long as the judge lived. . . . But when the judge died, the people returned to ways even more corrupt than those of their ancestors. . . . They refused to give up their evil practices and stubborn ways.

JUDGES 2:18–19

What pattern have you worked hard to establish? Working out after work? Reading the Bible at lunch? And what pattern have you worked hard to break? The unhelpful self-talk that too regularly plays in your mind?

Which is harder—establishing a good pattern or breaking a bad habit? The Israelites had only short-lived success with both! They were a picture of Albert Einstein's definition of *insanity*: "doing the same thing over and over again and expecting different results." The people of Israel looked pretty crazy: turn away from God, be invaded by a foreign army, repent, be rescued by God, turn away from God, be invaded by a foreign army, repent, be rescued . . . you get the idea.

God sent judges to lead his rescued people, only to see the people ignore the judges' leadership and "[prostitute] themselves to other gods" (Judges 2:17). And we're not all that different from them.

LORD, SHOW ME MY PATTERN OF
SIN—AND HELP ME BREAK IT!

GOD-GIVEN VICTORY

Now Deborah . . . was leading Israel at that time. . . . She sent for Barak . . . and said to him, "The LORD, the God of Israel, commands you: 'Go, take with you ten thousand men . . . and lead them up to Mount Tabor. I will lead Sisera, the commander of Jabin's army, with his chariots and his troops to the Kishon River and give him into your hands.'"

Barak said to her, "If you go with me, I will go; but if you don't go with me, I won't go."

JUDGES 4:4, 6–8

When have you insisted on having a partner for a project? Maybe you simply wanted companionship. But maybe you needed the expertise or encouragement or even protection that person offered. Would you have still needed that person if you had been given a guarantee of success?

Speaking through Judge Deborah, God had given Barak that kind of guarantee: "I will give Sisera into your hands." Scripture doesn't explain why Barak made his request, but it does say that Barak's ten thousand men faced Sisera's "nine hundred chariots fitted with iron" (Judges 4:13). And the Lord gave victory to his people.

PRAISE GOD FOR A VICTORY HE HAS GIVEN
YOU—AND BE ENCOURAGED ABOUT
THE CURRENT OR IMMINENT BATTLE.

TAKING A BOLD STEP

*Jael . . . picked up a tent peg and a hammer and went quietly
to [Sisera] while he lay fast asleep, exhausted. She drove the peg
through his temple into the ground, and he died.*

JUDGES 4:21

Patriotism is a powerful force. Love of country can compel individuals to find courage they didn't know they had and to risk
making the ultimate sacrifice. Love of God also increases one's willingness to take bold and risky steps. Maybe you've been privileged
to serve your country or your Lord in a way you never would have
imagined.

Jael probably never imagined doing what she did in honor
of her nation, her God's nation, and her nation's God. Exactly as
Deborah had said he would, the Lord gave his people victory over the
Canaanite army. Yet the honor for the victory was not Barak's: "For
the LORD will deliver Sisera into the hands of a woman" (Judges 4:9).

Under Barak's leadership, "all Sisera's troops fell by the sword;
not a man was left" (v. 16). Sisera fled to the tent of Jael. She welcomed him, covered him with a blanket, and gave him some water.
That's when the hospitality ended and the victory God gave the
Israelites was sealed.

BE OPEN TO HOW GOD MAY USE
YOU FOR HIS KINGDOM WORK IN
WAYS YOU NEVER IMAGINED.

HONESTLY!

"Pardon me, my lord," Gideon replied, "but if the LORD is with us, why has all this happened to us? Where are all his wonders that our ancestors told us about when they said, 'Did not the LORD bring us up out of Egypt?' But now the LORD has abandoned us and given us into the hand of Midian."

JUDGES 6:13

Some people have a gift for knowing what to say and how to say it. Others of us too often think after we speak! Some people are known for saying whatever is on their mind. Others overthink and end up not saying much at all.

Gideon was definitely a diplomat when the angel announced, "The LORD is with you" (Judges 6:12). "Pardon me, my lord" was Gideon's respectful lead-in to what may be a very innocent question (Gideon hadn't grown up in a believing culture) or a rather accusatory one: "If the LORD is with us, why has all this happened to us?"

Whatever its tone, Gideon's question may put words to thoughts you've had: *If God is with me, then why did (fill in the blank)?* Don't ever hesitate to be brutally honest with God. He already knows those feelings are there.

RELATIONSHIPS DEPEND ON HONESTY, AND YOUR RELATIONSHIP WITH GOD IS NO EXCEPTION.

DAY 97
DECISIONS, DECISIONS

Gideon said to God, "I will place a wool fleece on the threshing floor. If there is dew only on the fleece and all the ground is dry, then I will know that you will save Israel by my hand, as you said." And that is what happened. Gideon rose early the next day; he squeezed the fleece and wrung out the dew—a bowlful of water.

JUDGES 6:36–38

Of course you want to do what the Lord wants you to do. You're just as willing to choose Option A as Option B. *Just show me, Lord!*

If you've ever felt like that, you can understand Gideon. He hadn't grown up in the church; he didn't see role models who walked with the Lord; he didn't know how to determine God's will. Oh, Gideon had heard that the Lord led his ancestors out of Egypt, but was God really going to use him to save Israel from Midian?

The wet—very wet—fleece indicated that God indeed planned to use Gideon. And just to be sure, Gideon asked for the sign in reverse: this time dry fleece and dewy ground again suggested Gideon was the man for the job.

WHETHER FLEECE OR THE HOLY SPIRIT,
GOD'S CALL WILL ALWAYS REQUIRE FAITH.

TOO MANY MEN

The LORD said to Gideon, "There are still too many men. . . ."
So Gideon took the men down to the water. . . . Three
hundred of them drank from cupped hands, lapping like dogs. . . .
The LORD said to Gideon, "With the three hundred men that
lapped I will save you and give the Midianites into your hands."

JUDGES 7:4–7

Has another person ever gotten credit for something you actually did? As innocent as the mistake may be, the confusion that follows never feels right. It simply isn't fair when one person gets another's glory—and God wasn't about to let the Israelite army get credit for victory over Midian.

So began his whittling. "If you are afraid, leave" (see Judges 7:3)—and that trimmed the army by twenty-two thousand. Still, ten thousand soldiers was too big an army. The three hundred who lapped like dogs stayed; the 9,700 who knelt to drink were dismissed.

Now the army was down to three hundred soldiers. If victory over the Midianites came, it would clearly be due to the Lord's great power, not to the size of Israel's army. Remember Gideon's story when you find yourself facing a situation that you feel is insurmountable.

GOD'S POWER "WORKS BEST IN
WEAKNESS." (2 CORINTHIANS 12:9 NLT)

WHO GETS THE CREDIT?

Dividing the three hundred men into three companies, [Gideon] placed trumpets and empty jars in the hands of all of them, with torches inside. . . .

The three companies blew the trumpets and smashed the jars. Grasping the torches in their left hands and holding in their right hands the trumpets they were to blow, they shouted, "A sword for the LORD and for Gideon!" While each man held his position around the camp, all the Midianites ran, crying out as they fled.

JUDGES 7:16, 20–21

God's creativity can be seen in the wide variety of ways he provides for his people.

We first see this frightened thresher of wheat hiding in a winepress so the Midianites would not steal the grain—yet the angel addressed him as "mighty warrior" (Judges 6:12). God soon gathered a trimmed-down army of three hundred people to go against the Midianites. And the weapons of choice were trumpets to blow, jars to smash. Unlikely gear for battle!

Confused by the clamor, the Midianite soldiers turned on one another. The victory was—make no mistake—the Lord's.

TRUST GOD IN ALL YOUR BATTLES.
EVERY VICTORY IS HIS.

ONE KIND OF STRENGTH

Suddenly a young lion came roaring toward [Samson]. The Spirit of the LORD came powerfully upon him so that he tore the lion apart with his bare hands as he might have torn a young goat.

JUDGES 14:5–6

Maybe it can be applied to many situations, but the advice "Use 'em or lose 'em" definitely applies to one's physical muscles. The Israelite judge Samson had God-given physical strength that he used in remarkable ways, especially when the Holy Spirit added his power to the mix. That was the case when a young lion "came roaring toward him." Samson tore apart the beast with his bare hands.

Another time Samson "caught three hundred foxes and tied them tail to tail in pairs. He then fastened a torch to every pair of tails, lit the torches and let the foxes loose in the standing grain of the Philistines" (Judges 15:4–5). One day Samson grabbed "a fresh jawbone of a donkey" and killed a thousand Philistines (15:15).

Whatever skills or traits God has given us, we are to use those gifts to build up his kingdom. And just as his Spirit heightened Samson's physical strength, the Spirit will heighten your gifts as you yield them to him for God's great glory.

USE THE SKILLS AND TRAITS GOD GIVES YOU FOR HIS KINGDOM WORK.

BLIND AND DEAF AND PRIDEFUL

[Samson] told [Delilah] everything. . . . "If my head were shaved, my strength would leave me, and I would become as weak as any other man."

When Delilah saw that he had told her everything, she sent word to the rulers of the Philistines. . . . After putting him to sleep on her lap, she called for someone to shave off the seven braids of his hair. . . . And his strength left him.

JUDGES 16:17–19

Love can definitely be blind. Perhaps you learned this lesson the hard way. It's a lesson that can have lifelong repercussions. Sadly, not learning this very lesson led Samson to his death. As unbelievable as it sounds, he was blind to the fact that Delilah was not to be trusted.

How could he not see it coming? Three other times Delilah had asked him the secret of his strength, and each time she had clearly tried to rob him of that strength. Furthermore, each of those times the Philistines had arrived to take hold of Samson. Since he'd still had his strength, they had not succeeded. This time was different.

ASK GOD'S SPIRIT TO HELP YOU RECOGNIZE WHAT SAPS YOUR STRENGTH IN THE LORD SO THAT YOU CAN BE STRONG IN HIM.

OUT OF CONTROL

Samson prayed. . . . "Please, God, strengthen me just once more. . . ." Then Samson reached toward the two central pillars. . . . Bracing himself against them, his right hand on the one and his left hand on the other, Samson. . . . pushed with all his might, and down came the temple on the rulers and all the people in it. Thus he killed many more when he died than while he lived.

JUDGES 16:28–30

S in can be like a snowball—starting small enough, with a simple thought. But when we act on that thought, the ball starts rolling. As it gains in size and momentum, the damage starts happening in wider circles and at a faster pace.

Samson fell in love with Delilah, a Philistine, a longstanding enemy of God's people who wanted to learn the secret of his strength. Finally, worn down by her nagging, he told her the truth, and she had someone shave his head. Then the Philistines "seized him, gouged out his eyes" and threw him into prison (Judges 16:21).

The snowball of sin had quite the impact! Desperate, Samson cried out, "Sovereign LORD, remember me" (v. 28). The Lord did: the tragic last scene of Samson's life (above) was his sacrificial death that exacted revenge for his blinded eyes and killed many of the Lord's enemies.

HEED THE WARNING OF THE SNOWBALLING
IMPACT OF SAMSON'S SIN.

So a man from Bethlehem . . . with his wife and two sons, went to live for a while in the country of Moab.

Elimelek, Naomi's husband, died, and she was left with her two sons. They married Moabite women, one named Orpah and the other Ruth. After . . . about ten years, both Mahlon and Kilion also died, and Naomi was left without her two sons and her husband.

RUTH 1:1, 3–5

How much more can a person handle? Maybe you've had that thought for the dear family that always seems to be on the church's prayer request list, for a much-loved friend, a dear relative, or even yourself. If so, welcome to the club! Naomi is probably a card-carrying member as well. How much more would God give her to handle?

Naomi's story started in Bethlehem—"House of Bread"—where there was, ironically, a famine. Her family fled to Moab, a land occupied by a non-Jewish people whom Jews were not to marry. Naomi's husband died. Her sons married Moabite women. Her sons died. *How much more can a person handle?*

Times like that enable us to know the Lord's grace in a new and usually more substantial way. That was true for Naomi.

WHAT HAS GOD REVEALED TO YOU ABOUT HIMSELF DURING YOUR *HOW MUCH MORE CAN A PERSON HANDLE* SEASONS?

TWO ARE BETTER THAN ONE

Naomi said to her two daughters-in-law, "Go back . . . to your mother's home. May the LORD show you kindness, as you have shown kindness to your dead husbands and to me."

Then she kissed them goodbye and they wept aloud. . . . Then Orpah kissed her mother-in-law goodbye, but Ruth clung to her.

RUTH 1:8–9, 14

Thanks to Facebook, that cyberspace world of virtual everything, the concept of *friend* has been undermined. Facebook friends may know more about you than people you see seven days a week— and who aren't on Facebook. Ruth understood real friendship and the value of loyalty. She had known Naomi for more than a decade and seen her deal with the painful loss of her sons. Whatever else Ruth saw in Naomi made her want to journey with her back to Bethlehem, since the famine had ended.

Hear Ruth's beautiful words: "Where you go I will go, and where you stay I will stay. Your people will be my people and your God my God" (Ruth 1:16). Heartbroken Naomi and loyal Ruth started walking toward Bethlehem, each taking a step of faith into the unknown. Two are better than one at such times.

TODAY SEND A REAL NOTE TO A FRIEND
WHOSE LOYALTY HAS BEEN A BLESSING.
DON'T JUST FACEBOOK THAT PERSON!

AS IT TURNED OUT . . .

Ruth the Moabite said to Naomi, "Let me go to the fields and pick up the leftover grain behind anyone in whose eyes I find favor."

Naomi said to her, "Go ahead, my daughter." . . . As it turned out, she was working in a field belonging to Boaz, who was from the clan of Elimelek.

RUTH 2:2–3

S omeone has defined *coincidence* as "when God chooses to remain anonymous." Events in this world—disasters, blessings, tragedies, joys—don't happen randomly. Chance meetings aren't chance: they are divine appointments. What hope and peace we can know when we choose to rest in God's sovereignty.

So "as it turned out" was no coincidence. Ruth had walked to a barley field for a God-ordained appointment: to meet Naomi's relative Boaz. He immediately recognized her noble character, provided for her protection, and instructed his workers to leave some stalks for her to pick up.

When Ruth later told Naomi whose field she had been gleaning in, Naomi praised God for this "close relative" and his kindness (Ruth 2:20). God's providence shone brightly against the dark backdrop of Naomi's great losses.

GOD'S GRACE CAN BE EASIER TO SEE WHEN IT SHINES INTO A DARK SEASON OF LIFE.

GOD'S PLAN UNFOLDS

"I will do for you all you ask. . . . Although it is true that I am a guardian-redeemer of our family, there is another who is more closely related than I. . . . If he wants to do his duty as your guardian-redeemer, good; let him redeem you. But if he is not willing . . . I will do it."

RUTH 3:11–13

The Disneyland ride It's a Small World is a glorious celebration of the variety of the world's languages, dress, architecture, dance, and customs. If we somehow landed in a nation not our own, we might share—as the ride's song suggests—laughter, tears, hope, and fears, but we'd need certain aspects of the culture explained.

We also need an explanation of Bethlehem in Ruth's day. What, for instance, is a "guardian-redeemer"? It was Boaz being willing to come alongside of Naomi and Ruth, to redeem their difficult situation, but by law he first had to confirm that the closest relative did not want this role.

Naomi understood this cultural practice and knew of Boaz's fine character. She was seeing God at work.

GOD'S LOVE REACHES AROUND THE WORLD TOUCHING INDIVIDUALS IN PERSONAL, INTIMATE WAYS.

So Boaz took Ruth and she became his wife . . . and she gave birth to a son. . . .

Naomi took the child in her arms and cared for him. . . . They named him Obed. He was the father of Jesse, the father of David.

RUTH 4:13, 16–17

Okay, who's the best multitasker you know? Yes, trick question. God is: he multitasks for billions perfectly, never dropping a stitch or missing a beat or forgetting a name or getting tired and cranky.

God is the multitasking Author of the Upper Story (God's story) as well as of the Lower Story (humanity's story) that unfolds for every human being throughout time. In Ruth's story, he blessed her with a godly husband and a son in the line of Jesus. Yet in the Upper Story, God was teaching his chosen people, Israel, that he was not their exclusive property. This loyal, determined, lovely woman—from Moab!—became part of the lineage of King David and therefore of King Jesus. She illustrates the worldwide reach of God's gift of hope and life—his plan of salvation that is as broad and deep as his divine love.

PRAISE GOD WHO LOVES TO BLESS YOU IN WAYS FAR GREATER THAN YOU MIGHT ASK OR IMAGINE!

HEARTBREAK AND HOPE

*Eli the priest was sitting . . . by the doorpost of the LORD's
house. In her deep anguish Hannah prayed to the LORD,
weeping bitterly. . . . "LORD Almighty, if you will only look on
your servant's misery and . . . give her a son, then I will give him
to the LORD for all the days of his life." . . .*

*Eli answered . . . "May the God of Israel grant you what you
have asked of him."*

1 SAMUEL 1:9–11, 17

It's one thing to grieve when God answers a heartfelt prayer with
"no" or "not yet." That grief is heavier as you notice that everyone
around you seems to have exactly what you had requested of your
heavenly Father. *Yes,* your head says, *God's ways are good, his timing
is perfect, and he loves me.* But your heart still aches.

Hannah knew this kind of heartache. She had long wanted
children—as her husband's other wife had. Praying one morning,
Hannah again let the Lord know her heart's desire. She also offered
to dedicate to him the son she trusted him to give her. The Lord
heard Hannah's impassioned prayer, and this time said, "Yes."

DON'T STOP GOING TO THE LORD WITH
YOUR HEARTFELT HOPES AND PRAYERS.

TRUE TO HER WORD

In the course of time Hannah became pregnant and gave birth to a son. . . .

After he was weaned, she took the boy . . . to Eli, and she said to him, "Pardon me, my lord. . . . I prayed for this child, and the LORD has granted me what I asked of him. So now I give him to the LORD."

1 SAMUEL 1:20, 24–28

What is the greatest sacrifice you have ever made for another person? Don't tie yourself in knots patting yourself on the back. Instead, remember what happened in your heart when you made that sacrifice.

What is the greatest sacrifice you have ever made for the Lord? And what might he have you sacrifice today as an act of obedience? The greatest sacrifice Hannah made was—true to her vow—giving her son "to the LORD for all the days of his life" (1 Samuel 1:11). Samuel was probably three or four years old, probably at a stage of separation anxiety whenever Mom was out of sight. (How hard for Mom! Drop-off that first day of preschool is tough enough.) But faithful Hannah kept her promise and gave up her only son. She must have known that God the Father would understand the significance of her gift and her pain.

SACRIFICES YOU MAKE FOR GOD HONOR
HIM WHO SACRIFICED HIS SON FOR YOU.

Then Hannah prayed and said:
"My heart rejoices in the LORD. . . .
"There is no one holy like the LORD." . . .
Each year [Samuel's] mother made him a little robe and took it
to him. . . . The boy Samuel grew up in the presence of the LORD.

1 SAMUEL 2:1–2, 19, 21

Whether you've been gone for thirty seconds to get the mail or you've logged a ten-hour day at work, a golden retriever is ecstatic about your being home. His tail goes back and forth, he tries hard to keep all four paws on the ground, and sometimes he whimpers with delight. He'd turn cartwheels if he could; he'd sing as Hannah did if he could.

And how Hannah sang! She praised the Almighty for his power, his goodness, his authority over all the earth, and his faithfulness to those who trust him. She kept her vow: Samuel was the Lord's to raise. And the Lord honored her sacrifice: she who had long been barren "gave birth to three sons and two daughters" (1 Samuel 2:21). No, of course none was a replacement for Samuel, but each was a reminder of God's pleasure in Hannah.

REMEMBER THE UNFAILING JOY OF A DOG
GREETING HIS MASTER, AND LET THAT
UNBRIDLED GLEE BE A REMINDER OF THE
ENDLESS LOVE THAT GOD HAS FOR YOU!

GOD CALLS

Samuel went and lay down in his place.

The LORD came and stood there, calling as at the other times,
"Samuel! Samuel!"

Then Samuel said, "Speak, for your servant is listening."

1 SAMUEL 3:9–10

Think about your most recent *ah-hah!* moment. What dots did you finally connect? What insight did you suddenly have? It's a great feeling, isn't it? Now imagine the feeling that comes when the *ah-hah!* moment marks the realization that God is alive and present with you.

Three times Samuel had heard his name called, and three times he went to Eli the priest. Who else would have called him? Samuel said each time, "Here I am; you called me." The first two times Eli's response was, "I did not call; go back and lie down." The third time, though, "Eli realized that the LORD was calling the boy" (1 Samuel 3:8).

God is always alive and present and very active in his children's lives. We just aren't always expecting or aware of his calling.

WHEN YOU THINK GOD MAY BE
CALLING TO YOU, STOP AND LISTEN
CAREFULLY AND PRAYERFULLY.

BEARING—AND RECEIVING—HARD NEWS

The LORD said to Samuel . . . "I will carry out against Eli everything I spoke against his family. . . . 'The guilt of Eli's house will never be atoned for by sacrifice or offering.'"

Samuel lay down until morning. . . . He was afraid to tell Eli the vision.

1 SAMUEL 3:11–12, 14–15

God calls his people to be iron sharpening iron. That can mean the not-so-easy task of helping someone recognize his sin so he can repent—and the not-so-easy position of trying to respond with grace or gratitude when someone does the same for us.

Samuel was still a boy when the Lord gave him a message for Eli. Eli would experience consequences for his sin. Yet in the morning Eli insisted that Samuel tell him everything (1 Samuel 3:17). We can learn from both Samuel and Eli in what happened next: "Samuel told him everything, hiding nothing from him. Then Eli said, 'He is the LORD; let him do what is good in his eyes'" (v. 18).

If the Lord entrusts us, who are we to offer an edited version? And if the Lord speaks to us through one of his people, may we hear and accept it as God doing "what is good in his eyes."

MAY WE BOTH SPEAK GOD'S CONVICTING TRUTH IN LOVE AND RECEIVE IT WITH GRATITUDE.

GOOD LUCK

The LORD was with Samuel as he grew up. . . . And all
Israel . . . recognized that Samuel was attested as a prophet of
the LORD.

Now the Israelites went out to fight against the Philistines.

The Philistines fought, and the Israelites were defeated. . . . The
slaughter was very great; Israel lost thirty thousand foot soldiers.
The ark of God was captured, and Eli's two sons . . . died.

1 SAMUEL 3:19–20; 4:1, 10–11

People can do strange things in quest of good luck. A baseball
player may eat the same meal before a game or perform the same
routine as he steps up to bat. For others good luck comes from a rab-
bit's foot. A four-leaf clover. The ark of the Lord. *The ark of the Lord?*

Yes, the ark of the Lord, because that's how the people of God
treated it. The Israelites went out to fight the Philistines. No mention is made of their consulting God—which is always a good idea.
When four thousand Israelites died, the survivors wondered, "Why
did the LORD bring defeat on us today?" (1 Samuel 4:3) and decided
to take the ark of the Lord with them into the next battle. This time
Israel "lost thirty thousand foot soldiers" and, far worse, "the ark of
God was captured."

God Almighty is not his people's good luck charm.

HONOR THE LORD ALWAYS, CONSULT
HIM ALWAYS, OBEY HIM ALWAYS.

GIMME!

All the elders of Israel . . . came to Samuel. . . . "Appoint a king to lead us, such as all the other nations have."

This displeased Samuel; so he prayed. . . . And the LORD told him. . . . "Warn them solemnly . . . what the king . . . will claim as his rights." . . .

The people refused to listen. . . . "We want a king over us. Then we will be like all the other nations." . . .

The LORD answered . . . "Give them a king."

1 SAMUEL 8:4–7, 9, 19–20, 22

Kids can make some crazy requests, and parents sometimes have to say no in order to protect their kids. But when the answer is no, older children—like the people of Israel—may talk back rather than submit.

Israel requested a king, God said no, Israel talked back, and Samuel warned them that kings would—among other things—put their sons to work in the fields or in battle, force their daughters to work in the palace, and take their best vineyards, olive groves, servants, and livestock. And the warning continued: when you "cry out for relief from the king . . . the LORD will not answer you" (1 Samuel 8:18).

Still, they demanded a king!

CONSIDER CHOICES THAT YOU HAVE MADE WHILE TRYING TO BE LIKE THE WORLD INSTEAD OF LIKE CHRIST—AND THE IMPACT THEY ARE HAVING ON YOUR LIFE.

ENTER SAUL

*When Samuel caught sight of Saul, the LORD said to him, "This is
the man I spoke to you about; he will govern my people."*

*Saul approached Samuel . . . and asked, "Would you please
tell me where the seer's house is?"*

"I am the seer," Samuel replied. . . . "Today you are to eat with me."

1 SAMUEL 9:17–19

Some people command respect by their very presence. Certain
government officials, like England's queen and the US presi-
dent, don't arrive anywhere without pomp and circumstance. A
high-ranking military officer is saluted by standing-at-attention soldiers. But the future king Saul's entrance onto the biblical stage was
nothing like this.

When we meet Saul, he is looking for his father's lost donkeys—
and not succeeding. The servant, rather than the master who was
ready to return home, suggests a new strategy: "Let's consult a man
of God" (see 1 Samuel 9:6).

God had prepared that very man of God—Samuel—for this
encounter and commanded him to "anoint [Saul] ruler over my people Israel" (v. 16). And Saul objected: "Why do you say such a thing
to me?" (v. 21).

TO WHAT ASPECT OF GOD'S CALL
ON YOUR LIFE ARE YOU OBJECTING,
OR AT LEAST RESISTING?

ANOINTED AND CHANGED

"Go to Gibeah of God. . . . The Spirit of the LORD will come powerfully upon you, and you will prophesy with them; and you will be changed into a different person. Once these signs are fulfilled, do whatever your hand finds to do, for God is with you." . . .

As Saul turned to leave Samuel, God changed Saul's heart.

1 SAMUEL 10:5–7, 9

Maybe you've heard this said: God doesn't call the equipped; he equips the called. Perhaps you doubt that truth when God calls you to do something definitely beyond your reach—or at least out of your comfort zone. You aren't the first person to claim lack of ability, skill, or giftedness. Think, for instance, of Moses. And now consider Saul.

Samuel anointed Saul, told him that his father's donkeys had been found, and sent him on his way to Gibeah. Then Samuel explained that "the Spirit of the LORD will come powerfully upon you." How else could the reluctant Saul begin to handle the responsibilities of kingship? And how else could you do anything worth doing?

God doesn't call us to do something we can do on our own. He calls us to do something we can do only with his help.

CHANGE MY HEART SO THAT I AM YOUR
WILLING PARTNER IN MINISTRY.

MAKING A FIRST IMPRESSION

When Samuel had all Israel come forward by tribes, the tribe of Benjamin was taken by lot. . . . Finally Saul son of Kish was taken. But when they looked for him, he was not to be found.

1 SAMUEL 10:20–21

You thought you were clear: you requested the petite salad, dressing on the side, and, please, no tomatoes or green onions. Then the petite salad arrived, with the dressing on the side but garnished with diced tomatoes and green onions. Not exactly the salad you had in mind, but almost.

Similarly, Israel had been clear with God: "We want a king over us" (1 Samuel 8:19). Now it was time for them to meet their king.

Although the prophet Samuel knew whom God had selected, he used lots so that Israel could see that Saul was God's choice. That's exactly what the lots revealed—but where was Saul? "He has hidden himself among the supplies" was the Lord's response (1 Samuel 10:22). Really? Was this the king Israel had asked for? A hiding king was not exactly what they had in mind.

WE ARE TO PRAY SPECIFICALLY, BUT GOD'S GOOD AND PERFECT WILL MAY NOT PERFECTLY MATCH OUR REQUESTS.

EXTENDING GRACE

*Saul separated his men into three divisions; during the last watch
of the night they broke into the camp of the Ammonites and
slaughtered them until the heat of the day. . . .*

*Saul said, "No one will be put to death today, for this day
the LORD has rescued Israel."*

1 SAMUEL 11:11, 13

One aspect of leadership is knowing when to act and when not
to act. Consider the role of parent: When do we show grace?
When do we enforce consequences? No rule of thumb exists.

Leadership of a nation can also involve knowing when to act
and when not to act. Consider King Saul's position. Upon hearing
that Philistines were holding Israelites in Jabesh at their mercy, Saul
burned with Spirit-prompted righteous anger. Threatening to cut
into pieces the oxen of any Israelite who did not join him, Saul mus-
tered 330,000 men for the rescue mission—and the men succeeded.
Now, as some had asked, should Saul put to death those who had
objected to his kingship?

Let's choose to believe that Saul consulted God and then
extended grace. Saul would put no one to death who had earlier
objected to his kingship. Instead, all would celebrate the victory
over the Philistines that the Lord had given them.

CONSULT GOD—AND ERR IN
THE DIRECTION OF GRACE.

The people all said to Samuel, "Pray to the LORD . . . so that we will not die, for we have added to all our other sins the evil of asking for a king."

[Samuel replied] . . . "For the sake of his great name the LORD will not reject his people. . . . Be sure to fear the LORD and serve him faithfully. . . . If you persist in doing evil, both you and your king will perish."

1 SAMUEL 12:19–20, 22, 24–25

Sometimes we human beings need clear and concrete evidence in order to see what we haven't yet understood. We can know money is tight, but seeing the numbers—what is coming in and what is going out—helps us better understand.

The Israelites had known it was wrong to ask for a king because the Lord was their king, so when Samuel called on the Lord to send thunder and rain and the Lord did, "all the people stood in awe of the LORD" (1 Samuel 12:18). Now that the King of kings had the people's attention, Samuel reviewed some key points with them, points that are just as relevant to us today.

IF YOU FEAR THE LORD AND SERVE AND OBEY HIM . . . GOOD! BUT IF YOU DO NOT OBEY THE LORD . . . HIS HAND WILL BE AGAINST YOU. . . . (1 SAMUEL 12:14–15)

SAUL'S SINS

"You have done a foolish thing," Samuel said. "You have not kept the command the LORD your God gave you . . . now your kingdom will not endure."

1 SAMUEL 13:13–14

What are you waiting for right now? Maybe a loved one's salvation, your pastor's battle against cancer, or your nephew's reconciliation with your sister. God cares about whatever you are waiting for, but he cares even more about who you become as you wait.

And waiting is hard. Three thousand Philistine chariots, "six thousand charioteers, and soldiers as numerous as the sand on the seashore" had assembled against Israel (1 Samuel 13:5). King Saul had been waiting for Samuel, but with his men scattering and the Philistine presence seeming more ominous, Saul waited no longer and "offered up the burnt offering" himself (v. 9). That's when Samuel arrived and spoke the words above.

This time of waiting could have been a time for Saul to cry out to God, to remember the Lord's power and faithfulness, and to have his own faith and the faith of his people grown and strengthened. And none of that happened.

LET GOD USE SEASONS OF WAITING TO INCREASE YOUR ABILITY TO TRUST HIM.

HE MEANS IT!

Samuel said to Saul . . . "Go, attack the Amalekites and
totally destroy all that belongs to them. Do not spare them; put
to death men and women, children and infants, cattle and sheep,
camels and donkeys." . . .

But Saul . . . spared Agag and the best of the sheep and cattle,
the fat calves and lambs—everything that was good. . . . Everything
that was despised and weak they totally destroyed.

1 SAMUEL 15:1, 3, 9

When the speed limit sign says 65 MPH, that is the speed limit. When the umpire calls, "Strike three," there's no arguing. When the IRS says, "April 15," they're serious. And when God says to do something, he is very, very serious.

Apparently King Saul hadn't exactly grasped that concept. God's command was clear: destroy all of the Amalekite property as punishment for waylaying Israel as they left Egypt (1 Samuel 15:2). But Saul and his men destroyed what was not of value. Later, Saul would claim that he spared the good livestock to use as sacrifices to God (v. 15). To that Samuel said, "To obey is better than sacrifice" (v. 22). Saul had disobeyed. Saul had failed as king. It was time to find a successor.

GOD SAYS, "DON'T" AND "DO"—
AND THERE'S NO GRAY BETWEEN
THAT BLACK AND THAT WHITE.

TAKING THE NEXT STEP

The LORD said to Samuel . . . "I am sending you to Jesse of Bethlehem. I have chosen one of his sons to be king. . . .

"Do not consider his appearance or his height . . . The LORD does not look at the things people look at. People look at the outward appearance, but the LORD looks at the heart."

1 SAMUEL 16:1, 7

We all know that the best-looking apple may not be the sweetest. Some good books have unappealing covers, and some great covers far surpass the quality of the book's content. The tall man with his dashing good looks and magnetic charm may not be the best leader. That's what God needed to remind Samuel.

Samuel was still grieving over King Saul's failure to obey God and lead Israel in the way of the Lord, but God had already determined who the next king of Israel would be. So Samuel headed to Bethlehem—specifically to the family of Jesse—to anoint the chosen man.

THERE IS A TIME TO MOURN (ECCLESIASTES 3:4), THERE IS A TIME TO TAKE THE NEXT STEP, AND GOD WILL BE WITH YOU IN BOTH SEASONS AND IN BETWEEN.

A SURPRISING CHOICE

[Jesse sent for his youngest son.] He was glowing with health and had a fine appearance and handsome features.

Then the LORD said, "Rise and anoint him; this is the one."

So Samuel took the horn of oil and anointed him . . . and from that day on the Spirit of the LORD came powerfully upon David.

1 SAMUEL 16:12–13

Being chosen is a pretty good feeling, isn't it? It's great to have friends who have chosen you even as you have chosen them. And it's pretty incredible to be someone whom God has chosen to receive salvation from sins and enjoy eternity with him.

It was also pretty incredible when Jesse's youngest son was called home from his shepherding duties. The prophet Samuel had seen seven of Jesse's sons, but none was the Lord's chosen. When Samuel asked Jesse if he had any other sons, Jesse summoned David. And Samuel anointed him the next king of Israel. Yes, David had a "fine appearance and handsome features," but we know "the LORD looks at the heart" (1 Samuel 16:7).

The choice of young David may have surprised some people, but he was God's choice.

REJOICE WHOLEHEARTEDLY AND HUMBLY THAT YOU ARE GOD'S CHOICE TOO!

WHAT GIANT ARE YOU FACING?

A champion named Goliath . . . came out of the Philistine camp.
His height was six cubits and a span. He had a bronze helmet on
his head and wore a coat of scale armor of bronze. . . .

[Goliath shouted to Israel], "Choose a man. . . . If he is
able to fight and kill me, we will become your subjects; but if I
overcome him and kill him, you will become our subjects and
serve us." . . . Saul and all the Israelites were dismayed and
terrified.

1 SAMUEL 17:4–5, 8–9, 11

Who is the most terrifying person you have ever seen? Maybe it was the neighbor who never smiled, the bully who ruled at recess, the boss who was never satisfied. Those people were giants in your life, but maybe you are facing other giants as well. Maybe your giant is an addiction, fear of failure, loneliness, worry about the future. Whatever your giant, you can learn from David's confrontation with his.

The Philistines' spokesman was nine-foot, nine-inch Goliath, and he was wearing armor that weighed 125 pounds. Intimidating, to say the least. That "Saul and all the Israelites were dismayed and terrified" is understandable. Dangers are real; certain threats should not be ignored.

DON'T DENY THE GIANT IN YOUR LIFE—
BUT DON'T CONFRONT IT ALONE.

THE RIGHT PERSPECTIVE

David said to Saul . . . "When a lion or a bear . . . carried off a sheep . . . I went after it, struck it and rescued the sheep from its mouth. When it turned on me, I seized it by its hair, struck it and killed it. . . . The LORD who rescued me from the paw of the lion and the paw of the bear will rescue me from the hand of this Philistine."

1 SAMUEL 17:34–35, 37

Famed Green Bay Packers football coach Vince Lombardi once said, "Fatigue makes cowards of us all." And he's right. But other things can sap our confidence as well: standing alone in front of a giant can make that giant seem twice the size. Unless, like David, you know the Lord is present and powerful.

Saul did not understand that at all. David volunteered to fight the Philistine, but Saul objected: "You are only a young man, and he has been a warrior from his youth" (1 Samuel 17:33).

Granted, David didn't have specific experience with a nine-foot, nine-inch heavily armed and highly skilled soldier, but he did know from experience with a lion and a bear that God was with him. David had grabbed attacking wild animals and killed them. David's strength came from his God. And he knew that.

YOU AREN'T ALONE WHEN YOU CONFRONT YOUR GIANT. REMEMBER WHO FIGHTS FOR YOU!

NO LEVEL PLAYING FIELD HERE

[Saul] put a coat of armor on [David] and a bronze helmet on his head. . . .

"I cannot go in these," he said to Saul, "because I am not used to them." So he took them off. Then he took his staff in his hand, chose five smooth stones from the stream, put them in the pouch of his shepherd's bag and, with his sling in his hand, approached the Philistine.

1 SAMUEL 17:38–40

Fighting fire with fire isn't a bad strategy. And it only makes sense that if someone is coming at you with real bullets, you aren't relying on a squirt gun.

So, whether he was convinced that David could defeat Goliath or he simply realized he had no other option, Saul put his own fighting clothes on David. David "was not used to them," so rather than leveling the playing field, that equipment would be a liability. Besides, David didn't need armor. Goliath had prepared for the duel with all that the world offered, but David was relying on the power of the Creator of the world.

YOU CAN'T FIGHT THE WORLD WITH THINGS OF THIS WORLD AND WIN.

GOD'S PLAN, GOD'S GLORY

David said . . . "You come against me with sword and spear
and javelin, but I come against you in the name of the LORD
Almighty. . . . This day the LORD will deliver you into my
hands." . . .

Reaching into his bag and taking out a stone, he slung it and
struck the Philistine on the forehead. The stone sank into his
forehead, and he fell facedown on the ground.

1 SAMUEL 17:45–46, 49

t's not about you." So begins Rick Warren's best-selling book *The Purpose-Driven Life*. Contrary to the message our culture sends with its various self-help methods and encouragement toward self-fulfillment, life is not all about you.

Similarly, the battle against Goliath was not about David. Goliath taunted him: "Am I a dog, that you come at me with sticks?" (1 Samuel 17:43). David calmly and confidently proclaimed, "You come against me with sword and spear and javelin, but I come against you in the name of the LORD Almighty." That being the case, the single stone, slung with skill and blessed by God, found Goliath's weak spot. This was God's way, and God received the glory.

CONFRONTING YOUR GIANT IN GOD'S
WAY WILL MEAN VICTORY FOR YOU
AND GREAT GLORY FOR HIM.

A DIVINE TOUCH

Saul was afraid of David, because the LORD was with David but had departed from Saul. So he sent David away from him and gave him command over a thousand men. . . . In everything he did he had great success, because the LORD was with him.

1 SAMUEL 18:12–14

Occasionally we hear of a businessperson who has "the golden touch." Whatever he gets involved in flourishes. Whatever company she leads prospers. A golden touch in the economic world is, however, less significant than a God-blessed role in the spiritual world. As one of God's children, whatever you do for God—and for others in his name—matters whether you are front and center or behind the scenes.

David was definitely front and center, and God graciously blessed him (1 Samuel 18:5). The women celebrated David's accomplishments with songs of praise, and this chorus fueled Saul's paranoia and jealousy—and his rage. Then "an evil spirit from God came forcefully on Saul. . . . David was playing the lyre. . . . Saul had a spear in his hand and he hurled it. . . . But David eluded him twice" (vv. 10–11).

Saul's attempts to take David's life failed, and David's efforts on the battlefield prospered: God was with one, but not the other.

WHAT A PRIVILEGE TO WALK WITH
GOD AND SHARE WITH OTHERS A
DIVINE TOUCH OF HIS LOVE.

POURED-OUT FEARS

Deliver me from my enemies, O God;
be my fortress against those who are attacking me.

PSALM 59:1

Whether it's a murder mystery, an action-packed movie, or everyday life in the twenty-first century, the plot can thicken. Protagonists can find themselves very puzzled, in extreme danger, beaten down, or defeated by circumstances. Whatever the specific situation, these individuals can feel very much alone. If that's you, follow David's example.

Fearing for his life, David was running from Saul. Six hundred loyal men had joined him. Also in his corner and serving as a double agent from inside the palace was Jonathan, Saul's son and David's kindred spirit (1 Samuel 18:1, 3). As Saul's army neared David and his small band of soldiers, David poured out his fears to God and prayed for help.

Do the same—and join David in the last chorus of this song (Psalm 59:17): "You are my strength, I sing praise to you; you, God, are my fortress, my God on whom I can rely."

AS HE WAS FOR DAVID, GOD IS
YOUR FORTRESS, REFUGE, AND
STRENGTH IN TIMES OF TROUBLE.

HONORING GOD—ALWAYS

David crept up unnoticed and cut off a corner of Saul's robe.
Afterward, David was conscience-stricken. . . . He said . . .
"The LORD forbid that I should do such a thing to my master, the
LORD's anointed . . . for he is the anointed of the LORD."

1 SAMUEL 24:4–6

Perched on one shoulder of the cartoon hero is a bright, white angel; perched on the other, a red devil with his pitchfork and bad ideas. One wonders who was perched on Saul's shoulders . . .

Taking three thousand men with him, the enraged and jealous Saul pursued David without any hesitation, any twinge of conscience, or any sense of guilt. And when Saul stopped in a cave, the young soldier could easily have taken the life of his murderous enemy. That was the devil on David's shoulder, but the angel won out—yet, from David's perspective, not entirely.

David was "conscience-stricken," acutely aware that, by cutting off a corner of Saul's robe, he had dishonored "the anointed of the LORD." David wanted to honor God even in a life-or-death battle.

STAY CLOSE TO THE LORD
SO YOUR CONSCIENCE STAYS
SENSITIVE TO HIS GUIDANCE.

CHOOSING GOD'S WAY

David . . . called out to Saul, "My lord the king! . . . Why
do you listen when men say, 'David is bent on harming you'?
This day . . . the LORD delivered you into my hands in the
cave. . . . Look at this piece of your robe in my hand! I cut off
the corner of your robe but did not kill you." . . .
"You are more righteous than I," [Saul] said.

1 SAMUEL 24:8–11, 17

Think about a time when you chose to do God's way that prompted people around you to notice and scratch their heads. David made just such a head-scratching decision in the darkness of the cave when he could have slain Saul. But he didn't—and Saul recognized David's mercy. In a lucid moment, the crazed king from whom God's Spirit had removed himself acknowledged David's righteousness, recognized God's deliverance in David's sparing his life, and even spoke words of blessing over his rival (1 Samuel 24:18–19).

When we choose to do what is right in the Lord's eyes rather than the world's ("Why not kill Saul? He's been trying to kill you!"), God is greatly honored—and people notice. That kind of choice can pique people's interest in the God who leads you to live life so differently.

WHEN GOD'S PEOPLE CHOOSE
GOD'S WAY, THE WORLD WONDERS—
AND SOMETIMES INQUIRES!

A REFLEX ACTION

The LORD is my rock, my fortress and my deliverer;
my God is my rock, in whom I take refuge,
my shield and the horn of my salvation.
He is my stronghold, my refuge and my savior.

2 SAMUEL 22:2–3

We are concerned about a person or situation. We pray fervently and ask others to join us in praying. We remind God of his promises in Scripture. We look at the cross and thank him for his immeasurable love. But when he graciously responds, is our reflex action heartfelt praise and impassioned thanksgiving? Probably not often enough.

Delivered from Saul, David celebrated God's goodness with a joyous psalm, but the Lord doesn't require original songs of praise from us. Like any parent, he simply loves to hear, "Thank you!"

And, wonderfully, we can pray David's words of praise as our prayer of thanks. After all, the same God who protected David from Goliath and Saul is our Rock, our Fortress, and our Deliverer, saving us from our enemies and protecting us from "torrents of destruction" (v. 5). Thank *you*, David, for giving us words that express our hearts!

LORD, TRANSFORM MY HEART SO
THAT IT REFLEXIVELY GIVES THANKS
WHEN I NOTICE YOUR BLESSINGS.

JUST ONE SCENE

David went to bring up the ark of God . . . to the City of David with rejoicing. . . . Wearing a linen ephod, David was dancing before the LORD with all his might, while he and all Israel were bringing up the ark of the LORD with shouts and the sound of trumpets.

2 SAMUEL 6:12, 14–15

Take a minute and think about which one scene from your life offers a snapshot of what you most value and what you live for.

If King David had to choose, this scene from 2 Samuel just might be the one. The Philistines had killed Saul and his sons. David was made king over the house of Judah and, seven years later, over all of Israel. He twice led the Israelites in decisive victories over the Philistines, and he defeated the Jebusites living in Jerusalem, making that city Israel's national and spiritual capital.

David loved God and wanted his people to love God, so he brought the ark of the covenant into Jerusalem. What a joyous celebration! And what a snapshot of all that David most valued and what he lived for: honoring and rejoicing in his almighty God and King!

GUIDE MY HEART AND MY STEPS, LORD, THAT MANY SCENES FROM MY LIFE WILL REFLECT MY FAITH AND JOY IN YOU.

GOD'S GOOD PLANS

King David went in and sat before the LORD, and he said: "Who am I, Sovereign LORD, and what is my family, that you have brought me this far?"

2 SAMUEL 7:18

We choose to believe by faith that God's plans for us are plans for good (Jeremiah 29:11) and that his faithfulness will indeed continue to future generations (Psalm 100:5). We can look back and celebrate his great faithfulness to us. Those backward looks can strengthen our hope for both the present and the future.

David experienced this kind of moment when he reflected on God's faithfulness to the Hebrew people in delivering them from slavery in Egypt, leading them into the promised land, and choosing the line of David to be his servants. And now David longed to build a house for God, but when the prophet Nathan revealed to him God's plan—that one of David's sons would build that house—David praised the Lord wholeheartedly.

Rejoicing in God's plan, David prayed, "You, Sovereign LORD, have spoken, and with your blessing the house of your servant will be blessed forever" (2 Samuel 7:29).

GREAT HAS BEEN GOD'S FAITHFULNESS—
AND GREAT IT WILL CONTINUE TO BE!

THE FIRST DOMINO

In the spring, at the time when kings go off to war, David sent Joab out with the king's men and the whole Israelite army. . . . But David remained in Jerusalem.

One evening David got up from his bed and walked around on the roof of the palace. From the roof he saw a woman bathing. The woman was very beautiful, and David sent someone to find out about her.

2 SAMUEL 11:1–3

Finding yourself at the right place at the right time—that's God's hand on your life. Words of praise are appropriate. Finding yourself at the wrong place at the worst possible time—that can be a sign that you're acting independently of God. A change of direction is critical.

Here David was at the wrong place at the wrong time. As king, he should have been at war alongside his men. Unable to sleep (perhaps a guilty conscience?), David walked around the roof of his palace home. We read that "he saw a woman bathing." Rather than turning away, he clearly paused to admire her beauty. Already the husband of six wives, David nevertheless "sent someone to find out about" the woman he had seen. Another bad idea, David.

WHEN YOU PAUSE AT THE THRESHOLD
OF SIN, TURN AWAY RATHER
THAN STEPPING ACROSS IT.

WHAT RED FLAG?

*The man said, "She is Bathsheba, the daughter of Eliam and the
wife of Uriah the Hittite." Then David sent messengers to get her.
She came to him, and he slept with her. . . . Then she went
back home . . . and sent word to David, saying, "I am pregnant."*

2 SAMUEL 11:3–5

Sometimes the momentum created by one false step is too
strong for us to stand against—at least in our own limited
human power. We may be able to do nothing to stop the downward
movement.

But sometimes we can put the brakes on. Did David have to
send someone to find out who the beautiful woman was? No. But
once David learned she was the wife of Uriah, why didn't that red
flag stop him? This information didn't serve as a wake-up call to
David or prompt even a slight twinge of conscience.

The king summoned, the woman went, "he slept with her," and
"[she] conceived." David had completely ignored the red flags.

"GOD IS FAITHFUL; HE WILL NOT LET YOU
BE TEMPTED BEYOND WHAT YOU CAN BEAR.
BUT WHEN YOU ARE TEMPTED, HE WILL
ALSO PROVIDE A WAY OUT SO THAT YOU
CAN ENDURE IT." (1 CORINTHIANS 10:13)

ADDING DECEIT

David sent this word to Joab: "Send me Uriah the Hittite." . . .
When Uriah came to him, David asked him . . . how the war was
going. Then David said to Uriah, "Go down to your house and
wash your feet." So Uriah left the palace . . . but Uriah . . . did
not go down to his house.

2 SAMUEL 11:6–9

Perhaps you could tell your own horror story about a step of rebellion against God's ways that started a journey of deceit and pain that you could have avoided.

David's immoral journey began in earnest when he slept with Bathsheba. The next leg of the journey involved misusing his military authority and calling Uriah home from battle. Dinner conversation—another aspect of the ruse—suggested David's concern for his soldiers. Then the king dismissed the soldier to go home.

The honorable Uriah did not go home: "My commander Joab and my lord's men are camped in the open country. How could I go to my house to eat and drink and make love to my wife?" (2 Samuel 11:11). What must King David have felt? Humiliation? Moral outrage directed at himself? Recognition of his sin and a sense of conviction? Apparently not. He simply issued Uriah another dinner invitation.

WE CAN LEARN FROM BOTH URIAH'S
HONORABLE EXAMPLE AND DAVID'S
LESS–THAN-HONORABLE EXAMPLE.

MURDEROUS HARD-HEARTEDNESS

In the morning David wrote a letter to Joab and sent it with Uriah.
In it he wrote, "Put Uriah out in front where the fighting is fiercest.
Then withdraw from him so he will be struck down and die." . .

When the men of the city came out and fought against Joab,
some of the men in David's army fell; moreover, Uriah the
Hittite died.

2 SAMUEL 11:14–15, 17

It is so easy to recognize sin in other people, even the exact sin we ourselves are guilty of, yet we are blind when we look in the mirror. We can also feel prideful when we watch others commit sins we think we would never commit!

David again tried to cover his sin by giving Uriah another opportunity to spend time with Bathsheba. When once again Uriah didn't go to his wife, David plotted his murder, even knowing that ensuring Uriah's death would mean the loss of other soldiers as well.

Before you settle into any smug self-righteousness, consider what Jesus taught: "I tell you that anyone who is angry with a brother or sister will be subject to judgment. . . . I tell you that anyone who looks at a woman lustfully has already committed adultery with her in his heart" (Matthew 5:22, 27–28).

WE ARE SLOW TO SEE OUR OWN SIN BUT
QUICK TO SEE—AND JUDGE—OTHERS'.

A CONSCIENCE AWAKENED

*"Now a traveler came to the rich man, but the rich man
refrained from taking one of his own sheep or cattle to prepare
a meal. . . . Instead, he took the ewe lamb that belonged to the
poor man and prepared it for the one who had come to him."*

*David burned with anger against the man and said to Nathan,
"As surely as the LORD lives, the man who did this must die!"*

2 SAMUEL 12:4–5

It's all in the delivery. Messages about one's faults, mistakes, and, yes, sin tend to be better received when they're delivered gently.

At God's prompting, the prophet Nathan took a gentle approach when he confronted King David after his affair with Bathsheba and murder of Uriah. The story began innocently enough, yet the punch line achieved the desired effect. The enraged David immediately recognized the rich man's wrongdoing: "The man who did this must die . . . because he did such a thing and had no pity" (2 Samuel 12:5–6). David wasn't as quick to see what Nathan next proclaimed—and proclaimed quite boldly: "You are the man!" (v. 7).

David's conscience was no longer in hibernation. He was the rich man in the story: he who had six wives had stolen Uriah's Bathsheba.

WE OFTEN CRITICIZE IN OTHER
PEOPLE CHARACTERISTICS AND
TRAITS THAT ARE OURS AS WELL.

THE TRUTH AND THE CONSEQUENCES

Nathan said to David . . . "The LORD, the God of Israel,
says . . . 'Why did you despise the word of the LORD by doing
what is evil in his eyes? You struck down Uriah the Hittite with the
sword [of the Ammonites] and took his wife to be your own.'" . . .
Then David said to Nathan, "I have sinned against the LORD."

2 SAMUEL 12:7, 9, 13

God's greatest commandments are to love him with all our heart, soul, and mind and to love our neighbors as ourselves (Matthew 22:37–39). None of us can obey these commandments perfectly, and that reality cannot be ignored.

Neither can the reality that failing to love our neighbors is failing to obey God's commandment to love them. Any sin we commit against another person is a sin we commit against God himself. And that is a sobering truth.

The God of Israel alluded to that truth using these chilling words to David: "You despised me" (2 Samuel 12:10).

"The thing David had done displeased the LORD" (2 Samuel 11:27) and would not—could not—go unpunished.

> JESUS ASSUMED THE SPIRITUAL
> CONSEQUENCES OF OUR SIN. WE
> MUST DEAL WITH THE TEMPORAL
> CONSEQUENCES OF OUR SINS.

"AGAINST YOU HAVE I SINNED"

Have mercy on me, O God. . . .
Against you, you only, have I sinned
and done what is evil in your sight.

PSALM 51:1, 4

Since the garden, we human beings have struggled to take responsibility when we blow it—and blowing it can range from disappointing someone with a poorly cooked steak to gossiping to stealing to having someone murdered. Is anything we ever do completely our fault—and our fault alone? We don't like to think so!

King David was different. Psalm 51 shows that he was not a man looking to blame others. He didn't try to explain away his sin as the result of a bad upbringing; neither was he trying to justify his sin in any way. Instead, we see a humbled and heartbroken David shouldering the responsibility for his sin.

Furthermore, David understood that his sin—his irresponsibility, greed, lust, and murder—had broken his relationship with God. David's sin was a breach in a divine friendship, and that breach needed to be repaired.

We do well to follow David's example. Let's take responsibility for our sin and then ask the Lord's forgiveness.

CLEANSE ME WITH HYSSOP. . . . BLOT OUT ALL MY INIQUITY. CREATE IN ME A PURE HEART, O GOD. (PSALM 51:7, 9–10)

THE HIGH COST OF CONTEMPT

Nathan replied, "The LORD has taken away your sin. You are not going to die. But because by doing this you have shown utter contempt for the LORD, the son born to you will die." . . .

The LORD struck the child that Uriah's wife had borne to David, and he became ill. . . . On the seventh day the child died.

2 SAMUEL 12:13–15, 18

If you've ever watched soccer, you may think you know a hand ball when you see it. Only goalies use their hands in soccer, so a hand ball is clearly accidental—except when it's intentional. And that call is the referee's. He has the authority to determine the player's intent, to decide whether it was ball to hand (unintentional) or hand to ball (intentional). The consequence of a direct free kick may seem extreme, but not if the touch was deliberate.

When you read that David and Bathsheba's child would die, you may have thought that was more than a little extreme. Death always brings grief; even the hope of heaven doesn't mean we don't cry at our loss. But the death of one's child brings a degree of grief beyond words. Yet, despite David's fasting and praying, despite his pleading, the child's death is what our all-wise, all-good, all-just, all-loving God deemed righteous for David's "utter contempt for the LORD."

> THAT GOD'S PUNISHMENT FOR SIN SEEMS SO HARSH INDICATES HOW LITTLE WE GRASP THE SERIOUSNESS OF OUR SIN.

THE GRACE OF GOD'S FORGIVENESS

> *Blessed is the one*
> *whose transgressions are forgiven,*
> *whose sins are covered.*
> *Blessed is the one*
> *whose sin the LORD does not count against them.*

PSALM 32:1–2

Have you discovered that God's commands are always for your good? Oh, at times he may sound like a real fun-sucker, but he puts limits on our behavior to spare us pain.

He calls us to confess our sin to him so that his forgiveness can cleanse the wounds from our sin. When a repentant David asked God to forgive him, God said *yes*. God values the person who respects his holiness and treasures his friendship. We show that kind of respect for him, and God continues to forgive us. It's no wonder, then, that on more than one occasion David expressed his gratitude for God's gift of forgiveness.

We who have been forgiven our sin as David was respond gladly to his invitation to celebrate with him:

REJOICE IN THE LORD AND BE GLAD, YOU RIGHTEOUS; SING, ALL YOU WHO ARE UPRIGHT IN HEART! (PSALM 32:11)

NEEDING PERSPECTIVE ON WHAT IS NEAR

Absalom happened to meet David's men. He was riding his mule, and as the mule went under the thick branches of a large oak, Absalom's hair got caught in the tree. He was left hanging in midair, while the mule he was riding kept on going. . . .

[Joab] took three javelins . . . and plunged them into Absalom's heart. . . . Ten of Joab's armor-bearers surrounded Absalom, struck him and killed him.

2 SAMUEL 18:9, 14–15

Parent-child relationships are complex, so we don't always see in our own family what is so obvious to us elsewhere.

King David was not exempt from that: his normally deep insight into human behavior failed him with respect to his son Absalom. David didn't act as Absalom subtly undermined his administration and courted the populace. Finally Absalom challenged David's political position: Absalom was a traitor, and war ensued.

David's army killed 20,000 of Absalom's troops. "The battle spread out over the whole countryside, and the forest swallowed up more men that day than the sword" (2 Samuel 18:8). One of those men was Absalom.

ASK GOD TO HELP YOU ACCURATELY SEE PEOPLE AND SITUATIONS THAT ARE CLOSE TO YOU.

A PARENT'S LOVE

The king asked the Cushite, "Is the young man Absalom safe?"

The Cushite replied, "May the enemies of my lord the king and all who rise up to harm you be like that young man."

The king was shaken. He went up to the room over the gateway and wept. As he went, he said: "O my son Absalom! My son, my son Absalom! If only I had died instead of you—O Absalom, my son, my son!"

2 SAMUEL 18:32–33

"This hurts me more than it hurts you," says the parent before the child's much-deserved spanking. "I would take a bullet for any one of my kids!" "I would trade places with my child in a heartbeat."

A parent's love for a child is hard to describe—and hard to understand from the outside. Only a parent can begin to understand David's response to news of Absalom's death. Yes, Absalom had schemed against David, undermined his administration, raised an army, and led an uprising in the kingdom, yet David reacted with heartache and grief to the news of his son's death.

THE LOVE AN EARTHLY PARENT HAS FOR A CHILD IS A MERE SHADOW OF THE LOVE YOUR HEAVENLY FATHER HAS FOR YOU, HIS CHILD.

PREPARING FOR A LABOR OF LOVE

[David] called for his son Solomon. . . .

"Now, my son, the LORD *be with you, and may you have success and build the house of the* LORD *your God. . . . May the* LORD *give you discretion and understanding when he puts you in command over Israel. . . . You will have success if you are careful to observe the decrees and laws that the* LORD *gave Moses for Israel. Be strong and courageous."*

1 CHRONICLES 22:6, 11–13

You couldn't attend the wedding, but you sent a gift. You couldn't be at the graduation, so you mailed a card and a check. You weren't able to be at the event, but you wanted to participate in some way. That was David's situation.

David would not build the Lord's house, but he could support his son Solomon's efforts. So David planned big and gathered lavish materials: "a hundred thousand talents of gold, a million talents of silver, quantities of bronze and iron too great to be weighed, and wood and stone" (1 Chronicles 22:14).

Supplies were key, but another thing had to be in order: "Devote your heart and soul to seeking the LORD your God" (v. 19).

MAY OUR CHILDREN DEVOTE THEIR
HEART AND SOUL TO SEEKING YOU.
WE REJOICE, LORD, IN THE KINGDOM
TASKS YOU CALL THEM TO DO.

A GRATEFUL, GENEROUS PEOPLE

The leaders of families, the officers of the tribes of Israel, the commanders of thousands and commanders of hundreds, and the officials in charge of the king's work gave willingly. . . . The people rejoiced at the willing response of their leaders, for they had given freely and wholeheartedly to the LORD. David the king also rejoiced greatly.

1 CHRONICLES 29:6, 9

When have you experienced that it truly is "more blessed to give than to receive" (Acts 20:35)? Maybe you were able to secretly mow the lawn for a neighbor, anonymously cover the month's rent for the struggling family, sit with the lonely widow in her grief, or help design the church's new website. We honor God when we give his people our time, talent, and treasures.

The leaders of Israel honored God and inspired joy in the people when they gave generously—190 tons of gold, 380 tons of silver, 675 tons of bronze, and 3,800 tons of iron—to the temple project (1 Chronicles 29:7–8).

Is it hard to consider giving so lavishly of your treasures? One wise Christ-follower advised, "Give until it hurts—and then give until it stops hurting!"

GOD IS GLORIFIED WHEN WE GIVE HIM THE ABSOLUTE BEST OF OUR TIME, OUR TALENTS, AND OUR TREASURES.

A HUMBLE KING

"Who am I, and who are my people, that we should be able to give as generously as this? Everything comes from you, and we have given you only what comes from your hand. LORD our God, all this abundance that we have provided for building you a temple for your Holy Name comes from your hand, and all of it belongs to you."

1 CHRONICLES 29:14, 16

Think of a moment in your life when your heart overflowed with joy. In the moment, did you acknowledge the role God played in providing the reason for that joy?

David clearly understood that everything we have comes from the hand of our gracious and generous God. Any reason we have for joy—people and experiences as well as material blessings—is a gift from the Lord. This truth that God gives us everything we have can free us to share—and share generously—those gifts with other people, including God's workers in this world.

The truth that God gives us everything we have also sets us free from pride. King David knew that all his riches and all his accomplishments as warrior and ruler were gifts from his Lord. This perspective fuels gratitude and joy, and this humble attitude of a servant honors the God we serve.

MAY THE JOY GOD BLESSES YOU WITH BE YOUR STRENGTH!

GOD AS PROTECTOR, FATHER, LORD

> *The LORD is my shepherd, I lack nothing. . . .*
> *He guides me along the right paths. . . .*
> *Surely your goodness and love will follow me*
> *all the days of my life.*

PSALM 23:1, 3, 6

No step you've ever taken is outside of God's sovereign reign or beyond the reach of his redeeming love. That means he oversaw your first job (mowing lawns? babysitting?), your put-yourself-through-school job (waiting tables? tutoring?), and your current job (parenting? teaching? medicine? retail? law?). And if we were all like King David, we might have looked for what God could teach us about himself in our jobs.

David was a shepherd before he was a warrior and a king, and at least looking back, he recognized what his shepherding revealed to him about God. Those lessons have offered comfort and hope to countless people.

David's poetry paints a beautiful picture of his relationship with God—with his Protector, Father, and Lord. And that relationship is available to you as well.

LET THE LORD BE YOUR SHEPHERD.
REST IN HIS PRESENCE, PROVISION,
GUIDANCE, AND CARE.

FINAL WORDS

When the time drew near for David to die, he gave a charge to
Solomon his son. . . .

"Be strong, act like a man, and observe what the LORD *your*
God requires: Walk in obedience to him, and keep his decrees
and commands. . . . Do this so that you may prosper in all you
do and wherever you go."

1 KINGS 2:1–3

Perhaps you've sat with a loved one about to take that final breath. And perhaps you were blessed to hear words of encouragement, love, and blessing.

Here King David gave his son Solomon exactly that kind of treasure: words of encouragement, love, and blessing. This scene is also a fulfillment of a promise God had made King David: "God has provided a successor for the throne of David, a throne upon which the resurrected and victorious Jesus will one day sit."

As we wait for his return, we would do well to heed King David's words to Solomon:

BE STRONG. OBSERVE WHAT THE LORD
YOUR GOD REQUIRES: WALK IN OBEDIENCE
TO HIM, SO THAT YOU MAY PROSPER.

A TEACHABLE HEART

"LORD my God, you have made your servant king. . . . But I am only a little child and do not know how to carry out my duties. . . . So give your servant a discerning heart to govern your people and to distinguish between right and wrong. For who is able to govern this great people of yours?"

1 KINGS 3:7, 9

We don't know what we don't know. Go ahead and read that with what may be a clarification: we don't know what it is that we don't know! And that's not a great position from which to govern.

So when the Lord said to Solomon in a dream, "Ask for whatever you want me to give you" (1 Kings 3:5), the new king very wisely asked for wisdom. Undoubtedly, Solomon was well set when it came to the tangibles, to the houses, clothes, household help, and extremely healthy bank accounts that many folks might request if they were asked that question. So perhaps not so surprisingly, Solomon requested an intangible. Aware of both his responsibilities as leader of God's people and his human limitations, Solomon unselfishly asked for wisdom so that he would be a better ruler.

And, of course, God was pleased.

MAY WE, LIKE SOLOMON, ACKNOWLEDGE HOW LITTLE WE KNOW AND ASK GOD FOR WISDOM.

WISDOM TO JUDGE

The king said, "Bring me a sword. . . . Cut the living child in two and give half to one and half to the other."

The woman whose son was alive was deeply moved out of love for her son and said to the king, "Please, my lord, give her the living baby! Don't kill him!"

But the other said, "Neither I nor you shall have him. Cut him in two!"

Then the king gave his ruling: "Give the living baby to the first woman. . . . She is his mother."

1 KINGS 3:24–27

Think about the toughest decision you've ever had to make. Even the most difficult probably didn't involve literal life or death.

When he faced one tough decision in particular, when two mothers each claimed the same child as her own, Solomon did bring up the matter of life and death. When Solomon wisely called for a sword, suddenly the case was easy to solve. Of course the child's mother would rather have her son raised by another than killed!

The nation "held the king in awe, because they saw that he had wisdom from God to administer justice" (1 Kings 3:28).

ASK THE LORD TO FILL THE LEADERS OF
YOUR NATION WITH GODLY WISDOM.

THE VALUE OF WISDOM

The proverbs of Solomon son of David, king of Israel:
for gaining wisdom and instruction;
for understanding words of insight;
for receiving instruction in prudent behavior,
doing what is right and just and fair;
for giving prudence to those who are simple.

PROVERBS 1:1–4

Do a quick Google search of "quotes about wisdom," and in 0.29 seconds about 58,000,000 results will appear on the screen. That's a lot of people thinking about, commenting on, and praising the value of wisdom—but those activities are very different from actually pursuing wisdom and living wisely.

King Solomon, however, wanted wisdom to be lived out. He wanted these thoughts he shared to help us gain wisdom for everyday life. Worth noticing is the wise king's starting point: "the fear of the LORD" (Proverbs 1:7). Pondering what that phrase means can be a step toward wisdom. When we choose to ground ourselves in a 24/7 awareness of our God and to live in a way that both blesses others and gives glory to him, we are putting ourselves in a position of being able to receive the wisdom that "the LORD gives" (2:6).

TEACH ME TO FEAR YOU, LORD, SO THAT
I WILL BOTH HEAR AND LIVE ACCORDING
TO THE WISDOM YOU LONG TO GIVE ME.

Trust in the LORD with all your heart
and lean not on your own understanding;
in all your ways submit to him,
and he will make your paths straight. . . .
The LORD disciplines those he loves,
as a father the son he delights in. . . .
There is no wisdom, no insight, no plan
that can succeed against the LORD.

PROVERBS 3:5–6, 12; 21:30

Wisdom often comes from personal experience: a person gains knowledge from experience and applies that lesson to future experiences. Think about these wisdom-applied-to-life experiences:

- When has trusting "in the LORD with all your heart" proven wise?
- When has leaning "not on your own understanding" proven to be prudent?
- When have you wisely chosen to receive the Lord's discipline as love and be blessed by what he wanted to teach you?

LIVING ACCORDING TO GOD'S WISDOM WILL
MEAN GREATER JOY, HOPE, AND PEACE.

Sluggards do not plow in season;
so at harvest time they look but find nothing. . . .
Do not love sleep or you will grow poor;
stay awake and you will have food to spare. . . .
Food gained by fraud tastes sweet,
but one ends up with a mouth full of gravel. . . .
A fortune made by a lying tongue
is a fleeting vapor and a deadly snare.

PROVERBS 20:4, 13, 17; 21:6

Have you somewhat to do tomorrow, do it today . . . Up, sluggard, and waste not life; in the grave will be sleep enough. Sloth (like Rust) consumes faster than Labour wears, while the key is always bright. No gains without pains. Poor Richard (a.k.a. Benjamin Franklin) shared these thoughts on work in his almanac, published from 1732 to 1758, and King Solomon addressed this same theme in the tenth century BC. Apparently human nature hasn't changed much!

Perhaps the key to living wisely is this: live your life for your audience of One. Do all that you do with the goal of honoring and pleasing God. Then being a sluggard or a fraud or a liar won't even be issues.

"WHATEVER YOU DO, WORK AT IT WITH ALL YOUR HEART, AS WORKING FOR THE LORD." (COLOSSIANS 3:23)

MORE WISDOM FOR REAL LIFE

"So give orders that cedars of Lebanon be cut for me. My men will work with yours, and I will pay you for your men whatever wages you set. You know that we have no one so skilled in felling timber as the Sidonians."

When Hiram heard Solomon's message, he . . . said, "Praise be to the LORD today, for he has given David a wise son to rule over this great nation."

1 KINGS 5:6–7

D o you have a knack for bargaining at a garage sale? Maybe, like Solomon, you are gifted with the ability to negotiate a good deal.

And because his father's military success had secured Israel's borders, King Solomon could focus on diplomacy, architecture, and temple construction. Solomon, for instance, approached Hiram, king of Tyre, and requested cedars for construction of the temple in exchange for 3,600 tons of wheat and 120,000 gallons of olive oil each year. The result was peace between Hiram and Solomon.

Clearly, Solomon made wise use of his God-given wisdom.

EXERCISING OUR GOD-GIVEN
WISDOM IN OUR WORK LIFE AS WELL
AS OUR DAILY LIFE CAN GIVE HIM
GLORY AND BRING US BLESSING.

A HOME FOR THE ALMIGHTY

The singers raised their voices in praise to the LORD and sang:
  "He is good; his love endures forever."
  Then the temple of the LORD was filled with the cloud . . . for
the glory of the LORD filled the temple of God.

2 CHRONICLES 5:13–14

Maybe you've seen St. Paul's Cathedral in London, the Taj Mahal in Agra, or the pyramids in Egypt. Human creativity and hard work are evident in the world's breathtaking architectural accomplishments.

Solomon's temple was every bit as remarkable as any of these, if not more so. Two bronze pillars led to the portico, and the Most Holy Place was overlaid in gold. Construction took seven years as 180,000 conscripted laborers worked for nearly 4,000 supervisors. King Solomon brought in the silver and gold that David had dedicated for that purpose.

And then, making the spectacular even more spectacular, "the glory of the LORD filled the temple of God." The Holy One took up residency in the home David had long wanted the Lord to have.

"I REJOICED WITH THOSE WHO SAID
TO ME, 'LET US GO TO THE HOUSE
OF THE LORD.'" (PSALM 122:1)

GOD'S GRACIOUS CONDESCENSION

"But will God really dwell on earth? The heavens, even the highest heaven, cannot contain you. How much less this temple I have built!"

1 KINGS 8:27

The immeasurable distance between God and human beings has been compared to the vast difference between human beings and ants. Despite this gap in intellect, power, and essence between the divine and the human, God entered our world simply because he loves us. Can you imagine caring that much about the planet's ant population, much less an individual ant?

As he saw the glory of the Lord fill the temple, Solomon knew that God had drawn near to his chosen people, Israel, and Solomon sang his praise (1 Kings 8:23–24). Then Solomon instructed his people: "May your hearts be fully committed to the LORD . . . to live by his decrees and obey his commands" (v. 61). Such is an appropriate response to God's gracious condescension.

MAY WE NEVER BECOME NUMB
TO THE INCREDIBLE TRUTH OF
EMMANUEL—"GOD WITH US"!

THE FIERY GLORY OF GOD

When Solomon finished praying, fire came down from heaven and consumed the burnt offering and the sacrifices, and the glory of the LORD filled the temple. . . . When all the Israelites saw the fire coming down and the glory of the LORD . . . they worshiped and gave thanks to the LORD.

2 CHRONICLES 7:1, 3

It is wise to respect fire. Confined to a birthday candle, fire is none too intimidating. But when a bonfire turns a pristine marshmallow into an ashy, sticky mess, we are reminded how quickly fire the friend can become fire the foe. And summertime news footage of wildfires that take lives and destroy homes hauntingly reminds us of fire's power.

At the dedication of Solomon's temple, "fire came down from heaven," and God's glory filled the place. And our glorious God is no more containable than fire. We find him unpredictable as he choreographs the unfolding of his good and perfect will. God is also a holy fire whose presence purges us of our sin. And he is a fire that guides and warms us as we travel through this fallen world. God's fire, though, will always be friend to those who call his Son "Lord."

WORSHIP THE LORD GOD'S
FIERY AND HOLY BEAUTY.

THE COST OF WORSHIP

Then the king and all the people offered sacrifices before the LORD.
And King Solomon offered a sacrifice of twenty-two thousand head
of cattle and a hundred and twenty thousand sheep and goats. So
the king and all the people dedicated the temple of God.

2 CHRONICLES 7:4–5

What does it cost you to worship? Believers in certain parts of the world risk their lives to gather in Jesus' name. Other believers work hard and save carefully in order to finally own the New Testament in their language. (How many Bibles do you have in your house?) Still other believers worry about missing the first half of a football game on Sunday morning. (Recording it is just not the same!)

Consider the cost of Solomon's worship. When he dedicated the temple, he sacrificed 22,000 head of cattle and 120,000 sheep and goats. And sacrificing an animal was not as simple as dropping a check into the offering plate. The temple workers would have worked hard to slay 142,000 cattle, sheep, and goats.

Clearly, worship cost God's people. It cost not just valuable animals but time and effort as well. But anything worth doing—and worshiping God is definitely worth doing—costs.

WHAT WE ARE WILLING TO SACRIFICE
IN ORDER TO WORSHIP GOD REVEALS
MUCH ABOUT OUR HEARTS.

DAY 161
WARNING!

"If you turn away and forsake the decrees and commands I have given you and go off to serve other gods and worship them, then I will uproot Israel from my land."

2 CHRONICLES 7:19–20

One relentless aspect of parenting is the necessary repetition of certain instructions: "Try everything on your plate"; "No TV until after all your homework is done"; "No cell phones at the dinner table"; "Did you put gas in Dad's car after you drove it?" Our heavenly Father also knows the need to repeat himself for his children, and he graciously does so.

Many times, for instance, the Lord has reminded us, "Obey my commands. Don't chase after other gods. Walk faithfully before me, and I will bless you. If you follow your own desires, live according to your own rules, make something, someone, or *yourself* more important than me, I will bring disaster upon you rather than blessings."

We need to hear this message from the Lord. After all, as the classic hymn puts it, our hearts *are* prone to wandering. We also need to learn from the Lord's delivery: may we extend to others the kind of patience and grace he extends to us.

WE LEARN FROM THE LORD'S
WORDS OF INSTRUCTION AS WELL
AS HIS WAYS OF GRACE.

A NOBLE REPUTATION

"In wisdom and wealth you have far exceeded the report I heard. How happy your people must be! . . . Praise be to the LORD your God, who has delighted in you and placed you on the throne of Israel. . . . to maintain justice and righteousness."

1 KINGS 10:7–9

What's the MPG on that vehicle?" "Is he serving constituency or self? Reputations—of cars, and politicians, for instance—tend to be based on performance.

But consider Solomon's reputation. Interestingly, "the queen of Sheba heard about the fame of Solomon and his relationship to the LORD" (1 Kings 10:1). Did you see that? She had heard about Solomon's relationship to the Lord. What an amazing reputation to have!

The queen also understood that the Lord himself had made Solomon king (v. 9). She knew, too, of his wisdom and arrived with many questions for him, and Solomon answered every one. She had heard of his wisdom, his achievements, and undoubtedly his wealth. But rich in her own right, she wasn't interested in the stuff as much as the person. Curiosity about this wise ruler may have prompted her journey, but before she left to return home, she was praising the God whose reputation was intertwined with Solomon's.

MAY OUR REPUTATION ENHANCE
THE LORD'S REPUTATION.

SOLOMON'S FOOLISHNESS

King Solomon . . . loved many foreign women . . . Moabites,
Ammonites, Edomites, Sidonians and Hittites. They were from
nations about which the LORD had told the Israelites, "You must
not intermarry with them, because they will surely turn your hearts
after their gods." Nevertheless, Solomon held fast to them in love.

1 KINGS 11:1–2

It's been said that the Bible is not a kids' book. (Can you say "Bathsheba"?) In fact, certain aspects sound like a twenty-first-century reality TV series. Certain aspects like Solomon's love life.

In Solomon's day, polygamy was considered normal in the culture; it did not, however, have God's blessing. Solomon had a large harem: "seven hundred wives . . . and three hundred concubines" (1 Kings 11:3). And just as God had warned, Solomon's wives from other nations "turned his heart after other gods, and his heart was not fully devoted to the LORD" (v. 4). These foreign wives led Solomon to relax his guard against pagan worship. Not a wise decision by a fellow known for his wisdom.

Solomon was vigilant against idol worship early on, but he failed to maintain that vigilance. On this matter of idolatry, wise Solomon failed to have wisdom for himself. May we learn from his missteps.

LORD, KEEP OUR HEARTS LOYAL
AND OUR EYES FIXED ON YOU.

A FATHER'S WRATH

Solomon did evil in the eyes of the LORD; he did not follow
the LORD completely. . . . The LORD became angry with
Solomon because his heart had turned away from the LORD.

1 KINGS 11:6, 9

A toddler's time-out. A teenager's curfew. The lost privilege of computer games. A revoked driver's license. As we get older, our disobedience can result in greater harm and longer-lasting consequences. Underage drinking can result in a DUI and loss of life, and many people can pay the price of that driver's disobedience.

Similarly, Solomon's disobedience—his sinful turning away from God—cost many people dearly. Solomon followed his rebellious heart, broke the covenant with God, and disobeyed the Lord's commands. These serious crimes called for severe consequences: God took the kingdom away from Solomon, causing Solomon's sin to have a ripple effect throughout the chosen people of Israel for generations, right up to the present day. Clearly and ironically, as Solomon himself observed, "The LORD disciplines those he loves, as a father the son he delights in" (Proverbs 3:12).

IF WE CHOOSE TO DISOBEY
GOD'S COMMANDS, WE MAY FIND
OURSELVES FACING CONSEQUENCES
WE CANNOT IGNORE.

JUDGMENT AND MERCY

The LORD said to Solomon, "Since . . . you have not kept
my covenant and my decrees . . . I will most certainly tear the
kingdom away from you. . . . For the sake of David your father,
I will not do it during your lifetime. I will tear it out of the hand of
your son. . . . but will give him one tribe for the sake of David my
servant."

1 KINGS 11:11–13

W e've all done it. We start a new year with great goals to eat
better, exercise regularly, read a book a month, memorize
a verse of Scripture each week . . . and usually our resolve has dis-
solved long before the groundhog checks for its shadow.

And wise King Solomon was no exception. He was unable to
keep his earlier pledge to follow God and obey his commands.

Yet the Lord kept his pledge to "establish the throne of
[Solomon's] kingdom forever." But God had also promised this:
"When he does wrong, I will punish him with a rod wielded by men"
(2 Samuel 7:13–14)—and Solomon had done wrong.

Judgment: Solomon's son would rule over only a single tribe.
Mercy: the Lord would wait until after Solomon's death to enforce
that judgment.

PRAISE GOD WHO JUDGES FAIRLY
AND EXTENDS MERCY.

CONSIDER THE SOURCE

Rejecting the advice given him by the elders, [King Rehoboam]
followed the advice of the young men and said, "My father
made your yoke heavy; I will make it even heavier. My father
scourged you with whips; I will scourge you with scorpions." So
the king did not listen to the people.

1 KINGS 12:13–15

Wikipedia or *Encyclopedia Britannica*? The *National Enquirer* or the *Wall Street Journal*? Consider the source! Be aware of both the source's knowledge and motive.

After Solomon died, his son Rehoboam assumed the throne. Much of the population had resented Solomon's heavy taxation and conscripted labor for his grand projects, and they let their complaints be known. The new king asked for three days to consider their position.

Rehoboam first consulted the elders who had served Solomon. They advised, "If today you . . . give them a favorable answer, they will always be your servants" (1 Kings 12:7). Not liking this advice, Rehoboam went to the young men he had grown up with. Their unwise input was very different, and theirs was the input he followed.

CHOOSE COUNSELORS WISELY: CONSIDER
THEIR LIFE EXPERIENCE, KNOWLEDGE,
HISTORY WITH THE LORD, AND MOTIVES.

CORPORATE AMNESIA

Jeroboam thought . . . "If these people go up to offer sacrifices . . . in Jerusalem, they will again give their allegiance to . . . Rehoboam. . . ."

After seeking advice, the king made two golden calves. He said to the people . . . "Here are your gods, Israel, who brought you up out of Egypt."

1 KINGS 12:26–28

Certain experiences in life are important for us to remember, and we help ourselves remember when we retell the story. Apparently, the people Jeroboam ruled hadn't reviewed often enough the account of God's appearance at Mount Sinai—and of his anger.

As Rehoboam ruled the tribes of Judah and Benjamin in the south, Jeroboam ruled over the remaining tribes in the north. Already divided in worship practices, the nation was now also divided in politics, in priesthood, in security, and in safety. And Jeroboam wanted it divided.

So Jeroboam made two golden calves that he presented as the "gods who brought you up out of Egypt." And that didn't remind anyone about God's anger and his sentencing that generation to forty years in the wilderness and banning them from the promised land?

LORD, PLEASE REINFORCE MY FAITH
BY HELPING ME REMEMBER SPECIFIC
INSTANCES OF YOUR FAITHFULNESS TO ME.

A SLOW LEARNER

[Jeroboam] stretched out his hand . . . and said, "Seize him!" But the hand he stretched out . . . shriveled up, so that he could not pull it back. . . .

Then the king said to the man of God, "Intercede with the LORD your God and pray for me that my hand may be restored." So the man of God interceded with the LORD, and the king's hand was restored.

1 KINGS 13:4, 6, 33

Some people are slow learners, and maybe all of us are slow to learn one thing or another: maybe algebra or Spanish verbs or the importance of following the Lord.

King Jeroboam appeared to be slow to learn about the power of God. As he stood at the altar making sacrifices to his golden calves, a man of God began denouncing the pagan worship. Crying, "Seize him!" Jeroboam pointed at the man. Not only did his hand shrivel up, but "the altar was split apart and its ashes poured out" (1 Kings 13:5).

Graciously, the man of God healed Jeroboam's hand, but still he "did not change his evil ways" (v. 33). Jeroboam was slow to learn that the Lord is serious when he forbids idolatry.

TWENTY-FIRST CENTURY IDOLS ARE MORE SUBTLE THAN A GOLDEN CALF, BUT JUST AS DEADLY TO ONE'S RELATIONSHIP TO THE HOLY GOD.

"You have done more evil than all who lived before you. You have made for yourself . . . idols of metal; you have aroused my anger and turned your back on me. Because of this . . . I will burn up the house of Jeroboam as one burns dung, until it is all gone. . . . The LORD has spoken!"

1 KINGS 14:9–11

W ho's on first. What's on second. I Don't Know is on third . . ." The clever humor of this famous Abbott and Costello sketch is timeless. In this section of 1 Kings, we don't have the humor, but we do have the potential confusion.

Both Rehoboam and Jeroboam had a son named Abijah. Jeroboam's son died; Rehoboam's son became king after Rehoboam died. And there was a prophet named Ahijah in Rehoboam's court.

Jeroboam's son Abijah was sick, so he sent his wife to Ahijah, the prophet, to find out what would happen to the boy. Prompted by the Lord, Ahijah greeted the disguised woman with, "Come in, wife of Jeroboam" (1 Kings 14:6), then boldly proclaimed the Lord's anger at Jeroboam for the evil he had done, announced that the boy would die, and explained that the line of Jeroboam would end because of his sin.

> SIN IMPACTS THE SINNER. IT CAN ALSO IMPACT GENERATIONS TO COME AND EVEN ENTIRE NATIONS.

EVIL IN THE SOUTH AS WELL

Judah did evil in the eyes of the LORD. By the sins they committed they stirred up his jealous anger more than those who were before them had done.

1 KINGS 14:22

When relationships end, we may use the term *breaking up*. But one insightful person has observed that people don't *break*; people *tear*. *Breaking* suggests clean, quick, and painless; *tearing*, however, suggests a lot of pain and a slower process. And *tear* was the word the Lord spoke to Solomon: "I will most certainly tear the kingdom away from you" (1 Kings 11:11). People in both parts of the kingdom broke God's heart by turning to idols. And these brothers not only turned away from God, but they turned on each other: "There was continual warfare between Rehoboam and Jeroboam" during their lifetimes (14:30). After Rehoboam died, "there was war between [his son] Abijah and Jeroboam throughout Abijah's lifetime" (15:6).

The Middle Ages' bubonic plague was nothing compared to the spiritual plague of God's kingdom once it had been torn in two.

WE PROTECT OURSELVES FROM SPIRITUAL
PLAGUE WHEN WE MAKE IT A PRIORITY
TO SPEND TIME WITH JESUS.

ISRAEL'S PATTERN, OUR PATTERN

Asa did what was right in the eyes of the LORD, as his father David had done. He . . . got rid of all the idols his ancestors had made. . . . Although he did not remove the high places, Asa's heart was fully committed to the LORD all his life.

1 KINGS 15:11–12, 14

Patterns of behavior reveal a lot about a person—or a people. Historical distance helps us see, for instance, the bad-out-weighing-the-good pattern of Israel's cycle of turning away from God, crying out for help, being delivered, and following God once again—until, for whatever reasons, they turned away.

Most kings who reigned in the divided kingdom did evil. Only a few rid the kingdom of idolatry.

And yes, the Lord had clearly warned them: obey his commands and know his blessing; rebel and know his displeasure. We can shake our heads over Israel not getting this, yet if we are honest, we just might see the same pattern in our own lives. We follow Jesus and know the blessing not of an easy life necessarily, but of a fulfilled one. When we go our own way, we can experience emptiness, purposelessness, and pain that we could have avoided. Why do we ever turn away?

LORD, TRANSFORM MY HEART, THAT I WILL FIND IT EASIER TO OBEY YOU.

ONCE UPON A TIME

Elijah . . . said to Ahab, "As the LORD, the God of Israel, lives,
whom I serve, there will be neither dew nor rain in the next few
years except at my word." . . .

[Elijah] did what the LORD had told him. He went to the
Kerith Ravine. . . . The ravens brought him bread and meat in
the morning and bread and meat in the evening, and he drank
from the brook.

1 KINGS 17:1, 5–6

"O nce upon a time" triggers the expectation of "happily ever
after." "There will be neither dew nor rain." The prophet
Elijah's message from God to evil King Ahab may not set up any
specific expectations, but a great story follows.

God, our Hero with a capital *H*, instructed Elijah, our lowercase
h hero, to go to Kerith Ravine where ravens would take him food and
God would preserve water in a brook for Elijah to drink. And we can
only imagine what transpired between the prophet and his God during the three years before he once again paid a visit to Ahab.

And Ahab was less than thrilled. Elijah didn't hold back: "You
have abandoned the LORD's commands" (1 Kings 18:18). Then Elijah
issued a challenge: "Have your almost one thousand false prophets
meet me on Mount Carmel—and call all of Israel as witnesses."

GOD'S WORD TELLS OF EVENTS MORE
REMARKABLE THAN WE COULD IMAGINE.

SHOWDOWN

> *Get two bulls for us. Let Baal's prophets choose one . . . and let*
> *them cut it into pieces and put it on the wood but not set fire to it.*
> *I will prepare the other bull and put it on the wood but not set fire*
> *to it. Then you call on the name of your god, and I will call on the*
> *name of the LORD. The god who answers by fire—he is God.*

1 KINGS 18:23–24

Hard evidence can help decision making. Which shoes? Try on a few pairs. Which car? Take a test drive. Which God? Elijah was after hard evidence for that decision.

In one corner, we have Elijah, "the only one of the LORD's prophets left" (1 Kings 18:22), and in the other, four hundred and fifty prophets of Baal and four hundred prophets of Asherah. And Elijah was pumped for the competition. "How long will you waver? . . . If the LORD is God, follow him; but if Baal is God, follow him" (v. 21).

Then Elijah got specific about this head-to-head confrontation. Each team—the prophets of Baal versus Elijah and God—would prepare a bull for sacrifice and then call on their god to send down fire to burn the offering. The prophets of Baal would go first.

Would this hard evidence—fire from heaven or its absence— compel the people of Israel to return to the one true God?

BE MINDFUL OF THE HARD EVIDENCE
OF HIS LOVE GOD HAS SHOWN YOU.

THE FRENZY OF IDOLATRY

*Then [false prophets] called on the name of Baal from morning
till noon. "Baal, answer us!" they shouted. But there was no
response; no one answered. And they danced around the altar
they had made.*

*At noon Elijah began to taunt them. . . . So they shouted
louder and slashed themselves with swords and spears . . . until
their blood flowed.*

1 KINGS 18:26–28

The rituals of another faith may not make much sense to an
outsider looking in. Consider the followers of Baal. Shouting
for their god was not too strange. And dancing around the altar was
not too unusual. But then came Elijah's taunts: "Perhaps [your god]
is deep in thought, or busy, or traveling. Maybe he is sleeping and
must be awakened" (1 Kings 18:27). This mockery prompted louder
shouts as these prophets of Baal "slashed themselves with swords
and spears . . . until their blood flowed." What does that behavior
suggest about the kind of god they worshiped, a god who would—by
his slow response—encourage such a frenzy?

From morning until evening—with the shouting getting louder,
the dancing more frantic—still "there was no response, no one
answered, no one paid attention" (v. 29). Now it was Elijah's turn.

WHAT THE DEMANDS OF FALSE GODS
REVEAL ABOUT THEMSELVES IS TERRIFYING.

NO DOUBT

> *The fire of the LORD fell and burned up the sacrifice, the wood, the stones and the soil, and also licked up the water in the trench.*
>
> *When all the people saw this, they fell prostrate and cried, "The LORD—he is God! The LORD—he is God!"*

1 KINGS 18:38–39

In June 2013, tightrope walker Nik Wallenda tried to cross the Grand Canyon—and succeeded. As suspenseful as that event was, it was neither as suspenseful or significant as the competition between Baal and the God of Israel.

The prophets of Baal had accepted Elijah's challenge, but despite their shouting, dancing, and bleeding, their god did not send down flames. Now it was Elijah's turn, and he upped the level of difficulty by pouring water on the wood and the offering as well as in the trench he had dug around his stone altar. Then Elijah simply and confidently prayed, "LORD . . . let it be known today that you are God in Israel" (1 Kings 18:36).

No sooner had Elijah finished praying than "the fire of the LORD fell and burned up the sacrifice, the wood, the stones and the soil, and also licked up the water in the trench."

IN LIFE'S SUSPENSEFUL MOMENTS, REMEMBER THE FAITHFULNESS OF YOUR ALWAYS-LISTENING GOD.

GOD'S AUTHORITY AND POWER

Elijah commanded [the people], "Seize the prophets of Baal.
Don't let anyone get away!" They seized them, and Elijah had
them brought down to the Kishon Valley and slaughtered there.

1 KINGS 18:40

Sometimes instructions sound brutal—until you understand their purpose. God's command to destroy the residents of the promised land sounds brutal—and it was brutal . . . for a very important reason. The need was to wipe out the evil influence of the pagan cultures that would draw the children of Israel away from their devotion to the one true God. That was Elijah's motive when, after the showdown between Baal and the Lord, he had all the prophets of Baal slaughtered. Elijah acted in God's authority to protect the chosen people.

Then, not too long after this demonstration of the Lord's authority, came a demonstration of his power. The three-and-a-half-year drought ended. At last, God sent long-awaited rain to the parched land.

What evil influence or sinful habit is God calling you to wipe out of your life? In what current situation do you long to see a demonstration of his power?

HONOR GOD'S CALL TO GET RID OF SIN
AND TRUST IN HIS POWER TO BRING LIFE
TO THE PARCHED PLACES IN YOUR SOUL.

YES, BUT . . .

Ahab told Jezebel everything Elijah had done and how he had killed all the prophets with the sword. So Jezebel sent a messenger to Elijah to say, "May the gods deal with me, be it ever so severely, if by this time tomorrow I do not make your life like that of one of them."

1 KINGS 19:1–2

Yes, God helped us make the mortgage payment last month, *but* . . . Yes, God protected me when I was driving in the blinding snowstorm, *but* . . . Not much time has to elapse after a great faith-building experience before we are wondering about whether God will be faithful *this* time!

What a spectacular faith-building experience it must have been at Mount Carmel, seeing God rain down fire that "burned up the sacrifice, the wood, the stones and the soil, and also licked up the water in the trench" during Elijah's showdown with the prophets of Baal (1 Kings 18:38). The evil queen Jezebel was infuriated that Elijah had killed all the prophets. She wanted that troublemaking man dead and gone. When Elijah heard her threat, he ran for his life. Yes, the living God had crushed the prophets of Baal, *but* . . .

But, Elijah may have wondered, *will God come through again and protect me from Jezebel and her hit men?*

ONLY ANOTHER STEP OF FAITH WILL
RESOLVE OUR "YES, BUT" MOMENTS.

"I HAVE HAD ENOUGH, Lord"

[Elijah] came to a broom bush, sat down under it and prayed that he might die. "I have had enough, Lord," he said. "Take my life. . . ." Then he lay down under the bush and fell asleep.

All at once an angel touched him and said, "Get up and eat." He looked around and there by his head was some bread baked over hot coals, and a jar of water. He ate and drank.

1 KINGS 19:4–6

'I've had enough!" Think about the circumstances that last prompted you to feel that way. And think about this: How tired were you?

Fleeing for his life, Elijah could hardly be calm or carefree. Outnumbered by any force Jezebel would send, he couldn't stop and rest. Yet exhaustion overcame him, and he slept—until an angel awakened him and fed him. And then he slept again. The angel again woke Elijah and fed him. Then we read, "strengthened by that food, he traveled forty days and forty nights until he reached Horeb, the mountain of God" (1 Kings 19:8).

When we're at our breaking point, sometimes simple food can help us—physical food and/or spiritual food. The angel provided Elijah with physical food after his strenuous showdown and escape. Now Elijah was ready for the forty-day journey.

WHEN YOU'VE HAD ENOUGH, FEED
YOUR SOUL AS WELL AS YOUR BODY.

ARE YOU LISTENING?

*A great and powerful wind tore the mountains apart and
shattered the rocks before the LORD, but the LORD was not in the
wind. After the wind there was an earthquake, but the LORD was
not in the earthquake. After the earthquake came a fire, but
the LORD was not in the fire. And after the fire came a gentle
whisper. . . . Elijah heard it.*

1 KINGS 19:11–13

If you've raised kids, you undoubtedly know that toddlers and
teens and kids in between can *hear* an adult voice ("Waaa-waaaa-
waaa-waaaaaa-waa") but not *listen* (translation: "We need to leave
in ten minutes. Are you ready to go?"). A related phenomenon is
selective listening. Kids hear "Waaa-waaaa-waaa-waaaaaa-waa"
when the topic is getting ready for bed, but they hear the words very
clearly when the topic is going out for frozen yogurt. Are we—God's
kids—any different?

Let's see how Elijah did. He endured a powerful wind but heard
nothing. He survived an earthquake and fire but heard nothing.
The Almighty had made his presence known in three big ways, but
he used "a gentle whisper" to make a heart connection with his
faithful servant.

God often speaks to his children in a "gentle whisper." May we
be listening—and not selectively.

BE LISTENING WITH ALL YOUR HEART.

[Elisha] took his yoke of oxen and slaughtered them. He burned the plowing equipment to cook the meat and gave it to the people, and they ate. Then he set out to follow Elijah and became his servant.

1 KINGS 19:21

Some things in life are easier if they don't happen gradually. For instance, if the swimming pool water seems cold, don't try to get used to it a toe at a time. It's much easier if you jump in and get all wet all at once.

When, in obedience to God, Elijah threw his cloak around Elisha, signifying that he would be the next of God's prophets, Elisha showed himself to be all in. This was the scene: When Elijah arrived, Elisha was hard at work "plowing with twelve yoke of oxen" (1 Kings 19:19), a detail that suggests he was hardly poor. Responding to what he understood Elijah's action to mean, Elisha "took his yoke of oxen and slaughtered them. He burned the plowing equipment to cook the meat." Having used his plow as firewood, and having fed the people the barbecued oxen that had been key to his now-former livelihood, Elisha was all in as Elijah's servant—as God's servant.

WHAT, IF ANYTHING, IS KEEPING YOU FROM BEING ALL IN AS GOD'S SERVANT? ASK HIM. HE WILL NOT ONLY SHOW YOU, BUT HE WILL HELP YOU ESCAPE ITS HOLD ON YOU.

As they were walking along and talking together, suddenly a chariot of fire and horses of fire appeared and separated the two of them, and Elijah went up to heaven in a whirlwind. Elisha saw this and cried out, "My father! My father! The chariots and horsemen of Israel!" And Elisha saw him no more.

2 KINGS 2:11–12

It's pretty hard to grasp that no two people among the more than seven billion (7,000,000,000) on this planet have the same fingerprints. It's also pretty hard to grasp the fact that the God who keeps the planets in order (and we're just talking about *this* solar system) knows you by name—and, in fact, knew you even before you were born (Psalm 139:13).

This God knows you personally, and he loves you as an individual, not as a member of the human race or of a particular nationality, ethnicity, denomination, or congregation. He extends love and common grace to all his children; he blesses every human being with the beauty of this earth. And this God, who knows each of us intimately, treats each of us uniquely. No one else has ever ridden a chariot of fire into heaven, but that was God's plan for Elijah. And God has a unique plan for you.

GOD, MAY I LIVE IN EAGER ANTICIPATION
OF THE PLANS YOU HAVE FOR ME.

ELIJAH'S CLOAK

Elisha then picked up Elijah's cloak . . . and went back and stood on the bank of the Jordan. He took the cloak . . . and struck the water with it. [The water] divided to the right and to the left, and he crossed over.

The company of the prophets from Jericho, who were watching, said, "The spirit of Elijah is resting on Elisha."

2 KINGS 2:13–15

What is the most Christlike act of love you have ever been blessed to witness? Was it the young woman who spent her life caring for her new husband who contracted polio and spent the three decades of their marriage in an iron lung? Was it the wife who gave a kidney to her husband when she was a better match than either of their sons?

Our actions reveal more than our words do about the person each of us is at the very core of our being. In fact, renowned UCLA basketball coach John Wooden said, "The true test of a man's character is what he does when no one is watching." Often people are watching, though, and it is very sobering to realize that—as one wise person put it—your life may be the only Bible some folks ever read. And God can help that be a good read!

MAY WE LIVE GOD'S LOVE SO THAT PEOPLE
SEE THAT HIS SPIRIT IS RESTING ON US.

JOY AND TRAGEDY

The child grew, and one day he went out to his father, who was with the reapers. He said to his father, "My head! My head!"

His father told a servant, "Carry him to his mother." After the servant had lifted him up and carried him to his mother, the boy sat on her lap until noon, and then he died.

2 KINGS 4:18–20

What is your reflex action when something horrible happens? Worry? Rage? A mad search for help? Maybe you call friends for advice. Or maybe you go to the Lord in prayer.

This woman was a friend of the prophet Elisha. She and her husband had set aside a bedroom for this itinerant prophet who had been named to carry on Elijah's work. Clearly, God's power was on Elisha. He purified a spring to provide water for an entire town. He supplied a poor widow with a bottomless jar of oil. And he prophesied that this childless friend would have a son—and she did. But now the son was dead. Clearly, Elisha's God was one of unspeakable power.

In the face of death, this heartbroken mother had no earthly source of help. What advice could any friend give her at this point? She knew she had to go to the man of God.

WHEN TRAGEDY STRIKES, GO TO MEN AND WOMEN OF GOD TO RECEIVE THEIR PRAYER SUPPORT AND LOVE.

RESURRECTION JOY

When Elisha reached the house, there was the boy lying
dead. . . . He went in, shut the door . . . and prayed to the
LORD. Then he got on the bed and lay on the boy. . . . As
he stretched himself out on him, the boy's body grew warm.
Elisha turned away and walked back and forth in the room and
then . . . stretched out on him once more. The boy sneezed seven
times and opened his eyes.

2 KINGS 4:32–35

Good-natured teasing can be great fun and even build bridges between people. But sometimes teasing can be downright cruel and can destroy relationships.

Teasing can also raise expectations that, when not fulfilled, will mean even greater disappointment. That's why Elisha's childless friend immediately objected when he said, "About this time next year . . . you will hold a son in your arms" (2 Kings 4:16–17). She did not want to be teased about such a tender topic.

The teasing, however, was actually prophecy: she had a son. But then, when he was only a boy, he died. Feeling like her short time with her son was a cruel tease, this mother was heartbroken and angry—but she was soon blessed with resurrection joy!

IT'S ACCEPTABLE AND WISE AND HEALTHY
TO TELL GOD YOU ARE ANGRY WITH
HIM! HE ALREADY KNOWS YOU ARE.

HEAVEN'S ARMY

An army with horses and chariots had surrounded the city. "Oh no, my lord! What shall we do?" the servant asked.

"Don't be afraid," the prophet answered. "Those who are with us are more than those who are with them."

And Elisha prayed, "Open his eyes, LORD." . . . [The servant] looked and saw the hills full of horses and chariots of fire all around Elisha.

2 KINGS 6:15–17

It's a well-known optical illusion—but what is it a picture of? A vase—or the side profile of two women facing each other? We don't always see clearly things right in front of us. How much harder to see the unseen!

The apostle Paul was aware of the unseen: "Our struggle is . . . against . . . the spiritual forces of evil in the heavenly realms" (Ephesians 6:12). Elisha was also aware of the unseen, and he asked God to help his servant see it. And God showed Elisha and his servant that fighting for God's people were—to paraphrase Paul—the spiritual forces of good in the heavenly realms.

We may not be privileged to ever see God's army on the hills, but they are fighting in those heavenly realms for the good of God's people and his glory.

BE COMFORTED. TO QUOTE DAVID, "THE BATTLE IS THE LORD'S!" (1 SAMUEL 17:47)

A BETTER STRATEGY

When the king of Israel saw them, he asked Elisha, "Shall I kill them, my father? Shall I kill them?"

"Do not kill them," he answered. . . . "Set food and water before them so that they may eat and drink." . . . So he prepared a great feast for them, and after they had finished eating and drinking, he sent them away, and they returned to their master. So the bands from Aram stopped raiding Israel's territory.

2 KINGS 6:21–23

Have you played the game Battleship? The goal is to figure out where on the grid the ships in your opponent's fleet are located and sink them.

Battleship and war require a strategy. Elisha's strategy against the army of Aram was unique. With the enemy army fast approaching, Elisha asked the Lord to blind the soldiers—and God did. Then, although the now-blind soldiers were in search of Elisha, the prophet was able to serve as tour guide. Elisha took them to Samaria, and when they arrived, Elisha asked God to enable them to see—and they saw they were in enemy territory.

The king of Israel then consulted Elisha, whose plan was unexpected: "Feed them." And the results were probably just as unexpected: "The bands from Aram stopped raiding Israel's territory."

TRUST GOD'S STRATEGY FOR LIFE—OBEY! TRUST! SERVE!

A MESSAGE OF JUSTICE AND JUDGMENT

Hear this word, people of Israel, the word the LORD has spoken
against you—against the whole family I brought up out of Egypt:
> *"You only have I chosen*
> *of all the families of the earth;*
> *therefore I will punish you*
> *for all your sins."*

AMOS 3:1–2

"With privilege comes responsibility"—this is a parent's mantra and a lesson for life. With the privilege of being God's chosen people, for instance, comes the responsibility to obey him in everything. And that didn't happen in Old Testament times, just as it doesn't happen today.

Before Elisha died, he named Jehu as his successor, and Jehu was zealous for the Lord. Not all of the many kings who came and went in Israel and Judah were, however. Jeroboam II, for instance, secured Israel's borders, but he never guarded Israel's soul. During this prosperous period of idol worship, a prophet named Amos arose with a message of justice and judgment.

Notice the almost-paradox: "I have chosen you" and "I will punish you." The punishment comes because of the love (Proverbs 3:12).

MAY I RECEIVE YOUR DISCIPLINE
AS A SIGN OF YOUR LOVE.

DON'T MISS THE GRACE

Seek the LORD and live. . . .
Seek good, not evil,
that you may live. . . .
Hate evil, love good.

AMOS 5:6, 14–15

It's strange, how a song gets stuck in your mind. And not necessarily a song you want to have running through your brain: the oldie you hear in the grocery store, the couple of notes you catch as you change stations. Why can't your favorite praise song or hymn stick instead? And why can't you program that part of your brain?

The children of Israel certainly hadn't programmed the chorus God has sung since Abraham. The words are simple: "Seek the LORD and live. . . . Seek good, not evil. . . . Hate evil, love good." But God's chosen people—then and now—haven't chosen this as their theme song. The more ominous notes apparently haven't stuck either: "Sweep through . . . like a fire; it will devour. . . . I will destroy it from the face of the earth" (5:6; 9:8).

The bright notes haven't made an impression; the dark notes apparently don't threaten. And the note of grace may have been overlooked: "I will not totally destroy the descendants of Jacob" (9:8).

HOLD ON TO GOD'S NOTES
OF HOPE AND GRACE.

AN ANCIENT MIRROR FOR MODERN TIMES

> *Hear the word of the LORD. . . .*
> *Return, Israel, to the LORD your God.*
> *Your sins have been your downfall! . . .*
> *Say to [the Lord]:*
> *"Forgive all our sins*
> *and receive us graciously."*
>
> HOSEA 4:1; 14:1–2

What did Grandpa always say? Even when the wording is a bit dusty, true wisdom—like the ancient truths of God's Word—is timeless and often all too relevant today.

"There is . . . no acknowledgment of God in the land" (Hosea 4:1).

"There is only cursing, lying and murder, stealing and adultery" (4:2).

"They do not acknowledge the LORD" (5:4). What country do these sentences remind you of?

The words of the prophet Hosea serve as a mirror for life in the twenty-first century. We suffer from the same illness—sin—and the same symptoms—no acknowledgment of the Lord—that the northern kingdom of Israel did. The cure is the same: "Forgive all our sins." Will we repent?

WHAT DOES GOD WANT YOU PERSONALLY TO CLEAN UP?

HOW BAD CAN THINGS GET?

The king of Assyria captured Samaria and deported the Israelites to Assyria. . . . The Israelites had sinned against the LORD their God. . . . They worshiped other gods. . . . They did wicked things. . . . The LORD warned Israel and Judah . . . "Turn from your evil ways." . . . But they would not listen.

2 KINGS 17:6–7, 11, 13–14

Their suits were awfully tight. Their hair was definitely long. The drums almost overpowered their—using the term loosely—music. And those lyrics were profound: "Yeah, yeah, yeah." What was the (music) world coming to? What did people see in those mop-top British singers?

In a far, far more serious vein, the angels of heaven must have been appalled. What was happening with God's chosen people? They weren't obeying God's commands; they weren't listening to his warnings. What did Israel see in the handcrafted, absolutely powerless idols they were choosing to worship?

The people of Israel were not willing to stop their downward spiral, so the Assyrians would be—in the Lord's words—"the rod of my anger, in whose hand is the club of my wrath!" (Isaiah 10:5).

GOD WILL HELP YOU BOTH RECOGNIZE AND TURN FROM YOUR EVIL WAYS. JUST ASK HIM.

LEARNING THE HARD WAY

[Hezekiah] did what was right in the eyes of the LORD, just as his father David had done. . . . The LORD was with him; he was successful in whatever he undertook. He rebelled against the king of Assyria and did not serve him.

2 KINGS 18:3, 7

B e honest. What lesson have you had to learn the hard way? More specifically, what did you have to experience for yourself before you understood the value of that guideline, family rule, or law?

Fortunately for the people of Judah, their king, Hezekiah, did not have to learn the hard way the lesson that God punishes sin and idolatry. After Israel's defenses crumbled, Hezekiah watched Sargon II of Assyria deport more than 27,000 people to distant cities, ensuring that no organized rebellion would happen. Any semblance of a nation was gone.

And now the tiny nation of Judah had the greatest army in the world camped on its northern border. Hezekiah did not want Judah to face God's wrath for their sin. What could he do?

DON'T LEARN THE HARD WAY THE TRUTH THAT YOUR JUST GOD HATES SIN.

A HEARTFELT CRY TO GOD

Hezekiah prayed to the LORD. . . . "The Assyrian kings have laid waste these nations and their lands. . . . Now, LORD our God, deliver us . . . so that all the kingdoms of the earth may know that you alone, LORD, are God."

2 KINGS 19:15, 17, 19

You've undoubtedly experienced tough situations and difficult relationships that put you face-to-face with your human limitations, with your finite understanding and power, with your sin. Hezekiah knew these truths about himself—and the Assyrian army just on the other side of the border kept the young king mindful of his limitations and needs.

The commander of the Assyrian army shouted to the people of Judah: "Hezekiah . . . is misleading you when he says, 'The LORD will deliver us.' Has the god of any nation ever delivered his land from the hand of the king of Assyria?" (2 Kings 18:32–33).

Hezekiah wasn't intimidated. The "god of any nation" wasn't fighting for him. The Lord of all the earth would be fighting for Judah.

> WHATEVER BATTLE YOU'RE FACING,
> YOU CAN KNOW—AS HEZEKIAH DID—
> THAT THE LORD IS ON YOUR SIDE.

HOPE VERSUS HOPE IN GOD

"Therefore this is what the LORD says concerning the king of Assyria. . . .

> *" 'He will not enter this city,*
> *declares the LORD.*
> *I will defend this city and save it,*
> *for my sake and for the sake of David my servant.' "*

2 KINGS 19:32–34

There's hope—and then there's *real* hope! The world's hope is an optimism about a particular event or a vague yearning for something good.[7] Not addressed is who or what will make that good happen. Christian hope is different because it is grounded in God. Knowing him gives us confidence that what we hope for will be fulfilled according to his perfect plan.

And that kind of hope is what King Hezekiah needed and what he received when, in response to his prayers, the Lord sent Isaiah with a hope-filled message (2 Kings 19:32–34).

He assured Hezekiah that God would "defend this city and save it." And God did: "That night the angel of the LORD went out and put to death a hundred and eighty-five thousand in the Assyrian camp" (v.35).

ARE YOU PREPARED TO "GIVE AN ANSWER . . . FOR THE HOPE THAT YOU HAVE" (1 PETER 3:15)?

GOD'S CALL; OUR RESPONSE

"Woe to me!" I cried. "I am ruined! For I am a man of unclean lips, and I live among a people of unclean lips, and my eyes have seen the King, the LORD Almighty."

Then one of the seraphim flew to me with a live coal. . . . With it he touched my mouth and said . . . "Your guilt is taken away and your sin atoned for."

ISAIAH 6:5–7

God is holy; we aren't. No wonder we who are sinful can't serve the Lord well without receiving his forgiveness—as Isaiah's life illustrates.

Isaiah helped King Hezekiah stand down the Assyrian threat by relying on God alone, and God came through. Such a strategy was founded on Isaiah's faith in God. Key to that faith was the transformational experience of seeing "the Lord, high and exalted, seated on a throne. . . . Above him were seraphim. . . . and they were calling to one another: 'Holy, holy, holy is the LORD Almighty'" (Isaiah 6:1–3).

Seeing God's glorious holiness made Isaiah's own sin far too apparent to him. He called out, "Woe to me!" and in response, God sent one of the seraphim to take away the prophet's guilt. So when Isaiah heard the Lord ask, "Whom shall I send?" he didn't hesitate: "Here am I. Send me!" (v. 8).

LOOK TO THE CROSS AND KNOW YOUR SINS ARE FORGIVEN.

"JUDAH IS FALLING!"

Jerusalem staggers,
Judah is falling;
their words and deeds are against the LORD,
defying his glorious presence. . . .
They have brought disaster upon themselves.

ISAIAH 3:8–9

Oh, at times most of us may have wished for a crystal ball, for at least a hint of what the future held. But not having a crystal ball is actually a blessing. Would you have wanted to know at sixteen that you wouldn't get married until you were twenty-nine? Or how many losses the Cubs would suffer before making it just to the playoffs? Would you want a sneak preview of the hard times?

Well, that preview was exactly Isaiah's message: hard times are coming. Isaiah boldly proclaimed the bad news the Lord had called him to share: Jerusalem would fall. In fact, a few chapters later, Isaiah's message became more specific: "The LORD Almighty is mustering an army for war. They come from faraway lands . . . to destroy the whole country" (Isaiah 13:4–5). And since Isaiah was a spokesman of God, what he prophesied would definitely happen.

WE CAN'T KNOW THE FUTURE, BUT WE CAN REST IN JESUS' PROMISE: "SURELY I AM WITH YOU ALWAYS" (MATTHEW 28:20).

A MESSAGE OF HOPE

"In the time of my favor I will answer you,
and in the day of salvation I will help you;
I will keep you and will make you
to be a covenant for the people." . . .
For the LORD comforts his people
and will have compassion on his afflicted ones.

ISAIAH 49:8, 13

Maybe you've heard accounts of amazing human beings who survived Auschwitz in Poland or the Hanoi Hilton in Vietnam. These survivors did so not knowing how long their captivity would last, without being certain they would survive. We human beings do better when we can be confident that circumstances will improve.

And that's one message Isaiah proclaimed in Judah. Yes, the people had turned away from God. Yes, they now faced the consequences of exile and oppression. But Isaiah reassured them that God would not forget them, that the Lord longed to lavish compassion and grace on his people. After judgment, Isaiah proclaimed, the Israelites would return home from Babylon and rebuild their nation. After all, the gracious and powerful Lord God was in control.

HEAR AND BELIEVE ISAIAH'S MESSAGE FROM THE LORD: "THOSE WHO HOPE IN ME WILL NOT BE DISAPPOINTED" (ISAIAH 49:23).

GOD'S GREATER PLAN

He had no beauty or majesty to attract us to him,
nothing in his appearance that we should desire him.
He was despised and rejected by mankind,
a man of suffering, and familiar with pain.
Like one from whom people hide their faces
he was despised, and we held him in low esteem.

ISAIAH 53:2–3

Some people just look the part. There's no mistaking, for instance, the college dean for a student, and athletes tend to carry themselves with a certain presence. Yet at other times, physical appearance reveals nothing accurate about a person's position or status. The Messiah that Isaiah described would not necessarily resemble anyone's idea of a deliverer for God's chosen people. Few, if any, would expect Isaiah's suffering Servant to play such a pivotal role in the unfolding of God's plan for all mankind.

Yet he would do exactly that. In describing the return of the kingdom of Judah, Isaiah was foreshadowing the more glorious future arrival of God's eternal kingdom when the Messiah would usher in a glorious kingdom without end.

SO THAT YOU CAN BE PART OF THAT KINGDOM, JESUS CHOSE THE CROSS ON HIS WAY TO THE THRONE.

THE SERVANT'S SUFFERING

He was pierced for our transgressions,
he was crushed for our iniquities. . . .
We all, like sheep, have gone astray . . .
and the LORD has laid on him
the iniquity of us all.

ISAIAH 53:5–6

I t's paradoxical, but some of life's loneliest moments can be at times when you're not alone. Walk into a crowded party where everyone is talking, laughing, and relaxing, and you can feel very much alone.

Now imagine the eternal God, who exists in relationship as Father, Son, and Holy Spirit, who has never been alone, volunteering for a time of separation and utter isolation. The lashings, the nails driven through his hands, the gasping for breath as he hung from the cross—this indescribable physical pain was nothing compared to the absolute separation from the heavenly Father that Jesus had chosen. He had made this choice—to take on himself the sin of the world and be the ultimate sacrifice once and for all—so that he could be in relationship with sinful people like us, people loved by Father, Son, and Spirit.

PONDER THE CROSS—CHRIST'S SEEN
AND UNSEEN SUFFERING, CHOSEN OUT
OF LOVE FOR YOU AND GUARANTEEING
AN ETERNAL RELATIONSHIP WITH YOU.

SINKING EVEN LOWER

*[Manasseh] did evil in the eyes of the LORD. . . . He sacrificed his
own son in the fire, practiced divination, sought omens, and consulted
mediums and spiritists. . . . Manasseh led [the people] astray.*

2 KINGS 21:2, 6, 9

Accounts of how evil we human beings can be are horrifying.
Concentration camps, suicide bombings, ethnic cleansing,
human trafficking—and those are the big-scale things. What
about behind closed doors? Alcoholism, incest, pornography, rage,
shame—people destroy their children and their spouses as well as
themselves.

Manasseh was a master of evil who, during his fifty-five-year
reign, led God's chosen people to abandon his holy ways. Placing idols
and altars to false gods in the Lord's temple, Manasseh was guilty of
"much evil in the eyes of the LORD" (2 Kings 21:6).

But before we feel even a twinge of "holier than thou," we need
to remember that God doesn't rank sins the way we do. Our cruel
words and unspoken kindness, our envy and anger, our jealousy and
self-centeredness offer us up-close-and-personal evidence of how evil
we human beings can be.

WE ARE BLESSED TO HAVE A
LONGSUFFERING GOD, BUT OUR JUST
AND RIGHTEOUS GOD IS ANGERED
BY SIN, AND HE WILL JUDGE.

WARNING, ANGER, PUNISHMENT

The LORD said . . . "Manasseh King of Judah has committed
these detestable sins. . . . I will wipe out Jerusalem. . . . I will
forsake the remnant of my inheritance and give them into the
hands of enemies. . . . They have done evil in my eyes and have
aroused my anger."

2 KINGS 21:10–11, 13–15

M aybe she purses her lips. Maybe he takes a very long, deep
breath. Kids have a way of knowing when they have pretty
much pushed Mom or Dad to the limit—and they also know it's
never good to make a parent angry!

Likewise, there is nothing good about making our heavenly
Father angry. Yes, our holy God had every right to be angry with
Manasseh & Co. (He also has every right to be angry with us for
our sin.) Rather than pursing his lips or breathing deeply, God sent
prophets, men of God who clearly reported his message. The prophets
were neither subtle nor apologetic; they didn't worry about being tact-
ful or ruining the people's self-esteem. God had commanded them to
communicate a very straightforward message: the people had done
wrong; God was angry; punishment would come.

LORD GOD, I HAVE DONE WRONG. THANK
YOU THAT YOU SENT YOUR SON TO TAKE THE
PUNISHMENT THAT WAS RIGHTFULLY MINE.

THE LAST ON THE LIST

In his distress he sought the favor of the LORD his God and
humbled himself greatly before [God]. . . . And when he prayed
to him, the LORD was moved by his entreaty and listened to his
plea; so he brought him back to Jerusalem and to his kingdom.
Then Manasseh knew that the LORD is God.

2 CHRONICLES 33:12–13

Were you surprised to see that the "he" who had humbled himself was Manasseh? What a testimony to God's grace. Manasseh had led many people astray, desecrated the temple of God, and paid no attention when the Lord warned again and again that punishment would come. So, "the LORD brought . . . the army commanders of the king of Assyria, who took Manasseh prisoner, put a hook in his nose, bound him with bronze shackles and took him to Babylon" (2 Chronicles 33:11).

The humiliation that Manasseh knew at the hands of Assyria opened his eyes to his sinfulness and evil—and he cried out to God. We don't know Manasseh's words, but God knew his heart. He allowed Manasseh to return to Jerusalem, where he did his best to make right what he had destroyed.

MAY WE—LIKE MANASSEH—DO
WELL TO MAKE RIGHT ALL THAT
OUR SIN MADE WRONG.

LIKE FATHER . . . AND UNLIKE FATHER

Amon was twenty-two years old when he became king, and
he reigned in Jerusalem two years. He did evil in the eyes of
the LORD, as his father Manasseh had done. Amon worshiped and
offered sacrifices to all the idols Manasseh had made. But unlike his
father Manasseh, he did not humble himself before the LORD.

2 CHRONICLES 33:21–23

Human development has its mysteries. Great parents, for instance, can have great kids—or prodigals. Self-centered, immoral parents can raise self-centered, immoral kids—or kids who choose to walk with the Lord. In this case, Amon witnessed both the evil ways of his father, and, after Manasseh's captivity in Babylon, the humbled, reformed, and godly once-again-king.

Whatever our influence as parents, our children have their own free will. Amon chose the way of evil, just as his father had initially. But "unlike his father Manasseh, he did not humble himself before the LORD."

HUMBLY CHOOSING JESUS AS LORD
OF OUR LIFE HAPPENS NOT JUST
ONCE, BUT COUNTLESS TIMES A DAY
WITH EVERY DECISION WE MAKE.

THE PATTERN CONTINUES

Jehoiakim was twenty-five years old when he became king, and he reigned in Jerusalem eleven years. . . . And he did evil in the eyes of the LORD, just as his predecessors had done.

2 KINGS 23:36–37

What patterns, if any, have you seen in your family? Maybe everyone in the past five generations has graduated from college. Or maybe there is a strong heritage of following Jesus.

You've undoubtedly noticed the roller-coaster pattern of God's chosen people following him, turning away, following him, and turning away. Manasseh turned away and then became a follower. His son Amon turned away. Then Amon's eight-year-old son, Josiah, brought thirty-one years of spiritual renewal to God's people. When the ancient Book of the Law of Moses was discovered, Josiah put his heart and soul into rediscovering for all the people God's way of living.

After Josiah's death, the old pattern of father-not-like-son continued. Josiah's son Jehoahaz was pathetic, lasting only three months as king. The next king, Jehoiakim, was no better. When the Lord sent foreign raiders into Judah, Jehoiakim died. His son Jehoiachin reigned for three months, continuing in his father's evil ways.

WE MAKE GOOD CHOICES AND BAD
CHOICES, AND GOD CONTINUES TO LOVE US.

NOT EMPTY THREATS

"Some of you will escape the sword when you are scattered among the lands and nations. Then in the nations where they have been carried captive, those who escape will remember me. . . . They will loathe themselves for the evil they have done and for all their detestable practices. And they will know that I am the LORD; I did not threaten in vain to bring this calamity on them."

EZEKIEL 6:8–10

The world is a complicated web of international connections; rarely does what happens in one country not impact what happens in another. So when nations flex their muscles, what is the role of other nations? Could those leaders be bluffing?

God does not bluff; his words are not empty threats. He desperately wanted his people to choose to leave their idols once and for all. So, "as the LORD had declared, Nebuchadnezzar . . . carried all Jerusalem into exile: . . . a total of ten thousand" (2 Kings 24:13–14).

When a second group of Israelites was taken to Babylon, Ezekiel was among them. His message was stern: this was the beginning of God's judgment, the beginning of the end of Jerusalem. Ezekiel's theme was not new: unbelief leads to doom.

GOD, SHOW ME WHERE I AM BEING AS
DEAF TO YOUR CALL TO REPENT OF MY
SIN AS THE PEOPLE OF JERUSALEM WERE.

YET ANOTHER MESSAGE OF DOOM

Doom has come upon you. . . .
The time has come! The day is near . . .
I am about to pour out my wrath on you. . . .
I will judge you according to your conduct
and repay you for all your detestable practices.

EZEKIEL 7:7–8

When have you found yourself the bearer of bad news? Whenever we have to share bad news, we need to be sure not only of its accuracy but also of our responsibility to speak out.

Our gracious God assured his prophets of both their responsibility and their authority when he called them into his service. When he called Ezekiel, the Lord opened the heavens: "Spread out above . . . was what looked something like a vault, sparkling like crystal. Above the vault . . . was what looked like a throne of lapis lazuli, and high above on the throne was a figure like that of a man. . . . [From] his waist up he looked like glowing metal, as if full of fire, and . . . from there down he looked like fire; and brilliant light surrounded him. . . . This was the appearance of the likeness of the glory of the LORD" (Ezekiel 1:22, 26–28). God blessed Ezekiel with an unforgettable moment of commissioning. Ezekiel would now begin his ministry . . . as another of God's messengers of doom.

REFLECT ON A TIME WHEN GOD MADE
CLEARER TO YOU HIS CALL ON YOUR LIFE.

NO FEAR! NO EXCUSES!

"Sovereign LORD," I said, "I do not know how to speak; I am too young."

But the LORD said to me, "Do not say, 'I am too young.' You must go to everyone I send you to and say whatever I command you. Do not be afraid of them, for I am with you and will rescue you."

JEREMIAH 1:6–8

Perhaps you've encountered situations in life that you didn't feel prepared to tackle. Maybe you've felt intimidated by expectations or demands. You can probably empathize with Jeremiah.

When God first explained to Jeremiah that God had set him apart before he was born "as a prophet to the nations" (Jeremiah 1:5), Jeremiah wasn't convinced. But—in Jeremiah's own words—God "reached out his hand and touched my mouth and said to me, 'I have put my words in your mouth'" (v. 9). As things were going from bad to worse in Jerusalem, Jeremiah was to be yet another voice for the Lord who continued to pursue and warn his people.

Knowing God was with him, Jeremiah proclaimed his unwelcome message about the coming destruction of Jerusalem, about God's judgment for the people's sins of idolatry and pride. But Jeremiah also spoke another truth: God's mercy would never fail even toward the nation that had forsaken him.

SPEAKING ABOUT OUR FAITH GETS
EASIER THE MORE OFTEN WE DO SO.

THE PROPHET'S PAIN

If you do not listen,
I will weep in secret . . .
my eyes will weep bitterly . . .
because the LORD's flock will be taken captive.

JEREMIAH 13:17

We honor God when we serve him in all that we do. Jeremiah honored God as he served, leaving us an example to follow. Known as the "weeping prophet," Jeremiah truly invested his heart and soul in the task God had called him to. He felt deeply the burden of both the people's sin and the judgment that would come. He so wanted the people to hear and repent.

Jeremiah boldly proclaimed the Lord's message to the people who had "exchanged their glorious God for worthless idols," his chosen people who had "forsaken" him (Jeremiah 2:11, 13). The Lord's message could be stated no more clearly: "I am bringing disaster from the north, even terrible destruction" (4:6).

Jeremiah then encouraged the people to, in response, "put on sackcloth, lament and wail, for the fierce anger of the LORD has not turned away from us" (4:8).

HOLY GOD, HELP US SEE THE FILTH OF
OUR SIN, THE EVIL IN OUR HEARTS,
THAT WE MIGHT TRULY REPENT.

"THERE WAS NO REMEDY"

The LORD . . . sent word to [his people] through his messengers
again and again, because he had pity on his people and on his
dwelling place. But they mocked God's messengers, despised his
words and scoffed at his prophets until the wrath of the LORD was
aroused against his people and there was no remedy.

2 CHRONICLES 36:15–16

Ask teenagers why they did something dumb, and their answer will be "I don't know"—because they really don't know! The part of their brain that can reason, control impulses, and anticipate possible future events or consequences—the prefrontal cortex—has not yet developed. Hopefully by the time they're twenty-five, it will. So why did the *adults* of Judah continue to do the same dumb thing of disobeying God and pursuing idols?

Isaiah spoke clearly. Ezekiel spoke clearly. Jeremiah spoke clearly. But the kings and the people to whom they spoke refused to listen. Especially in Jeremiah's day, the kings grew increasingly brash, ignoring the prophet's warnings and wisdom.

The book of 2 Chronicles contains one of the saddest statements in Scripture: "The wrath of the LORD was aroused against his people and there was no remedy." Nebuchadnezzar was on the move, a tool of judgment in God's sovereign and righteous hands.

TRANSFORM MY HEART BEFORE I
REACH THE POINT OF "NO REMEDY."

TOO LITTLE TOO LATE

"This is what the LORD, the God of Israel, says: . . . I myself will fight against you with an outstretched hand and a mighty arm in furious anger and in great wrath."

There is something remarkable about the human spirit. Against the worst odds, even if there is no logical basis, we can somehow still hope.

Consider King Zedekiah as Nebuchadnezzar's attack became imminent. Like many kings before him, he "did evil in the eyes of the LORD" (2 Kings 24:19). Yet he sent messengers to Jeremiah: "Perhaps the LORD will perform wonders for us as in times past so that [Nebuchadnezzar] will withdraw from us" (Jeremiah 21:2). Zedekiah was not repentant, but he was hoping! And the Lord was adamant: "Absolutely not."

The Lord then allowed a commander in Nebuchadnezzar's army to enter Jerusalem where he "set fire to the temple of the LORD, the royal palace and all the houses of Jerusalem. . . . The whole Babylonian army . . . broke down all the walls around Jerusalem" (Jeremiah 52:13–14).

Jerusalem had fallen. On the surface, it appeared that God had abandoned his people. Where was his mercy now?

MERCY HAS BEEN DEFINED AS "NOT GETTING WHAT YOU DESERVE."

HEARTBREAK

How deserted lies the city.
The LORD has done what he planned. . . .
He has overthrown you without pity,
he has let the enemy gloat over you.

LAMENTATIONS 1:1, 2:17

"Let my heart be broken by the things that break the heart of God." Maybe you've heard those compelling words of Bob Pierce, founder of World Vision and Samaritan's Purse. Imagine the weeping prophet's response to the destruction of the holy city . . .

Jeremiah was grief-stricken as, from Egypt, he mourned the destruction of the holy city of his beloved homeland. (Jeremiah had been one of the Jews still in Judah when the governor whom Nebuchadnezzar had appointed was assassinated. Afraid of Babylon's reprisals, many of those Jews fled to Egypt, and they had forced Jeremiah to go with him.)

So from afar, Jeremiah grieved as he thought about the streets of Jerusalem—now empty and still. And Jeremiah wept bitterly for his people: "Joy is gone from our hearts" (Lamentations 5:15). Yet Jeremiah's ministry continued. The prophesied destruction had come, but he continued to trust in God's mercies.

"THE LORD HAS DONE WHAT HE PLANNED"
CAN BE A PEACE-GIVING TRUTH.

GRIEF YET HOPE

Because of the LORD's *great love we are not consumed,*
for his compassions never fail.
They are new every morning;
great is your faithfulness. . . .
The LORD *is good to those whose hope is in him.*

LAMENTATIONS 3:22–23, 25

Have you noticed the grace of a good night's sleep? It is a gift from God when we awaken with a lighter heart, a clearer mind, and a renewed sense of hope. No, circumstances didn't necessarily change overnight, but God changed us, enabling us to awake and confidently sing to him, "Great is your faithfulness!"

And God's faithfulness—his doing what he says he will do—is evident in his enforcing consequences as well as in his pouring out mercy and grace. Through the army of Babylon, for instance, God's wrath came to Judah. Jeremiah witnessed this tragedy and—even though he knew God's people had brought it on themselves, even though they had been warned judgment would come—felt heartbroken. Yet the faithful, weeping prophet chose to trust in God's mercies. You can make the same decision.

LIKE JEREMIAH, YOU CAN CHOOSE TO
TRUST IN GOD'S MERCIES WHEN TRAGEDY
STRIKES AND YOUR HEART BREAKS.

UNEARNED AND UNDESERVED GIFTS FROM GOD

"I will gather you from all the countries and bring you back into your own land. . . . I will remove from you your heart of stone and give you a heart of flesh. And I will put my Spirit in you and move you to follow my decrees. . . . Then you will . . . be my people, and I will be your God."

EZEKIEL 36:24–28

Don't let it go to your head! The only reason you have that car is because your grandfather is very generous. You're able to sing like that because God gave you the talent. The school didn't have to let you in when you were late applying. God's grace is behind all the blessings we receive, so we can't let those gifts go to our head!

And the Lord told the exiles in Babylon that same thing. Yes, his people would receive his grace and mercy, and the Almighty explained why: "It is not for your sake, people of Israel, that I am going to do these things, but for the sake of my holy name, which you have profaned among the nations where you have gone" (Ezekiel 36:22). And in case they didn't get it the first time, God repeated himself: "I want you to know that I am not doing this for your sake" (v. 32).

IT IS BY GRACE YOU HAVE BEEN
SAVED, THROUGH FAITH . . . IT IS THE
GIFT OF GOD. (EPHESIANS 2:8)

THE STRENGTH OF ONCE-BROKEN BONES

The LORD . . . set me in the middle of a valley; it was full of bones. . . . Then he said to me: "Son of man, these bones are the people of Israel. They say, 'Our bones are dried up and our hope is gone; we are cut off.'"

EZEKIEL 37:1, 11

Maybe you've heard that broken bones grow back stronger than they were before they were broken. Yes and no. As a broken bone heals, an extra-thick band of bone forms at the point of the fracture, making that part of the bone stronger than it was before the break. Over time the body absorbs the calcium in that extra band, and the bone becomes only as strong as it was before the break.

Now, back to the dry bones representing God's people. The Lord said to them: "I will bring you back to the land of Israel" (Ezekiel 37:12). Certainly their faith in God would be stronger after this great act of mercy!

But faith becomes faithlessness. Like the broken bone with the thicker band, Israel's faith would be extra strong for a while. But the cares of the world and self-centeredness would absorb the passion, and then their faith would be only as strong as it was before the exile.

ALMIGHTY GOD, USE MY TIMES OF BROKENNESS TO STRENGTHEN MY FAITH—PERMANENTLY!

TAKING A STAND

Daniel then said to the guard . . . "Please test your servants
for ten days: Give us nothing but vegetables to eat and water to
drink. Then compare our appearance with that of the young men
who eat the royal food."

DANIEL 1:11–13

Jesus said, "It is the one who is least among you all who is the greatest" (Luke 9:48), and "The greatest among you will be your servant. . . . Those who humble themselves will be exalted" (Matthew 23:11–12). Clearly, followers of Jesus take certain positions that the world will not understand.

Such was the case for four young Jews exiled to Babylon. Chosen to one day serve the king, Daniel and his three friends were given the best of Babylonian education, training, and food. Non-kosher food. Daniel boldly said, "No, thank you!" and offered to be part of an experiment. The guard agreed, and "at the end of the ten days they looked healthier and better nourished than any of the young men who ate the royal food" (Daniel 1:15).

Immersed in a pagan culture, these four young men stayed true to the one true God. Key was the fact that they had one another. Theirs was a small but clearly adequate community of fellowship and support in this strange, new world.

BEING PART OF A CHRISTIAN COMMUNITY
WILL HELP YOU TAKE A STAND FOR JESUS.

*The king . . . found none equal to Daniel, Hananiah, Mishael
and Azariah; so they entered the king's service. In every matter
of wisdom and understanding about which the king questioned
them, he found them ten times better than all the magicians and
enchanters in his whole kingdom.*

DANIEL 1:19–20

I t was a take-away from a sermon: "Being a Christian isn't permission to be weird." We are wearing the Lord's name, and we shouldn't be noticed because we dress or talk weirdly. We should be noticed because we are loving others and doing all things with excellence to honor and glorify our God.

In Babylon, Daniel, Hananiah, Mishael, and Azariah honored God not only by observing the kosher diet he had outlined for his people but also by working hard at every opportunity presented to them. As they honored God by doing their best, he honored and blessed their efforts by giving them "knowledge and understanding of all kinds of literature and learning" (Daniel 1:17).

Standing out can be good or bad depending on what about us is attracting people's attention. May people be drawn to the light of Christ shining through us as we live for him and walk in his ways.

IF I'M STANDING OUT IN A CROWD,
LORD, MAY IT ONLY BE BECAUSE
PEOPLE ARE NOTICING YOU IN ME.

USING GOD'S GIFTS
FOR GOD'S GLORY

The king asked Daniel . . . "Are you able to tell me what I saw
in my dream and interpret it?"
  Daniel replied, "No wise man, enchanter, magician or diviner
can . . . but there is a God in heaven who reveals mysteries. He has
shown King Nebuchadnezzar what will happen in days to come."

DANIEL 2:26–28

It's a head-scratcher, those teachers, coaches, bosses, and even parents who don't set up for success their students, athletes, employees, and children. Why not offer some guidelines as to what's on the test, what drill to be ready for, what the quarterly report should look like, or what behavior is expected at Grandma's house?

That, however, was not King Nebuchadnezzar's way either. He wanted to know what a disturbing dream meant, but (head scratching time!) he wanted his advisers to first tell him what he had dreamed. When (of course) they couldn't, Nebuchadnezzar sentenced all the wise men in Babylon to death.

When Daniel heard about this pronouncement, he and his three friends prayed for insight. During the night, God set Daniel up for success and revealed the mystery of the king's dream. When he stood before the king, Daniel gave God the credit and the glory.

LIKE DANIEL, USE FOR GOD'S GLORY
THE GIFTS HE HAS GIVEN YOU.

A LESSON FOR ALL

Then King Nebuchadnezzar fell prostrate before Daniel and paid
him honor and ordered that an offering and incense be presented
to him. The king said to Daniel, "Surely your God is the God of
gods and the Lord of kings and a revealer of mysteries, for you
were able to reveal this mystery."

DANIEL 2:46–47

Amazing performances can earn respect from all who witness them. Think Harlem Globetrotters, half-pipe snowboarders, and freestyle skiers. Think also about a mother with her special-needs child and a father letting his three-year-old "help" paint the fence. These scenarios are hard to ignore.

And Nebuchadnezzar could not ignore the fact that Daniel had told him exactly what he had dreamed. Nor could he ignore Daniel's explanation of its meaning.

God directs history, and Babylon's power, prestige, and privilege formed only a short chapter in a much longer story. Such news at the height of an empire's influence was bound to create a strong response of some kind. This king's response was awe and humility.

FIND PEACE, HOPE, AND COMFORT IN
THE FACT THAT GOD DIRECTS HISTORY—
THE HISTORY OF THE WORLD AS WELL
AS YOUR PERSONAL HISTORY.

NOT CROSSING THE LINE

The herald loudly proclaimed . . . "As soon as you hear the
sound of the horn, flute, zither, lyre, harp, pipe and all kinds of
music, you must fall down and worship the image of gold that
King Nebuchadnezzar has set up. Whoever does not fall down
and worship will immediately be thrown into a blazing furnace."

DANIEL 3:4–6

Pick your battles. Okay, your daughter's room is a mess. Close the bedroom door and later discuss the importance of being respectful. Okay, it would be great if your son would occasionally wear something other than board shorts to church, but at least he's going to church without grumbling or making everyone late.

The Jewish exiles in Babylon also had to pick their battles. Shadrach, Meshach, and Abednego had come up against a matter they knew they had to fight. King Nebuchadnezzar had erected a ninety-foot-tall, nine-foot-wide image of gold that the people of Babylon were to worship. Refusal to do so would mean death.

Shadrach, Meshach, and Abednego were not going to worship anything or anyone other than the God of Abraham, Isaac, and Jacob. So when the music played, these three men stood tall. They chose to obey God's law.

IT'S IMPORTANT TO KNOW WHICH
BATTLES ARE WORTH FIGHTING—
AND TO FIGHT THEM!

*Shadrach, Meshach and Abednego replied to him, "King
Nebuchadnezzar, we do not need to defend ourselves. . . . If we
are thrown into the blazing furnace, the God we serve is able to
deliver us from it. . . . But even if he does not, we . . . will not
serve your gods or worship the image of gold you have set up."*

DANIEL 3:16–18

*C*ourage. Who comes to mind when you hear that word? Maybe
the soldier who volunteers for another tour in the Middle
East. Or the middle-schooler who says "no" to drugs. The politician
who boldly announces that the emperor has no clothes on.

Daniel's friends Shadrach, Meshach, and Abednego offer a
striking example of courage. They knew the king's command and
the Lord's command. They knew that the consequences of obeying
God would be the consequences of disobeying the king. Yet the
three stood before Nebuchadnezzar, confident in their God.

Shadrach, Meshach, and Abednego did not want to perish in the
furnace, and they knew God could deliver them from the fire. But
they also understood that God is God. So with "even if he doesn't"
faith, Shadrach, Meshach, and Abednego told Nebuchadnezzar they
would not worship the gods of Babylon, or its king.

GOD WILL GIVE YOU THE COURAGE
YOU NEED IN YOUR "EVEN IF
HE DOESN'T" MOMENTS.

ONE, TWO, THREE . . . FOUR?

King Nebuchadnezzar leaped to his feet in amazement. . . . "Weren't there three men that we tied up and threw into the fire? . . . I see four men walking around in the fire, unbound and unharmed, and the fourth looks like a son of the gods."

DANIEL 3:24–25

Sometimes we are very aware of God's protection. His presence is the only reason you didn't get sideswiped and spin out. When everyone you knew on the cruise ship got the virus and you didn't, you praised God for his protection.

And God—who has been protecting his people since the garden—had no problem handling the fiery furnace. The soldiers who threw Shadrach, Meshach, and Abednego into the flames died, killed by the fire's intense heat, but the three Hebrews, standing exactly where the soldiers did, didn't perish.

Then an amazed Nebuchadnezzar noticed further evidence of God's protection of these three men: there in the roaring flames, alongside the unharmed and now unbound Shadrach, Meshach, and Abednego, stood a fourth figure who looked "like a son of the gods." Nebuchadnezzar—who had seen God reveal to Daniel his dream and its meaning—now saw God's protection of the three men.

MAY WE BE ALWAYS AWARE OF—AND
ALWAYS GRATEFUL FOR—THE LORD'S
PROTECTIVE PRESENCE WITH US.

NOT EVEN THE SMELL OF SMOKE

Shadrach, Meshach and Abednego came out of the fire, and the satraps, prefects, governors and royal advisers crowded around them. They saw that the fire had not harmed their bodies, nor was a hair of their heads singed; their robes were not scorched, and there was no smell of fire on them.

DANIEL 3:26–27

Sand in his hair and sunburned cheeks: evidence of beach time. Chocolate frosting on her face: evidence of a snack. A smoky scent: evidence of a campfire. Certain events leave evidence that they actually happened.

How, then, could there be absolutely "no smell of fire" on the three Hebrews when they came out of the furnace? Nebuchadnezzar knew right away: "Praise be to the God of Shadrach, Meshach and Abednego!" (Daniel 3:28). God got the credit and the glory: no burned skin, singed hair, scorched clothes, or clinging smell.

Nebuchadnezzar also understood why God had protected the three men: "They trusted in him . . . and were willing to give up their lives rather than serve or worship any god except their own God" (v. 28). This faith got the attention of the Babylonian king, and he forbade anyone in the land to speak against the Hebrews' God.

TAKE A STAND FOR GOD IN THIS UNBELIEVING WORLD. WHO KNOWS WHOSE SOUL GOD MIGHT SAVE AS A RESULT?

A NEW RULER AND JEALOUS COLLEAGUES

The administrators and the satraps tried to find grounds for charges against Daniel. . . . They could find no corruption in him, because he was trustworthy. . . . Finally these men said, "We will never find any basis for charges against this man Daniel unless it has something to do with the law of his God."

DANIEL 6:4–5

It was a setup. Oh, there are fun setups like being surprised on your birthday. But some setups are intended to cause trouble.

The officials in the court of new King Darius planned a setup. They suggested the king issue a decree that no one pray to any god or human being other than Darius; those violating the decree would be thrown into the lions' den. The king agreed; the faithful Daniel continued to pray to his God; the jealous officials caught him in the act. Setup successful! Daniel was on his way to an evening with the lions.

In something of a statement of faith, the king said to Daniel, "May your God . . . rescue you!" (Daniel 6:16). A stone sealed the opening; the king's signet ring guaranteed that no one would be rolling that stone away. Back in his palace, "the king . . . could not sleep" (v. 18).

IF YOU WERE ARRESTED FOR BEING
A FOLLOWER OF JESUS, WOULD
PEOPLE BE ABLE TO FIND ENOUGH
EVIDENCE TO CONVICT YOU?

At the first light of dawn, the king . . . hurried to the lions'
den. . . . He called to Daniel in an anguished voice, "Daniel,
servant of the living God, has your God . . . been able to rescue
you from the lions?"

Daniel answered . . . "My God sent his angel, and he shut
the mouths of the lions. They have not hurt me."

DANIEL 6:19–22

When in your life have you been most terrified? Step back into those feelings—your heart pounding, barely breathing, your prayer simply, "Help me, God!"

Now take those feelings into the lions' den with Daniel. These are *lions*. And they are carnivores that have not been fed recently, and you are a potential meal. Hear now the low rumble of their roar as they pace the den, circling their easy prey. Feel their warm breath. Smell their gamey scent. Notice their razor-sharp teeth and claws. This is the danger God delivered Daniel from—and "the king was overjoyed" (Daniel 6:23). After Daniel was lifted from the den, "no wound was found on him, because he had trusted in his God" (v. 23).

A footnote: "The men who had falsely accused Daniel were . . . thrown into the lions' den. . . . Before they reached the floor of the den, the lions overpowered them and crushed all their bones" (v. 24).

OUR VERY REAL GOD SAVES HIS
PEOPLE FROM VERY REAL DANGER.

LIVING IN RELATIONSHIP WITH JESUS

*"For he is the living God
and he endures forever. . . .
He rescues and he saves. . . .
He has rescued Daniel
from the power of the lions."*

DANIEL 6:26–27

Often these days, when prominent public figures come to name Jesus as their Savior or speak about their longtime love for him, these people get noticed—if not mocked and criticized. Undoubtedly aware of that risk, they are also aware that God has given them the platform, and they want to use it to glorify him.

King Darius himself took a stand for "the living God." The anguish he felt as he approached the lions' den after a sleepless night became joy when he saw that Daniel was safe. Clearly, Daniel's powerful God must be feared and revered, and that is what Darius decreed.

A law can call people to respect another's religion. A specific religion could be mandated by the state. But Christianity is about being in relationship with Jesus, not following a set of rules. Jesus came to restore a relationship between holy God and sinful human beings.

FOCUS ON LIVING IN RELATIONSHIP WITH JESUS.

"I WILL SURELY SAVE YOU"

*The LORD says: "When seventy years are completed . . . you will
call on me and come and pray to me, and I will listen to you. You
will seek me and find me when you seek me with all your heart. I
will be found by you . . . and will bring you back from captivity."*

JEREMIAH 29:10, 12–14

A promise kept is always a blessing and a joy. A promise made long
ago—a promise you thought might have been forgotten—can
be even a more precious blessing and a greater joy when it is kept.
Great-Grandma *did* remember to leave me the hope chest in her will.
Just as my uncle had said for twenty years, he got me a car when I
turned twenty-five.

Consider a promise made 1,500 years before its fulfillment, a
promise God repeated to his people again and again and again. Now
the count was seventy years before the fulfillment, before—just as the
prophet Jeremiah had said—their compassionate God would indeed
lead his people out of exile in Babylon and back to their homeland.

When mighty Babylon fell to Persian invaders in 539 BC,
King Cyrus issued a decree permitting Jewish exiles to return to
Jerusalem. This remnant of God's faithful people was going home.

GOD WILL NEVER FORSAKE YOU.

CYRUS'S INVITATION

This is what Cyrus king of Persia says:
"The Lord, the God of heaven, has given me all the
kingdoms of the earth and he has appointed me to build a temple
for him at Jerusalem in Judah. Any of his people among you may
go up . . . and may their God be with them."

EZRA 1:2–3

Throughout life, unexpected touches of grace from unexpected sources can turn an ordinary day into a memorable one.

Imagine the day that the people of Israel, exiled in Babylon and now ruled by Persia, heard from King Cyrus that they could return to Jerusalem to build a temple. What amazing news from an unexpected source! Notice, though, that—rightfully so—God gets the credit. The Lord, not Cyrus, is the hero of this story: "In the first year of Cyrus king of Persia, in order to fulfill the word of the Lord spoken by Jeremiah, the Lord moved the heart of Cyrus king of Persia to make a proclamation" (Ezra 1:1). The Lord had spoken through Jeremiah, and now the Lord spoke through Cyrus.

Any touch of grace in our life is a gift from the Lord, including grace from people who are not yet Christians. After all, "every good and perfect gift is from above, coming down from the Father of the heavenly lights" (James 1:17).

GOD IS BEHIND UNEXPECTED BLESSINGS.

THE TEMPLE RESTORED

When the builders laid the foundation of the temple of
the LORD, the priests . . . with trumpets, and the Levites . . .
with cymbals, took their places to praise the LORD. . . . With
praise and thanksgiving they sang to the LORD:
  "He is good; his love toward Israel endures forever."

EZRA 3:10–11

Painting the house is a big project. After you choose the color and gather the supplies, and when the weather allows, you can finally begin the project!

For fifty years the exiled people of Israel had grieved the destruction of the Lord's temple. So when King Cyrus gave them the opportunity to return to Jerusalem to rebuild the temple, 42,360 people headed back, taking with them 7,337 slaves. Before they left, Cyrus returned to these Jewish people the silver and gold articles that Nebuchadnezzar had carried away from the temple (Ezra 1:7). Then, once in Jerusalem, some among them gave free will offerings amounting to 1,100 pounds of gold and about 3 tons of silver (2:69).

The Israelites got to work—and worked diligently for their Lord's glory. When they saw that the foundation for the house of the Lord was complete, the people burst forth in thanksgiving: "All the people gave a great shout of praise to the LORD" (3:11).

DON'T TAKE FOR GRANTED THE FREEDOM
OR PLACES WE HAVE FOR WORSHIP.

OPPOSITION

*The peoples around them set out to discourage the people of
Judah and make them afraid to go on building. They bribed
officials to work against them and frustrate their plans during
the entire reign of Cyrus king of Persia and down to the reign of
Darius king of Persia.*

EZRA 4:4–5

Sometimes it's a backhanded compliment from the enemy—
God's enemy and therefore your enemy—who wants to
discourage you from doing what the Lord has called you to do. Or
you open the Bible for a quiet time, and the phone rings. You sign
up to teach Sunday school, and never have Sunday mornings been
so stressful for the family! Or you return to Jerusalem to rebuild the
temple, and the good start suddenly comes to a screeching halt.

The returnees' initial success alarmed the Samaritans and
other neighbors who feared what a rebuilt temple in a thriving
Jewish state might mean to political stability in the area. So vigor-
ously opposing the project, they slowed down the work for about six
years and completely stopped it for another ten. The Israelites were
discouraged, so they focused on settling into their own homes.

OPPOSITION JUST MAY MEAN THAT
YOU ARE DOING EXACTLY WHAT
GOD WANTS YOU TO BE DOING.

JUMP-STARTING THE TEMPLE PROJECT

This is what the LORD Almighty says: "These people say, 'The time has not yet come to rebuild the LORD's house.'"

Then the word of the LORD came through the prophet Haggai: "Is it a time for you yourselves to be living in your paneled houses, while this house remains a ruin?"

HAGGAI 1:2–4

Key to coaching is the ability to give an effective pep talk when the outcome looks dismal. Inspiring players to not give up—to keep getting up when they're knocked down, to believe they have a chance to win—can make a huge difference in a team's performances. Halftime talks and even brief time-outs can jump-start a team's performance.

God used Haggai to jump-start the Babylonian exiles who had returned to Jerusalem to rebuild the temple. With their efforts derailed by the opposition of neighboring nations, they started thinking that maybe the timing of the building project wasn't right after all. Haggai's message helped shake the people out of their complacency.

God spoke clearly about his unhappiness: "Give careful thought to your ways. . . . My house . . . remains a ruin, while each of you is busy with your own house" (Haggai 1:5, 9). The people heard the message and "obeyed the voice of the LORD their God" (v. 12).

GIVE CAREFUL THOUGHT TO YOUR WAYS!

GOD THE COVENANT KEEPER

"Just as I had determined to bring disaster on you and showed no pity when your ancestors angered me," says the LORD Almighty, "so now I have determined to do good again to Jerusalem and Judah. Do not be afraid. . . . Speak the truth to each other, and render true and sound judgment in your courts."

ZECHARIAH 8:14–16

Encouragement gives hope to tired hearts, shatters walls that isolate, and makes God's presence in our lives much more real as a human heart expresses God's heart to another human being.

Haggai continued his message of encouragement by proclaiming that God had not forgotten his covenant with Abraham, Isaac, and Jacob. God had not washed his hands of Israel. God would again bless his people and their city of Jerusalem. Haggai also hinted that would one day the Messiah would visit this very temple.

Like Haggai, the prophet and priest Zechariah wanted to encourage the temple rebuilding project. But also like Haggai, Zechariah wanted people to understand that the temple is important, but it's a sign and symbol of something greater yet to come. So, yes, work on the temple. That's important to the Lord. But also anticipate the day when God will bless Jerusalem once again.

TODAY ENCOURAGE SOMEONE
OR THANK SOMEONE FOR
ENCOURAGING YOU. OR BOTH!

PROTECTION GRANTED

*King Darius then issued an order, and they searched in the
archives stored in the treasury at Babylon. A scroll was
found . . . and this was written on it: . . . Let the temple be
rebuilt.*

EZRA 6:1–3

Sometimes a single question can have an unexpected impact. For example, "What do you think God wants you to do about that passion you have for victims of human trafficking?" And sometimes that question doesn't need to be particularly probing to bear fruit.

Thanks to Haggai's and Zechariah's encouragement, the people returned to their work on the temple, but their opposition got back to work too. Specifically, Governor Tattenai simply but not innocently asked, "Who authorized you to rebuild this temple?" (Ezra 5:3). King Darius did some research, learned that King Cyrus had indeed authorized the project, and sent a message to the governor: "Do not interfere with the work on this temple of God" (6:7).

Lest anyone doubt his resolve, Darius included this instruction: "I decree that if anyone defies this edict, a beam is to be pulled from their house and they are to be impaled on it" (v. 11). God's people could not have anticipated his provision of such protection!

PRAISE GOD FOR THOSE TIMES HE
MEETS YOUR NEEDS IN WAYS BEYOND
WHAT YOU COULD HAVE IMAGINED!

CELEBRATE!

The elders of the Jews continued to build and prosper under
the preaching of Haggai . . . and Zechariah. . . . They finished
building the temple. . . .

Then the people of Israel—the priests, the Levites and the rest of
the exiles—celebrated the dedication of the house of God with joy.

EZRA 6:14, 16

God's Word is full of celebrations—but what about your calendar? Undoubtedly you've noted a good number of birthdays and a few wedding anniversaries. Think about adding some celebrations of spiritual milestones. Celebrate occasions when God's work in your life was unmistakable.

That was what the people of Israel did when—by God's grace—they completed the rebuilding project. These one-time exiles celebrated God's provision, protection, and empowerment. They celebrated God's faithfulness to this remnant of his chosen people.

After the faithful Jews worked three and a half more years, and almost seventy years after its destruction, the temple was completed on March 12, 516 BC, commanded by God, facilitated by the decrees of Persian kings Cyrus, Darius, and Artaxerxes. This temple was not as large or as spectacular as Solomon's temple, but it was a home for their Lord!

CELEBRATE YOUR SPIRITUAL MILESTONES!

*For a full 180 days [Xerxes] displayed the vast wealth of his kingdom
and the splendor and glory of his majesty. . . . On the seventh
day . . . he commanded the seven eunuchs to bring before him
Queen Vashti . . . in order to display her beauty. . . . Queen Vashti
refused to come. The king became furious and burned with anger.*

ESTHER 1:4, 10–12

It's part of our human nature, our sin nature: we are perfectly content as long as things go our way on our schedule. When people
are cooperating with our wishes and serving us, when we enjoy people's respect and perhaps their envy, and when no one is annoying
us—life is good! Sounds like we're a lot like King Xerxes.

Imagine having 180 days to display your wealth—and imagine
having enough wealth to display for 180 days! It was quite the grand
event . . . until Queen Vashti said no.

The furious king consulted his advisers, and he approved of their
recommendation: Vashti would never again enter Xerxes's presence,
and someone would replace her as queen. When our ego is involved
(how humiliating that his wife said no,) and when we rationalize
our actions (we can't set a bad example for the kingdom, or all the
wives will rule the households), we—like King Xerxes—can agree to
excessive courses of action.

SHOW ME, LORD, WHERE I AM
RATIONALIZING MY SIN.

"LET A SEARCH BE MADE"

"Let a search be made for beautiful young virgins for the king. . . . Bring all these beautiful young women into the harem. . . . Let beauty treatments be given to them. Then let the young woman who pleases the king be queen instead of Vashti." This advice appealed to the king, and he followed it.

ESTHER 2:2–4

Some things never change! Men want their women beautiful. . . . Natural beauty is fine, but let's improve on nature. . . . Why be friends with other women when you can be competitors instead? . . . Are these fifth-century-BC issues or twenty-first-century-AD issues? Both.

After deposing beautiful Vashti, Xerxes was in search of another beautiful wife. So why not a beauty pageant? But consider being chosen! Maybe the spa treatment would be nice, but as Vashti's experience illustrated, even a queen's position was quite precarious.

Women outside the court were also subject to the king's ideas. His decree that girls from the kingdom be brought into his harem was irrefutable. The girls and their families had no say in the matter. If the king summoned, the family had no choice but to surrender their daughter to the king.

IT'S GOOD TO REMEMBER THAT THE
BIBLE TELLS OF REAL PEOPLE IN
REAL PLACES IN REAL TIMES.

A PROFILE OF ESTHER

Esther also was taken to the king's palace and entrusted to Hegai, who had charge of the harem. She . . . won his favor. . . . He provided her with her beauty treatments and special food . . . and moved her . . . into the best place in the harem.

ESTHER 2:8–9

Sometimes people skyrocket from virtual anonymity to fame overnight. Songs sung by Susan Boyle were suddenly heard across the US. Esther was suddenly in the king's harem! Who was this Esther?

The back story is that many Jews had chosen not to return to Judah. One of those, a man named Mordecai, was living in the city of Susa with his adopted daughter, Hadassah, also known as Esther. Through a series of miraculous events, they both became involved in a web of circumstances that involved King Xerxes, a royal decree, and a heinous plot of betrayal.

Esther became involved when she was chosen to be a candidate for King Xerxes's next wife. When she entered the palace, though, she did not reveal "her nationality . . . because Mordecai had forbidden her to do so" (Esther 2:10). Clearly, God guided Mordecai to offer wise advice that would keep Esther safe now and serve her well later; he placed Esther in the palace of the king; and he prompted Xerxes to choose her as queen.

CONSIDER WHERE GOD HAS PLACED YOU
AND WHAT HIS PURPOSES MIGHT BE.

HERO TO TARGET

During the time Mordecai was sitting at the king's gate . . . two of the king's officers . . . became angry and conspired to assassinate King Xerxes. But Mordecai found out about the plot and told Queen Esther, who in turn reported it to the king, giving credit to Mordecai.

ESTHER 2:21–22

The baseball player pitches a perfect game one day—and the next time he's on the mound, he costs the team the game. The politician is a rising star—until his mistress steps forward. Hero status can be quickly shattered, as Mordecai certainly learned.

First Mordecai was the hero, learning of a conspiracy against the king and then letting Esther know, thereby saving the king's life. This heroic act didn't gain Mordecai honor and attention from the king, but honor and attention were going to Haman (Esther 3:1). Now, per the king's command, the royal officials at the king's gate were required to kneel down before Haman.

Mordecai would have none of it. He knew the Lord's law: "You shall have no other gods before me" (Exodus 20:3). Mordecai was not going to bow to anyone or anything other than Yahweh. Mordecai refused to bow to Haman. And Haman was enraged.

HONOR GOD ABOVE ALL—ARE YOU BOWING ONLY TO HIM?

HAMAN'S CRUEL PLAN

When Haman saw that Mordecai would not kneel down or pay him honor, he was enraged. Yet having learned who Mordecai's people were, he scorned the idea of killing only Mordecai. Instead Haman looked for a way to destroy all Mordecai's people, the Jews, throughout the whole kingdom of Xerxes.

ESTHER 3:5–6

We human beings don't always think before we speak. We aren't always wise in the moment. We don't always exercise self-control when we most need to. We can overreact for many reasons, and these overreactions can be fueled by—among other things—sleep deprivation, hunger, stress, anger, and injured pride.

Haman's overreaction—his goal being "a way to destroy all Mordecai's people, the Jews"—was definitely fueled by anger, injured pride, and sin, if not outright evil.

Haman was not aware of either Esther's background or Mordecai's loyalty to the king. If Haman had been aware of their Jewish roots, he might not have so openly plotted against the Jews. Interestingly, Jewish tradition considers Haman a descendant of the Amalekite king Agag, an enemy of Israel during Saul's reign. So perhaps his confrontation with Mordecai and the decree he ultimately spearheaded was inevitable.

ASK A TRUSTED FRIEND OR RELATIVE
IF YOU TEND TO OVERREACT.

"FOR SUCH A TIME AS THIS"

When Esther's words were reported to Mordecai, he sent back this answer: . . . "If you remain silent at this time, relief and deliverance for the Jews will arise from another place, but you and your father's family will perish. And who knows but that you have come to your royal position for such a time as this?"

ESTHER 4:12–14

When you hear the word *courage*, you may think of big, dramatic moments like bungee-jumping or taking a bullet for someone. Courage can also be smaller and quieter. Bringing a child into the world is an act of courage. So is getting out of bed for the custody hearing or the oncologist's appointment. Where on that continuum would you place Esther's act of courage?

Esther's uncle had challenged her to approach the king and ask him to spare the Jews. Esther had reminded Mordecai that any uninvited person who approached the king risked being put to death. Now Esther would risk her life by appearing—uninvited—before the very king who had banished his queen from the throne and sent her away.

Esther asked Mordecai to have all the Jews in Susa fast for her for three days. "When this is done," she told Mordecai, "I will go to the king. . . . And if I perish, I perish" (Esther 4:16).

ESTHER WAS WILLING TO GIVE HER
LIFE TO SAVE THE LIVES OF MANY.
WHO DOES THAT REMIND YOU OF?

A DOMINO EFFECT

On the third day Esther put on her royal robes and stood in the inner court of the palace, in front of the king's hall. The king was sitting on his royal throne in the hall, facing the entrance. When he saw Queen Esther . . . he was pleased with her and held out to her the gold scepter. . . . So Esther approached.

ESTHER 5:1–2

Sometimes a chain of events can start when one seemingly innocuous domino falls.

Case in point: Esther approached Xerxes, who welcomed her rather than having her killed. She invited Xerxes and Haman to a banquet. After accepting the invitation, Haman was feeling good about himself—until at the king's gate he saw that Mordecai "neither rose nor showed fear in [Haman's] presence" (Esther 5:9). Haman was enraged! And the plot thickened.

That night Xerxes couldn't sleep, so at his request a servant read to him from the kingdom's chronicles, and he just "happened" to read about Mordecai foiling an assassination plot and saving Xerxes's life. Learning that Mordecai had never been honored, Xerxes asked Haman what should be done for him. Thinking Xerxes wanted to honor him, Haman described an elaborate and generous show of respect. Not so fast, Haman.

NO PLOT IS TOO THICK FOR GOD TO UNTANGLE.

"THIS VILE HAMAN!"

Queen Esther answered, "If I have found favor with you, Your Majesty, and if it pleases you, grant me my life—this is my petition. And spare my people—this is my request. For I and my people have been sold to be destroyed, killed and annihilated."

ESTHER 7:3–4

We all want to make a difference in life. Preventing the annihilation of a people—that's the opportunity that Queen Esther seized.

At her second banquet for Xerxes and Haman, Esther shared her concern about the planned destruction of her people. When Xerxes asked who was behind such evil, Esther didn't hesitate: "This vile Haman!" (Esther 7:6). And Haman was impaled on the pole he had set up for Mordecai.

Still, the irrevocable decree—such was the Persian way—posed a threat to the rest of the Jews. Haman's overthrow and Mordecai's elevation offered no real comfort as long as the decree against the Jews still stood. So Esther made another request: "Let an order be written overruling the dispatches that Haman . . . wrote to destroy the Jews" (8:5). In response, Xerxes issued an edict allowing the Jews to defend themselves on the scheduled day of annihilation. When the Persian armies attacked, God's people were ready.

BE READY TO DEFEND WHATEVER OR
WHOMEVER GOD CALLS YOU TO DEFEND.

"TEST ME IN THIS"

"You are under a curse . . . because you are robbing me. Bring the whole tithe into the storehouse. . . . Test me in this," says the LORD Almighty, "and see if I will not throw open the floodgates of heaven and pour out so much blessing that there will not be room enough to store it."

MALACHI 3:9–10

A godly parent's love can give children a hint about their heavenly Father's unconditional and unfailing love for them. Mom and Dad want life to go well for their son and daughter—so they don't keep consequences from teaching important lessons. Mom and Dad want to show their love for their son and daughter—so sometimes they wisely say no.

The heavenly Father is the perfect parent, and his "Test me" may sound odd. Of course God wants to give good gifts to his children, and some gifts are entirely grace. We don't deserve and we could never earn those gifts. But some gifts come only after we repent and start behaving the way God wants us to behave. So God says, "Test me. If you give me the entire tithe I've commanded you to give . . ."

When that tithe comes—when his children once again obey their heavenly Father's command—the floodgates of his heavens will open!

PRAISE GOD FOR HIS PERFECT
PARENTAL LOVE.

GOD'S TREASURED POSSESSION

*Those who feared the L*ORD *talked with each other, and
the L*ORD *listened and heard. A scroll of remembrance was written
in his presence concerning those who feared the L*ORD *and honored
his name. "On the day when I act," says the L*ORD *Almighty,
"they will be my treasured possession. I will spare them."*

MALACHI 3:16–17

We disappoint people. We break promises. We are self-centered. We are well-intentioned people who pledge lifelong loyalty to God but wander. And nothing in this list surprises our Creator. Oh, these behaviors don't please him, but they don't catch him off guard either.

Nor have these human behaviors—behaviors that have gone on since the garden—compelled God to invalidate his covenant promises to us. At the end of a long Old Testament journey, now speaking through Malachi, the ever-faithful God declared, "I the LORD do not change. So you, the descendants of Jacob, are not destroyed" (Malachi 3:6). Continuing to speak through Malachi, the holy Lord acknowledged, "Ever since the time of your ancestors you have turned away from my decrees and have not kept them" (v. 7). Yet again came a declaration of covenant promise keeping. The Lord knows who fears him and honors his name, and so he declares, "I will spare them."

RESPOND TO GOD'S GREAT
COVENANT WITH PRAISE.

GOD'S SET TIME

When the set time had fully come, God sent his Son, born of a woman, born under the law, to redeem those under the law, that we might receive adoption to sonship.

GALATIANS 4:4–5

Four hundred years ago North America was wilderness. No United States of America. Just the beginnings of colonies. The English founded Jamestown in 1607; the French, Quebec in 1608; and the Spanish, Santa Fe in 1609. It's an understatement, but a lot has happened on this continent in the intervening four centuries.

And four centuries is the length of time after Malachi's prophecies that God did not speak anything new. That's why this intertestamental period is sometimes referred to as the "silent years." These years of social and political upheaval were anything but silent for the Jews, God's on-again, off-again chosen people to whom he had pledged his never-ending love and faithfulness.

Furthermore, this period void of prophets and messages from the Almighty didn't mean that God's story was finished. Not at all! After four centuries, God's people would see his gracious, compassionate, unfailing love personified in Jesus. All the purposes of God came together in Jesus and his mission on planet Earth.

THIS CARPENTER FROM GALILEE, NAMED JESUS, WAS GOD'S FINAL WORD.

He has shown you, O mortal, what is good.
And what does the Lord require of you?
To act justly and to love mercy
and to walk humbly with your God.

MICAH 6:8

THE NEW
TESTAMENT

"IN THE BEGINNING"

In the beginning was the Word, and the Word was with God, and the Word was God. He was with God in the beginning. Through him all things were made; without him nothing was made that has been made. In him was life, and that life was the light of all mankind.

Some people like riddles; others don't. Some like biographies; others don't. Some like to analyze literature; others just want to read it. And what do those statements have to do with the first four verses of John's gospel?

First, where else in God's Word have you read "In the beginning"? Yes, Genesis 1:1. As we learned in elementary school, biographies are nonfiction, and these four biographies of Jesus—the gospels according to Matthew, Mark, Luke, and John—whatever your opinion of the genre, cannot be ignored. Finally, this passage can sound something like a riddle, but here comes the *ah-ha!* moment.

The Old Testament opens with "In the beginning God"; the gospel of John, with "In the beginning was the Word." In John's gospel, "the Word" *is* God who came in the flesh to dwell on this earth. Of course that statement raises all kinds of questions—when, how, and, most importantly, why. Keep reading!

AS FAMILIAR AS JOHN 1:1–4 MAY BE, TRY TO HEAR THIS TRUTH AFRESH—AND BE AWED.

UPSIDE DOWN

"Do not be afraid, Mary; you have found favor with God. You will conceive and give birth to a son, and you are to call him Jesus. He will be great and will be called the Son of the Most High. . . . His kingdom will never end."

D on't worry!" triggers worry. "Don't laugh" can prompt the giggles. And "Don't be afraid" means you have good reason to be afraid. Such was the case here as the angel Gabriel appeared to Mary, a young virgin pledged to marry a man named Joseph, yet chosen by God to play a unique and crucial role in history.

The angel began with, "Greetings, you who are highly favored!" (Luke 1:28). The account says that Mary was "greatly troubled" (v. 29), which is hardly synonymous with feeling "highly favored"! And those troubled feelings undoubtedly increased as this bride-to-be learned that she was to give birth to the Son of the Most High.

How would she begin to explain this to Joseph—or her mom? What about her engagement? And what would the neighbors think? "Don't be afraid"? How could Mary be anything *but* afraid? The angel's message turned her world upside down.

GABRIEL'S ANNOUNCEMENT CHANGED NOT ONLY MARY'S WORLD BUT ALSO THE COURSE OF WORLD HISTORY.

A WILLING SERVANT

"I am the Lord's servant," Mary answered. "May your word to
me be fulfilled." Then the angel left her. . . .
  "My soul glorifies the Lord
  and my spirit rejoices in God my Savior. . . .
  From now on all generations will call me blessed,
  for the Mighty One has done great things for me—
  holy is his name."

LUKE 1:38, 46–49

How well do you change gears? "But I just made dinner, and now you want to go out?" "I had an outfit planned, and now it's raining."

The news the angel Gabriel brought Mary didn't mean a mere change of gears. It meant a complete change of expectations for the entire course of her life. And her reaction was remarkable: "I am the Lord's servant. May your word to me be fulfilled."

What an example to those of us who prefer familiarity to spontaneity! Mary humbly accepted this radical change of direction in her life. In trust, she yielded herself—her dreams, her plans, her very body—to the Lord. And then she celebrated in song the privilege of being used by him in his kingdom plan.

LORD, TEACH US TO YIELD WITH GRACE
AND WITH FAITH TO YOUR PLANS FOR US.

KUDOS TO JOSEPH

An angel of the Lord appeared [to Joseph] in a dream and said, "Joseph son of David, do not be afraid to take Mary home as your wife, because what is conceived in her is from the Holy Spirit. She will give birth to a son, and you are to give him the name Jesus, because he will save his people from their sins."

MATTHEW 1:20–21

Y ou are absolutely glowing!" "We want to throw you a shower!" "Where are you registered?" A pregnancy tends to be much more about Mom than Dad, more about Mary than Joseph.

But let's consider Joseph's situation. He probably wanted to believe Mary, but he was in the difficult situation of being engaged to a woman whom his family and friends would now despise. And staying with Mary would definitely cost him his standing in the community, his success as a carpenter, and his future role in the synagogue. Certainly breaking off the engagement was the best option. But then Joseph had a visitor. And Joseph chose to do "what the angel of the Lord had commanded him and took Mary home as his wife" (Matthew 1:24).

JOSEPH'S ROLE DURING MARY'S PREGNANCY INDICATES THE FAITH AND GODLY CHARACTER OF THIS REMARKABLE MAN.

AUTHOR OF HISTORY, PROMISE MAKER, PROMISE KEEPER

In those days Caesar Augustus issued a decree that a census should be taken of the entire Roman world. . . . And everyone went to their own town to register. So Joseph also went up from the town of Nazareth in Galilee to Judea, to Bethlehem the town of David, because he belonged to the house and line of David.

LUKE 2:1, 3–4

The Lord works in mysterious ways. Some of that mystery lies in the fact that he is sovereign. He must always be at work to accomplish his good and perfect purpose for the world and, simultaneously, for individuals. Three verses from Luke 2 offer a clear illustration of God moving.

First, Caesar Augustus decreed that a census should be taken. Whatever his purposes were, a much bigger purpose was being accomplished. God was moving Joseph and his pregnant wife to Bethlehem—and he was doing so very near her due date!

Second, that the Baby would be born in Bethlehem had been prophesied approximately seven hundred years earlier (see Micah 5:2) and was now being fulfilled. And that the Son was born to a virgin fulfilled another prophecy, Isaiah 7:14.

Nothing that happens in God's universe is random.

CHRISTIANITY IS ROOTED IN
CONFIRMED HISTORICAL EVENTS.

PAUSE AT THE MANGER

While they were there, the time came for the baby to be born, and she gave birth to her firstborn, a son. She wrapped him in cloths and placed him in a manger, because there was no guest room available for them.

LUKE 2:6–7

Sometimes a close look at something familiar helps us see it in a new light and appreciate it in a new way. So let's take a look at the manger in Bethlehem.

We who understand who the Baby is need to pause and ponder, to be awed and amazed. This newborn was the Son of God; the infinite and eternal God came to this earth as a finite human being for a limited time—and a very specific purpose. He came to die, the unblemished Lamb of God as the ultimate sacrifice for mankind's sins.

God came as a helpless baby, totally dependent on Mary and Joseph to provide for his every need. And as a baby, God burped, he cried, and he had to learn to talk and to walk. As a toddler he probably bumped into the edge of a table, unaware of how tall he had gotten. Yes, Jesus with a knot on his forehead and certainly some skinned knees along the way. Jesus may also have wanted to "help" Joseph in the wood shop—and he may have frustrated Joseph who had promised the finished stool to the customer by sundown.

PAUSE AT THE MANGER AND PONDER GOD AS A BABY.

The angel said . . . "Do not be afraid. I bring you good news
that will cause great joy for all the people. Today in the town
of David a Savior has been born to you; he is the Messiah, the
Lord. This will be a sign to you: You will find a baby wrapped in
cloths and lying in a manger."

LUKE 2:10–12

Every birth is unique just as every baby is. But what God planned for the birth of his Son takes unique to a new level.

First, the Almighty arranged world events for Jesus' birth to the virgin named Mary to happen in Bethlehem, the city of David. For birth announcements, the Almighty chose a heavenly messenger rather than the post office. As for the site, rather than a rose-garden ceremony or a Super Bowl halftime show, he had the messenger share the news with a handful of shepherds out in the fields. And shepherds in those days were as respected as migrant workers picking strawberries or homeless people scavenging for food behind a restaurant.

Yet it was to shepherds that the Lord's glorious angel appeared. Of course the shepherds were terrified, so the angel first said, "Do not be afraid." Then came the big news: "A Savior, the Messiah, the Lord has been born!"

REJOICE THAT OUR SAVIOR HAS BEEN BORN!

ANGELIC PRAISE, HUMAN WONDER

Suddenly a great company of the heavenly host appeared with the
angel, praising God and saying,
   "Glory to God in the highest heaven,
      and on earth peace to those on whom his favor rests."
   When the angels had left . . . the shepherds . . . hurried off and
found Mary and Joseph, and the baby, who was lying in the manger.

LUKE 2:13–16

Some news is just too good to keep to yourself! Besides, joy shared is definitely joy multiplied.

Having seen the baby the angels had announced and celebrated, the shepherds did not keep the night's amazing events a secret. Luke wrote, "They spread the word . . . about this child, and all who heard it were amazed" (2:17–18). When the shepherds returned to their field and flocks, they praised and glorified God!

Some news, however, is just too good to share. Its beauty seems too fragile; the wonder, so delicate. Even the most gentle of words might somehow diminish the moment. The birth of her first child—God's Son—was such a moment for young Mary. As she watched the night's events unfold around her, she "treasured up all these things and pondered them in her heart" (v. 19).

> THE GOOD NEWS THAT SALVATION
> IS AVAILABLE TO ALL IS TOO
> GOOD NOT TO SHARE.

MOOD MUSIC

After Jesus was born in Bethlehem in Judea, during the time of
King Herod, Magi from the east came to Jerusalem and asked,
"Where is the one who has been born king of the Jews? We saw
his star when it rose and have come to worship him."

MATTHEW 2:1–2

You've noticed how a movie soundtrack can build suspense, heighten joy, invite worry, or intensify excitement. In your mind, add music to this account of the Magi's visit to Herod, Herod's unsettledness and deceit, and the wise men's visit to the Christ Child.

These wise men must have entered Herod's court with great excitement and anticipation: they were close to the spot where the star had led them. The mood and the music must have darkened as they spoke with Herod.

But the mood and music were once again joyful as the Magi arrived at the house and "saw the child with his mother Mary" (Matthew 2:11). Their worship and their gifts of gold, frankincense, and myrrh added to the celebration—but then came dark music and the warning to return home not via the palace and a visit with Herod but another way.

THINK BACK OVER YOUR JOURNEY WITH
JESUS AND ADD A SOUNDTRACK.

DIVINE GUIDANCE

An angel of the Lord appeared to Joseph in a dream. "Get up,"
he said, "take the child and his mother and escape to Egypt. Stay
there until I tell you, for Herod is going to search for the child to
kill him."

MATTHEW 2:13

Some people you just don't argue with. They say, "Jump!" and you say, "How high?" They say, "No!" and the case is closed. Maybe you had a coach, teacher, parent, or army drill instructor like that. Joseph had an angel of the Lord who undoubtedly warranted the same response: "Sir, yes, sir!"

The instructions were clear: "Go to Egypt with Mary and Jesus." The reason, rock-solid: "Herod wants to kill the child." Joseph immediately obeyed. The young family fled in the dark of night—and not long after that, Herod raged. The furious madman "gave orders to kill all the boys in Bethlehem and its vicinity who were two years old and under" (Matthew 2:16).

After Herod's death and more middle-of-the-night instructions from an angel, the young family returned to Israel. Then, in still another dream, an angel directed Joseph to settle in a town called Nazareth.

PREPARE YOUR HEART TO OBEY
WITHOUT HESITATING THE NEXT
TIME GOD SAYS, "GO!"

HIS FATHER'S HOUSE

"Why were you searching for me?" [Jesus asked his parents.] "Didn't you know I had to be in my Father's house?" But they did not understand. . . .

He went down to Nazareth and was obedient to them. . . . Jesus grew in wisdom and stature, and in favor with God and man.

LUKE 2:49–52

Inquiring minds want to know! Specifically, inquiring spiritual minds want to know more: Was Jesus an easy baby? What was the most challenging aspect of parenting him?

The Bible doesn't report on the first twelve years of Jesus' life. Most likely he studied in the synagogue and learned carpentry from Joseph. We learn that Jesus traveled to Jerusalem with his family to celebrate Passover. Afterward, Jesus' parents headed home, thinking he was among the large group. When they realized after a day that he wasn't, they returned to Jerusalem to look for their son. And where was Jesus? "In the temple courts, sitting among the teachers, listening to them and asking them questions. Everyone . . . was amazed at his understanding and his answers" (Luke 2:46–47). Clearly, Jesus was very much at home in his Father's house!

JESUS WAS GOD IN HUMAN FLESH—FULLY HUMAN AND FULLY DIVINE. WHAT MIGHT HIS FIRST TWELVE YEARS HAVE BEEN LIKE?

A TIMELESS MESSAGE

In those days John the Baptist came, preaching in the wilderness of Judea and saying, "Repent, for the kingdom of heaven has come near." . . . People went out to him from Jerusalem and all Judea and the whole region of the Jordan. Confessing their sins, they were baptized by him.

MATTHEW 3:1–2, 5–6

The Savior of the world was announced by a bohemian prophet known as John the Baptist who wore clothes "made of camel's hair," tied "a leather belt around his waist," and ate "locusts and wild honey" (Matthew 3:4). Such was Jesus' entrance into the ministry.

While still in the womb, John leaped when Mary—pregnant with Jesus—entered the room and greeted Elizabeth (Luke 1:41). John's father was the priest named Zechariah who had been told that John would "bring back many of the people of Israel to the Lord their God" (v. 16).

John's message was more timely than any other in Jesus' day when he first preached it, and it's still relevant today, twenty-one centuries later: "Repent, for the kingdom of heaven has come near."

REPENTANCE REQUIRES THE
RECOGNITION OF OUR SIN.

HEAVEN WAS OPENED

As soon as Jesus was baptized, he went up out of the water. At that moment heaven was opened, and [John] saw the Spirit of God descending like a dove and alighting on him. And a voice from heaven said, "This is my Son, whom I love; with him I am well pleased."

MATTHEW 3:16–17

Certain things just aren't done. The players don't decide the starting lineup. The students don't assign the homework. And John the Baptist does not baptize Jesus—but he did!

At first John protested (Matthew 3:14)—and wouldn't you? Imagine the calm authority in Jesus' voice when he said, "It is proper for us to do this to fulfill all righteousness" (v. 15). John consented—and wouldn't you? When God's Son speaks of the importance of fulfilling God's plan, you cooperate.

And what a blessing John received when he obeyed: "At that moment heaven was opened" (v. 16). Then John heard the voice of God and saw the Spirit of God, in the form of a dove, alight on Jesus. The Lord gloriously confirmed John's ministry and message. What a touchstone moment for the time when that ministry and message would be challenged.

THANK GOD FOR THOSE TOUCHSTONE MOMENTS WHEN HE BLESSED YOU WITH REASSURANCE OF HIS LOVE FOR YOU.

STANDING STRONG AGAINST TEMPTATION

After fasting forty days and forty nights, [Jesus] was hungry. The tempter came to him and said, "If you are the Son of God, tell these stones to become bread . . . . Throw yourself down. . . . Bow down and worship me." Jesus said to him, "Away from me, Satan!"

MATTHEW 4:2–3, 6, 9–10

What a sweet time with the Lord this morning, the sun warming your back as God's truth warmed your heart—and then came the phone call: "I got a pink slip, honey." The enemy's timing can be too perfect. Too horribly perfect. A rich time with Jesus can fade to nothingness when the world crashes in.

In Matthew's gospel, "This is my Son, whom I love; with him I am well pleased" is immediatcly followed by, "Jesus was led by the Spirit into the wilderness to be tempted by the devil" (Matthew 3:17; 4:1). Soul-wrenching temptation by the too-clever devil crashed in after Jesus' empowering baptism and forty-day communion with the Father.

Yet, despite physical weakness after a forty-day fast, Jesus stood strong in God's truth, countering Satan's temptations with the Lord's Word, and finally commanding the tempter to leave. "The devil left him, and angels came and attended him" (Matthew 4:11).

THE SAME WEAPON BY WHICH JESUS
DEFEATED SATAN IS AVAILABLE
TO YOU: THE WORD OF GOD.

QUESTIONS AND ANSWERS

The Jewish leaders in Jerusalem sent priests and Levites to ask [John] who he was. . . . John replied in the words of Isaiah the prophet, . . . "I am the voice of one calling in the wilderness, 'Make straight the way for the Lord.' . . . But among you stands one you do not know . . . the straps of whose sandals I am not worthy to untie."

JOHN 1:19, 23, 26–27

It can be more than a little unnerving when circumstances or people don't match—or even come close—to expectations.

After being tested in the wilderness, Jesus began his public ministry. John the Baptist continued to point to Jesus. The religious elite wondered: Who was this Jesus? A new prophet? A charismatic leader who would free Israel from Rome? John's answers to their questions may not have been especially helpful, yet his bold proclamations continued.

The day after the interrogation, John saw Jesus and said, "Look, the Lamb of God, who takes away the sin of the world!" and testified that "I saw the Spirit come down from heaven as a dove and remain on him. I have seen and I testify that this is God's Chosen One" (John 1:29, 32, 34).

BE READY TO SHARE YOUR TESTIMONY
WHEN SOMEONE ASKS, "WHO IS JESUS?"

LOOK! FOLLOW!

When [John] saw Jesus passing by, he said, "Look, the Lamb of God!" . . .

Andrew . . . heard what John had said. . . . The first thing Andrew did was to find his brother Simon [Peter] . . . and he brought him to Jesus. . . .

The next day Jesus decided to leave for Galilee. Finding Philip, he said to him, "Follow me."

JOHN 1:36, 40–43

Different things motivate different people—and not all motives are made equal. A medical diagnosis tends to prompt a healthier diet than an upcoming reunion does!

Now imagine the wide range of experiences that have motivated people through the centuries to follow Jesus. Perhaps threats of fire and brimstone, Mother Teresa-type love, or that quiet voice in your heart prompted you to name Jesus as your Savior. Maybe you had to hit rock bottom before turning to Jesus.

Or someone may have cried, as John the Baptist did, "Look!" and helped you recognize Jesus. Others may have gone after you and brought you face to face with Jesus. Or maybe Jesus found you as he found Philip and said, "Follow me"—and you did.

WHETHER YOU HEARD, "LOOK!" OR
"FOLLOW!" THANK JESUS FOR YOUR
SALVATION—AND ASK HIM TO SHOW YOU
WHO NEEDS TO HEAR YOU SAY, "LOOK!"

WATER INTO WINE

Jesus said to the servants, "Fill the jars with water." . . . *Then he told them, "Now draw some out."* . . . *The master of the banquet tasted the water that had been turned into wine.* . . . *He called the bridegroom aside and said* . . . *"You have saved the best till now."*

JOHN 2:7–10

It's a simple fact that actions can speak louder than words. We can say we care, but that's hard to believe if we are never available to help, to listen, to serve.

At this early point in Jesus' ministry, his actions would start to reinforce the truth that he was the Son of God. Yet what an interesting first miracle Jesus chose to perform!

Consider the setting: a wedding reception as opposed to a life-or-death situation. Consider the need—or was it more of a want? The wine was running low. And Jesus—fully God, fully man—acted. It was not a crisis or an emergency or a necessity, yet Jesus showed his concern. And he was concerned enough to act, yet he kept his action pretty low profile. The servants and his mother knew the source of the wine. The master of the banquet and the bridegroom might not even have known the wine was running low.

JESUS CONSTANTLY SHOWS HE CARES ABOUT THE DETAILS OF OUR LIVES. MAY WE NOT MISS SEEING HIS ACTS OF LOVE.

"BORN OF WATER AND THE SPIRIT"

Jesus replied, "Very truly I tell you, no one can see the kingdom of God unless they are born again. . . . Very truly I tell you, no one can enter the kingdom of God unless they are born of water and the Spirit. Flesh gives birth to flesh, but the Spirit gives birth to spirit."

JOHN 3:3, 5–6

C louds, *cookies,* and *spam* meant something different before technology co-opted those terms. Technology has meant new meanings for familiar words, and a new way to look at the world.

Jesus also brought new meanings for familiar words, and a new way to look at the world. And Nicodemus wanted to know more. Approaching Jesus at night, Nicodemus acknowledged that "no one could perform the signs you are doing if God were not with him" (John 3:2). Jesus responded that a full understanding of God's kingdom would come only if Nicodemus were born again—and, Jesus added, "born of water and the Spirit."

Baptism cleanses us from our sin once we recognize and confess that sin. Admitting our need for a Savior opens us to God's Spirit working in us to give us a new perspective on life—evidence of our entrance into God's kingdom.

REFLECT ON THE MOST SIGNIFICANT CHANGES YOU EXPERIENCED WHEN YOU WERE BORN AGAIN INTO GOD'S KINGDOM.

THE MOST IMPORTANT CHOICE YOU'LL MAKE

"For God so loved the world that he gave his one and only Son, that whoever believes in him shall not perish but have eternal life. . . . Whoever believes in him is not condemned, but whoever does not believe stands condemned already because they have not believed in the name of God's one and only Son."

JOHN 3:16, 18

*C*ause and effect is not as simple as that phrase may suggest. After all, one cause can have several effects and sometimes multiple causes can lead to a single effect.

Yet the cause-and-effect relationship of John 3:16 is pretty straightforward. Believing in Jesus (cause)—believing that Jesus is God's Son who died on the cross as payment for our sins and then rose from the dead victorious over sin and death—means eternal life (effect). Not believing this truth about Jesus (cause) means perishing (effect).

Yet not everyone chooses life. John explained why: "Light has come into the world, but people loved darkness instead of light because their deeds were evil" (John 3:19). The bright light of truth can be harsh at first, but light brings life. And in this case, life eternal.

GOD, WHAT A BLESSING TO WALK
IN YOUR LIGHT AND YOUR LOVE—
NOW AND FOR ETERNITY!

THE WATER OF ETERNAL LIFE

When a Samaritan woman came to draw water, Jesus said to her, "Will you give me a drink?" . . .

The Samaritan woman said to him, "You are a Jew and I am a Samaritan woman. How can you ask me for a drink?"

JOHN 4:7, 9

In our world of garage-door openers and earphones, we can easily live a solitary life in a cocoon of our own making. So it can be a little jarring when someone strikes up a conversation. And it was more than a little jarring for the Samaritan woman at the well when a Jewish man asked her for a drink of water. In the culture of that day, women were second-class citizens. Furthermore, there were longstanding historical reasons why Jews would not associate in any way with Samaritans, let alone a woman.

Yet here was Jesus initiating a potentially life-changing conversation. But at first the two were talking at cross purposes. The woman didn't understand the metaphorical and spiritual significance of the water Jesus offered: "Whoever drinks the water I give them will never thirst" (John 4:14). Never being thirsty? Never coming to this well?

"Sir, give me this water" (v. 15). Little did she know whom she was talking to and what she was asking for.

NOTHING IN THIS WORLD CAN
SATISFY THE WAY THE LIVING
WATER JESUS OFFERS US DOES.

"COULD THIS BE THE MESSIAH?"

*The woman said, "I know that Messiah" (called Christ) "is
coming." . . .*

Then Jesus declared, "I, the one speaking to you—I am he."

*Leaving her water jar, the woman went back to the town and
said to the people, "Come, see a man who told me everything I
ever did. Could this be the Messiah?"*

JOHN 4:25–26, 28–29

I hope you're hearing what I think I'm saying!" We've all felt like
that before. Communication is challenging. Consider the conversation between Jesus and the Samaritan woman at the well. The
woman wasn't always hearing what Jesus was saying as they discussed water, husbands, places of worship, and the Messiah.

Yet how they got to the woman's recognition that Jesus was
the Messiah is not as important as the fact that she did get there—
and when she did, she wanted to share the news. This woman with
many husbands who had gone to the well at noon to avoid people
was now heading back into town to tell as many people as she could
about the amazing conversation she'd had with Rabbi Jesus.

And "many of the Samaritans from that town believed in
[Jesus] because of the woman's testimony" (John 4:39).

JESUS LOVES YOU DESPITE
EVERYTHING YOU EVER DID!

FIRST THINGS FIRST

Very early in the morning, while it was still dark, Jesus got up,
left the house and went off to a solitary place, where he prayed.

MARK 1:35

Even when we know what the right thing to do is, we don't always do it. This is true about eating and exercising, treating others the way you want to be treated, and making our relationship with God our top priority.

We all know the value of spending regular time with the Lord. We know that his Word is the bread of life and the light for our path. We know the blessing that comes with asking him to show us what he has for us in Scripture. We understand the privilege and responsibility of prayer: we are to intercede for the church, the unsaved, our nation, our neighbors and coworkers, our friends and family. We recognize the importance of memorizing God's Word, of hiding his truth in our hearts. We want to learn to better listen for his still, small voice. *And* we have experienced the soul-refreshment that comes when we spend time simply praising him and worshiping him.

But it is all too easy to *not* get alone with God and pray. Consider, though, that Jesus himself—fully God and fully man— made his quiet times with the Almighty a priority.

MAY WE, AS JESUS DID, MAKE OUR QUIET
TIMES WITH THE ALMIGHTY A PRIORITY.

"IF YOU ARE WILLING"

A man with leprosy came to him and begged him on his knees, "If you are willing, you can make me clean."

Jesus was indignant. He reached out his hand and touched the man. "I am willing," he said. "Be clean!" Immediately the leprosy left him and he was cleansed.

MARK 1:40–42

In Jesus' day, the society legally isolated those individuals suffering from leprosy—and that rejection made the suffering even worse. As if the disease weren't horrifying enough, the victims were forbidden to be near people and forced to call out, "Unclean" to warn folks of their presence. No wonder this leper who approached Jesus said, "If you are willing, you can make me clean." Why would he expect anyone to pay attention to him, to not run from him, much less to heal him?

We read above that "Jesus was indignant" (Mark 1:41) upon hearing the man's "If you are willing," but other translations report Jesus as being "moved with compassion" (NASB, NKJV, NLT) or "moved with pity" (ESV, NRSV). Jesus, who knows hearts, may have understood the man's tentativeness and felt indignant toward those people who had given the leprous man reason to think no one would ever care. Such indignation and compassion are not mutually exclusive: Jesus healed first with a touch and then with his words.

NEVER DOUBT JESUS' WILLINGNESS
TO MAKE YOU CLEAN.

THE ORDER MATTERS

"Which is easier: to say to this paralyzed man, 'Your sins are forgiven,' or to say, 'Get up, take your mat and walk'? But I want you to know that the Son of Man has authority on earth to forgive sins." So he said to the man, "I tell you, get up, take your mat and go home." He got up, took his mat and walked out.

MARK 2:9–12

So do you put both socks on and then both shoes on? Or do you put sock and shoe on one foot first and then sock and shoe on the other? In this case, the order doesn't matter—but sometimes it does.

Case in point: Four men brought their paralyzed friend to Jesus. When Jesus said to him, "Your sins are forgiven," the teachers of the law objected: "Who can forgive sins but God alone?" (Mark 2:5, 7).

And that was Jesus' point: he *was* God. Only God—as the teachers of the law clearly understood—can forgive sins. So Jesus first forgave the man of his sins, and *then* he healed the man's legs. And Jesus was very clear about why: "I want you to know that the Son of Man has authority on earth to forgive sins."

Jesus can and does heal. But first and foremost Jesus can and does forgive our sins.

ALL PRAISE TO YOU, "LAMB OF GOD, WHO TAKES AWAY THE SIN OF THE WORLD!" (JOHN 1:29)

WHOSE FAITH?

Some men came, bringing to him a paralyzed man. . . . Since they could not get him to Jesus because of the crowd, they made an opening in the roof above Jesus . . . and then lowered the mat the man was lying on. When Jesus saw their faith, he said to the paralyzed man, "Son, your sins are forgiven."

MARK 2:3–5

Often something big can overshadow something significant. It was big that the homerun won the game, but it was significant that the batter signed his bat and, with no cameras recording the moment, took it to his buddy in the pediatric cancer ward.

It was huge that the man carried to Jesus on a mat was both healed of his paralysis and forgiven for his sins. But notice a significant detail. Four of his friends had brought the paralyzed man to Jesus, and that is what impressed the Lord: "When Jesus saw *their* faith."

Believing that Jesus could heal their friend, those friends worked hard to get him into the presence of this remarkable rabbi. These friends had to be resourceful ("It's standing room only in the house! We'll never be able to get to Jesus!") and brave ("I'm sure the homeowner won't mind if we make a hole in the roof right here!"). Each step of the way, they clearly trusted in the Lord's power and love. Jesus saw the faith of these four friends and did his healing work.

LET YOUR FRIENDS CARRY YOU
TO JESUS IF YOU NEED HELP.

DINING WITH SINNERS

When the teachers of the law . . . saw [Jesus] eating with the
sinners and tax collectors, they asked his disciples: "Why does he
eat with tax collectors and sinners?"

On hearing this, Jesus said to them, "It is not the healthy who
need a doctor, but the sick. I have not come to call the righteous,
but sinners."

MARK 2:16–17

In the Alcoholics Anonymous Twelve Step program, Step 1 is the
first step to freedom. "I admit to myself that something is seriously wrong in my life."[8] In one's faith walk with Jesus, Step 1 is also
admitting that "something is seriously wrong in my life," and that
"something" has a name: sin.

Clearly, the teachers of the law didn't see themselves as sinners.
That label was for the tax collectors and other rabble eating with
Jesus. But earlier that day, the host of the meal—Levi—had stood
up from his tax collector table and followed Jesus (Mark 2:14). He'd
had an easier time seeing his sin. And Jesus was willing to dine
in the home of that sinner! Jesus was definitely a different kind of
rabbi. He put people before laws. His "new way" was forgiving and
kind. Jesus was a friend to people on the outside, people most religious leaders disliked. The Pharisees didn't get it!

JESUS, THANK YOU FOR HELPING ME
SEE MY SIN AND MY NEED FOR YOU.

DOING GOOD—EVEN ON THE SABBATH

Jesus asked them, "Which is lawful on the Sabbath: to do good or to do evil, to save life or to kill?" But [the Pharisees] remained silent. . . .

[He] said to the man, "Stretch out your hand." He stretched it out, and his hand was completely restored.

MARK 3:4–5

In general, rules, with their explicit guidelines, are less complicated than relationships. What a contrast to relationships. Relationships can't have set guidelines. No wonder the Pharisees liked their rules.

But Jesus cared more about people than rules. So when Jesus met a man with a shriveled hand that Sabbath day, Jesus didn't hesitate—or opt for low profile. Jesus said, "Stand up in front of everyone" (Mark 3:3).

All eyes were on Jesus and the man, meaning all ears were hearing Jesus' very direct question—but no mouth responded. Jesus was very direct: "Which is lawful on the Sabbath: to do good or to do evil?" The answer was obvious. No one would argue that the Sabbath was a day for evil deeds. But what did Jesus' point say about the value of the Law? The Pharisees didn't want to go there. So they "began to plot . . . how they might kill Jesus" (v. 6).

LIKE JESUS, MAY I PUT PEOPLE FIRST.

ANOINTED FOR WHAT?

Jesus went throughout Galilee, teaching in their synagogues,
proclaiming the good news of the kingdom, and healing every disease
and sickness among the people. . . . People brought to him all who
were ill . . . those suffering severe pain, the demon-possessed, those
having seizures, and the paralyzed; and he healed them.

MATTHEW 4:23–24

When Robby becomes Rob, we can have a hard time reeducating our tongue. It's not easy to change gears.

And that kind of change is nothing compared to the reeducating that Jesus needed to do regarding the word *Messiah*. It means "Anointed One"—but not anointed to free the Jewish people from the political oppression of mighty Rome. Jesus' purpose was much deeper, his intentions more significant, and his kingship infinitely more glorious than what the people were expecting.

The Jews must have been puzzled by Jesus' focus on "healing every disease and sickness." What an odd prelude to a military showdown! Teaching in the synagogues was fine, but they wanted to hear more about the kingdom he would establish after he toppled Rome. Religious people didn't get Jesus then; some religious people don't get him today.

LET US BE OPEN TO SEEING AND
ACCEPTING THE WAYS THAT JESUS
DEFIES OUR EXPECTATIONS.

[Jesus] called to him those he wanted, and they came to him. He appointed twelve that they might be with him. . . .

Jesus traveled about . . . proclaiming the good news of the kingdom of God. The Twelve were with him, and also some women.

MARK 3:13–14; LUKE 8:1–2

There is always something intriguing about an important person's inner circle. Imagine being accepted into that group. Now imagine the exponentially increased emotions if you belonged to Jesus' inner circle—an amazing but costly privilege.

So who were the people Jesus chose to pour himself into during his limited time on earth? Mark listed the twelve: "Simon (to whom he gave the name Peter), James son of Zebedee and his brother John . . . Andrew, Philip, Bartholomew, Matthew, Thomas, James son of Alphaeus, Thaddaeus, Simon the Zealot and Judas Iscariot, who betrayed him" (Mark 3:16–19). Luke provided the other half—the countercultural half—of the roster: "Mary (called Magdalene) from whom seven demons had come out; Joanna . . . Susanna; and many others" (Luke 8:2–3).

As amazing as membership in Jesus' inner circle would have been, consider this truth:

SEE WHAT GREAT LOVE THE FATHER HAS LAVISHED ON US, THAT WE SHOULD BE CALLED CHILDREN OF GOD. (1 JOHN 3:1)

"ARE YOU THE MESSIAH?"

[John] sent his disciples to ask [Jesus], "Are you the one who is to come, or should we expect someone else?"

Jesus replied, "Go back and report to John what you hear and see: The blind receive sight, the lame walk, those who have leprosy are cleansed, the deaf hear, the dead are raised, and the good news is proclaimed to the poor."

MATTHEW 11:2–5

J esus was not exactly the person his Jewish peers expected. Even John the Baptist didn't really understand who Jesus was. Yes, John had announced Jesus as the coming Messiah, but Jesus' work hadn't brought the results John evidently anticipated. So at one point he sent his disciples: "Jesus, are you the Messiah?"

Jesus' answer (above) offered some insight into his role as Savior and the Messiah. Jesus certainly wasn't (yet) the conquering warrior Messiah that many Jews had longed for. But people were nevertheless intrigued by this prophet and teacher, and they wanted to hear more.

GUIDED AND TAUGHT BY GOD'S SPIRIT, WE TOO CAN LEARN MORE ABOUT THIS HOLY ONE WHOM WE CALL SAVIOR AND LORD.

SOWING SEEDS OF TRUTH

[Jesus] taught them many things by parables. . . . "A farmer went out to sow his seed. . . . Some fell along the path. . . . Some fell on rocky places. . . . Other seed fell among thorns. . . . Still other seed fell on good soil. It came up, grew and produced a crop, some multiplying thirty, some sixty, some a hundred times."

MARK 4:2–5, 7–8

When you learned the alphabet, you learned it by singing a song, didn't you? Music can help us learn facts and memorize Scripture verses. Similarly, a good story can help us learn and remember key truths.

One of Jesus' well-known parables (stories that teach a moral lesson or spiritual truth) speaks clearly about different responses to the Word of God. Sometimes Satan snatches the truth before it can take root: that's the seed falling along the path. Sometimes trouble or persecution comes, and people not rooted in God's truth fall away: this is the rocky soil. Other people hear God's truth, but worries, wealth, and wants "choke the word" (Mark 4:19): this is the seed among thorns. Then there are those people who hear God's Word, accept it as truth, and see its fruit in their lives: this is the seed in good soil.

WHAT DO YOU DO TO PREVENT ROCKS AND THORNS FROM CHOKING OUT GOD'S WORD?

MUSTARD SEEDS, ACORNS, AND ABRAHAM

[Jesus] said, "What shall we say the kingdom of God is like, or what parable shall we use to describe it? It is like a mustard seed, which is the smallest of all seeds on earth. Yet when planted, it grows and becomes the largest of all garden plants, with such big branches that the birds can perch in its shade."

MARK 4:30–32

A visit to the Holy Land helps Scripture come to life as you walk where Jesus and the Twelve walked, wade into the Sea of Galilee, and look at gnarled olive trees and sturdy mustard plants. And that mustard prompted a parable.

The gist of Jesus' parable is simple: the smallest of seeds gets much bigger than its size suggests. The point of a well-sharpened pencil is about the size of a mustard seed. Of course, those seeds are easily overlooked and not noticed as they're blown by the wind or trampled on. Yet what that little seed grows into is unexpectedly large and strong.

Jesus was commenting on the small beginnings of God's kingdom—Noah's family, Abraham, the faithful remnant, the ragtag Twelve—and the huge end product: "descendants [of Abraham] as numerous as the stars in the sky and as countless as the sand on the seashore" (Hebrews 11:12).

MARVEL THAT GOD KNOWS YOU, ONE OF THOSE MANY STARS, BY NAME.

Jesus told [the Pharisees and tax collectors] this parable: "Suppose one of you has a hundred sheep and loses one of them. Doesn't he leave the ninety-nine in the open country and go after the lost sheep until he finds it? And when he finds it, he joyfully puts it on his shoulders and goes home."

LUKE 15:3–6

Speaking the truth in love is one way we can love others the way we want to be loved. Sometimes a story is an effective but gentle and loving way for Jesus to hold up a mirror to his listeners. But would the Pharisees and teachers of the law get the message?

As the tax collectors and sinners gathered around Jesus, the self-righteous Pharisees and teachers of the law muttered and complained, "This man welcomes sinners" (Luke 15:2). And that prompted Jesus to tell a story about a lost sheep.

The tax collectors, the gathered "sinners," and, yes, the self-righteous Pharisees and teachers of the law were all lost. All of us are lost (Romans 3:23), but that fact needn't be the end of anyone's story. It can be a joy-filled beginning. As Jesus taught, "there will be more rejoicing in heaven over one sinner who repents than over ninety-nine righteous persons who do not need to repent" (Luke 15:7).

"I AM THE GOOD SHEPHERD; I KNOW MY SHEEP AND MY SHEEP KNOW ME" (JESUS IN JOHN 10:14).

THE YOUNGER BROTHER: LESSON LEARNED

"But while [his son] was still a long way off, his father saw him and was filled with compassion for him; he ran to his son, threw his arms around him and kissed him. . . . 'For this son of mine was dead and is alive again; he was lost and is found.'"

LUKE 15:20, 24

In a story Jesus told about a father and two sons, the younger one had gone off and "squandered his wealth in wild living" (Luke 15:13). Then when a famine came and his money was gone, he found himself tending pigs and wishing they would share with him the pods they were eating. The emptiness of his stomach brought him to his senses, so he mentally drafted an apology and request for forgiveness, swallowed hard, and headed home. But he never had a chance to give his speech!

Now imagine the father's joy. He had been watching for his son (he hadn't given up hope); he ran toward the boy (hardly dignified); and he celebrated his son's return. What amazing grace!

Maybe your wandering was a lifestyle change or more a matter of the heart. If you've come to your senses, that past doesn't matter. Your heavenly Father runs toward you to celebrate your return.

"AMAZING GRACE! . . . I ONCE WAS LOST BUT NOW I'M FOUND, WAS BLIND BUT NOW I SEE!"

THE OLDER BROTHER: LESSON PRESENTED

"The older brother became angry and refused to go in [to the party for his younger brother]. . . . He answered his father, 'Look! All these years I've been slaving for you and never disobeyed your orders. Yet you never gave me even a young goat so I could celebrate with my friends.'"

LUKE 15:28–29

Did the goody-bag gift really need to be a boogie board for every sixth-grader at the birthday party? (Not making that up!) Did the bride really need two wedding dresses, one for the ceremony and one for the reception? Over the top!

And that's what the older brother thought about all this music and dancing, this feasting on the fattened calf. Hardly appropriate consequences for the disrespectful, ungrateful, selfish, wasteful younger brother!

Many of us can do a good imitation of this older brother. We can be prideful about how good we are; we can be jealous when, in our estimation, an undeserving person is treated well, and we can absolutely fail to rejoice with those who are rejoicing (Romans 12:15). And suddenly it sounds as if we need to mentally draft an apology and request for forgiveness.

THANK YOU, LORD, FOR THE TRUTH-TELLING MIRROR OF YOUR WORD.

LOVING YOUR NEIGHBOR: PEOPLE OR PROJECTS?

*"A priest . . . passed by on the other side. So too, a Levite . . .
passed by on the other side. But a Samaritan . . . took pity on
him . . . bandaged his wounds . . . put the man on his own donkey,
brought him to an inn and took care of him. . . . He took out two
denarii and gave them to the innkeeper. 'Look after him.'"*

LUKE 10:31–35

When have you received help from an unexpected source?
And when have tasks, jobs, or even privileges taken priority
over a person's needs?

Jesus told the story of a man who was attacked and left for dead
who then received help from a very unexpected source. The priest
passed by, pretending not to see; maybe he had temple duties. The
Levite passed by; maybe he didn't want to help a bleeding man and
become unclean. And maybe none of these reasons were reason
enough to walk past the man who desperately needed help.

Whatever was on the Samaritan's agenda, he stopped and
helped. And his help was not at all the bare minimum: it was selfless,
generous, and well-thought-out. This despised-by-Jews Samaritan
was treating the injured Jewish man the way he would have wanted
to be treated.

DON'T LET ME WALK BY SOMEONE
WHO NEEDS HELP.

HOW LITTLE CAN I DO?

"Which of these three do you think was a neighbor to the man who fell into the hands of robbers?"

The expert in the law replied, "The one who had mercy on him."

Jesus told him, "Go and do likewise."

LUKE 10:36–37

Perhaps it's an age or a stage; perhaps it's a personality trait; perhaps—and we may not like to admit this—it's just plain sin. *It* is that tendency to do the least possible work, to make the least possible effort, to let merely satisfying the letter of the law be good enough.

An expert in the law had "stood up to test Jesus": "Teacher . . . what must I do to inherit eternal life?" (Luke 10:25).

As he often did, Jesus answered a question with a question—"What is written in the Law?" (v. 26)—and the legal expert passed: "'Love the Lord your God' . . . and, 'Love your neighbor as yourself'" (v. 27).

Then came another question from the "expert": "And who is my neighbor?" (v. 29). Could this religious man be wanting to know all, why help anyone he really didn't *have* to help?

SHOW ME, LORD, NOT ONLY WHO MY NEIGHBOR IS BUT WHERE MY HEART IS COLD AND HARD.

"BLESSED ARE . . ."

"Blessed are the poor in spirit,
for theirs is the kingdom of heaven. . . .
Blessed are those who hunger and thirst for righteousness,
for they will be filled.
Blessed are the merciful,
for they will be shown mercy."

MATTHEW 5:3, 6–7

The secret to happiness!" "Live your dreams!" "All this can be yours!" The world's messages suggesting what matters most in life are very different from what Jesus taught.

Even a brief glance at three of the Beatitudes offers an important take-away: the world's ways and the Lord's ways are opposites.

"Poor in spirit"? The world doesn't want to be poor in any way! "Hunger and thirst for righteousness"? The world is hungry for a lot, and righteousness isn't even on the list. "Merciful"? The world values strength and a take-charge, can-do attitude.

But Jesus taught the value of being poor in spirit means seeing our need for the Lord. Hungering and thirsting for righteousness is the Christlike priority of wanting to know God in all his holiness. And showing mercy shines God's light into a world dark with self-centeredness.

FOLLOW JESUS' UPSIDE-DOWN VALUES
AND KNOW A RIGHT-SIDE-UP ETERNITY.

SALT AND LIGHT

"You are the salt of the earth. But if the salt loses its saltiness,
how can it be made salty again? It is no longer good for anything."

MATTHEW 5:13

We walk down the grocery store aisle, and we can choose name brand or store brand, iodized or not. We can too easily take salt for granted, but Jesus referred to properties of salt to teach truth.

First, salt enhances the flavor of food—and we believers are to enhance life in this world for the people we interact with. We can bring joy, kindness, hope, love, and peace into the lives of others.

Salt also preserves food—and God's people are preservatives in this fallen, sin-filled world. The decay is unmistakable: we call murder "pro-choice" and are redefining marriage.

Finally, salt makes us thirsty. (There's a reason movie theaters sell drinks with their popcorn!) May our presence in the world—may our joy and our hope despite circumstances, may our concern for others and our willingness to serve them—make people who notice thirsty for the Living Water, for the knowledge of Jesus, his forgiveness, and his love.

THANK YOU, JESUS—THE LIVING WATER—
FOR QUENCHING MY SOUL-THIRST!

"YOUR WILL BE DONE"

"Our Father in heaven,
hallowed be your name,
your kingdom come,
your will be done,
on earth as it is in heaven."

MATTHEW 6:9–10

We human beings can make things harder than they need to be. Simply say, "I blew it" rather than spinning the situation, making excuses, or trying to defend yourself. And here Jesus said, essentially, "Don't make prayer so hard" and offered a model prayer that is straightforward, basic, and direct. We ask for what we need to live (food, water, shelter); we ask for what we need to live eternally (forgiveness of our sins). We ask for what will make our journey through life easier: help us forgive those who sin against us; keep us away from temptation; and deliver us from the evil one's efforts to deceive and trip us up.

Before those requests, though, comes what is a lifelong, 24/7 prayer for human beings who want to live in a way that glorifies the Holy God: "Your will be done on earth." He is only truly our Lord if we let him call the shots and set the agenda, guide our steps and show the way.

MAY I KEEP MY PRAYERS SIMPLE, CONTINUAL,
AND ALWAYS SUBMITTED TO YOUR WILL.

WHERE IS YOUR TREASURE?

"Store up for yourselves treasures in heaven. . . . For where your treasure is, there your heart will be also. No one can serve two masters. . . . You cannot serve both God and money."

MATTHEW 6:20–21, 24

Your calendar and your checkbook register reveal *what* and *who* matter most to you. Or, to echo Jesus' words, your calendar and checkbook register reveal what treasures you are investing in.

Jesus spoke to our tendency to "store up . . . treasures on earth" (Matthew 6:19)—treasures that are tangible, that are seen and admired by others, and that make us feel pretty good about ourselves. Jesus then addressed the importance of instead storing up "treasures in heaven"—and how do we do that? By giving a cup of water to someone in Jesus' name. By sharing with a lost soul the good news of Jesus. By speaking a kind word, serving with a humble heart, dying to our own wishes, giving our tithes and offerings. The list continues, and each item is a matter of the heart, of a heart committed to glorifying God.

Storing up treasures in heaven happens more easily, Jesus taught, when we are serving only God rather than trying to serve money as well. We can't go both directions at the same time.

YOUR CHOICE: SERVE GOD OR SERVE MONEY.

ME? WORRY? PROBABLY.

"Do not worry about your life, what you will eat or drink; or about your body, what you will wear. . . . Can any one of you by worrying add a single hour to your life? . . . But seek first [your heavenly Father's] kingdom and his righteousness, and all these things will be given to you as well."

MATTHEW 6:25, 27, 33

W hy does worrying seem as natural as breathing? Rather than listing theories or circumstances, let's look more closely at what Jesus said.

Jesus understands this very human tendency, and he offered logic to counter the emotion and hard evidence to argue against worrying. First, the birds don't worry about food, and they have plenty to eat—straight from our heavenly Father's hand. How much more generously and faithfully will God provide food for you, whom he values more than a sparrow!

You can be assured that your heavenly Father knows what you need and finds joy in providing those things. Then comes the charge/promise: "Seek first [your heavenly Father's] kingdom and his righteousness, and all these things will be given to you as well."

WHAT ARE YOU SEEKING FIRST?

A SURE FOUNDATION

"Everyone who hears these words of mine and puts them into practice is like a wise man who built his house on the rock. The rain came down, the streams rose, and the winds blew and beat against that house; yet it did not fall, because it had its foundation on the rock."

MATTHEW 7:24–25

M aybe it was wooden blocks, Legos, or Lincoln Logs. Whatever the construction pieces were, they taught you early on the importance of having a strong, sturdy, solid foundation for a building. Jesus taught that a strong, sturdy, solid foundation is as important for our lives as it is for the buildings we live in.

We have options when it comes to physical foundations: patio stones, cinder blocks, super spikes, concrete footings, concrete pad. With Jesus, the choice is simpler: building on the rock of Jesus' teachings or on the sand of anything else we might choose. According to Jesus, the first is wise; the second, foolish. The first option can weather the storms of life; the second collapses.

The fact that a person's life will be built on something is a given. The storms of life are a given. The choice of where you build is yours.

NO BETTER FOUNDATION FOR LIFE EXISTS THAN THE TEACHINGS OF JESUS.

"DON'T YOU CARE?"

A furious squall came up, and the waves broke over the boat, so that it was nearly swamped. Jesus was in the stern, sleeping on a cushion. The disciples woke him and said to him, "Teacher, don't you care if we drown?" Jesus got up, rebuked the wind and said to the waves, "Quiet! Be still!" Then the wind died down and it was completely calm.

MARK 4:37–39

The unexpected pink slip. A broken arm. The death that came so suddenly.

Life's storms come in different forms. Yet our reaction to any and all of them can pretty much be the same: "Don't you care?"

We can feel pretty helpless. The largeness of the situation overwhelms. The reality of our human limitations is cold and sobering. Over the noise of the gale-force winds and crashing water, we yell to God, "Don't you care?"

Jesus showed the disciples that he cared by calming the storm, and he still does this. Maybe he's done that for you. Suddenly the situation has been resolved; the need, met; the path, cleared.

But sometimes Jesus shows you he cares by riding out the storm with you. He's in the boat with you and won't be leaving you—ever.

YOU AREN'T ALONE, BECAUSE,
YES, HE CARES.

JESUS' POWER OVER DEMONS

A man with an impure spirit came . . . to meet [Jesus]. . . . He
shouted . . . "What do you want with me, Jesus, Son of the
Most High God?" . . . For Jesus had said to him, "Come out of
this man, you impure spirit!" . . .

The demons begged Jesus, "Send us among the
pigs." . . . The impure spirits went into the pigs. The herd, about
two thousand in number, rushed down the steep bank into the
lake and were drowned.

MARK 5:2, 7–8, 12–13

This demon-possessed man lived in the tombs, where "he tore the chains apart and broke the irons on his feet" (Mark 5:4). Jesus immediately knew what the problem was and called out the impure spirit—who introduced himself: "My name is Legion . . . for we are many" (v. 9). The demons begged Jesus to send them into the herd of pigs, and the "herd, about two thousand in number, rushed down the steep bank into the lake and were drowned" (v. 13).

As this scene unfolded, the people weren't eating M&Ms and enjoying their stadium seating. They were terrified by what they had seen—and they begged Jesus to leave.

DARKNESS IS TERRIFYING—AND SO IS THE
MORE POWERFUL LIGHT THAT CONQUERS IT.

THE POWER OF YOUR TESTIMONY

[The townspeople] saw the man who had been possessed by the legion of demons, sitting there, dressed and in his right mind; and they were afraid. . . .

As Jesus was getting into the boat, the man . . . begged to go with him. Jesus . . . said, "Go home to your own people and tell them how much the Lord has done for you, and how he has had mercy on you."

MARK 5:15, 18–19

Credibility comes when you speak from your personal experience. You aren't merely sharing something you've read about or heard secondhand or seen on TV. And speaking of your personal experience makes for a powerful testimony about God's goodness, power, and love. And that's what this demon-possessed man had: he knew what it was to be lost, to be living among tombs, tearing apart chains that bound him, cutting himself with stones—and he knew what it was to be found.

Yes, this man wanted to go with the One who had found him and delivered him, but Jesus knew the value of this man's testimony. "So the man went away and began to tell . . . how much Jesus had done for him. And all the people were amazed" (Mark 5:20).

BE PREPARED TO SHARE YOUR TESTIMONY.

*When she heard about Jesus, she came up behind him in the
crowd and touched his cloak, because she thought, "If I just touch
his clothes, I will be healed." Immediately her bleeding stopped
and she felt in her body that she was freed from her suffering.*

MARK 5:27–29

Nineteenth-century British preacher Charles Spurgeon observed,
"To trust God in the light is nothing, but to trust him in the
dark—that is faith."

This woman's days were dark, and they had been dark for at
least the twelve years she had been "subject to bleeding" (Mark 5:25).
The hemorrhaging made her unclean, and that uncleanness meant
isolation and loneliness. By God's grace—there is no other explanation—she still believed: "If I just touch his clothes, I will be healed."

Breaking cultural rules regarding uncleanness, she made her way
through the crowd of people pressing in around Jesus and touched his
cloak. It was not an accidental brush-up-against type touch; it was
an intentional, deliberate, premeditated, faith-filled touch—and Jesus
recognized it as such. And she immediately realized that she had been
healed! She also realized she had to answer Jesus' question: "Who
touched my clothes?" (v. 30). She "fell at his feet and, trembling with
fear, told him the whole truth" (v. 33)—and received his blessing: "Go
in peace" (v. 34).

GOD IS HONORED BY OUR STEPS OF FAITH.

"PLEASE COME"

One of the synagogue leaders, named Jairus, came, and when he saw Jesus, he fell at his feet. He pleaded earnestly with him, "My little daughter is dying. Please come and put your hands on her so that she will be healed and live." So Jesus went with him.

MARK 5:22–24

Think about times when you've cried out to Jesus in faith—or at least in the closest thing to faith you could muster. What circumstances do you think of? Cries of faith come in simple words as well as eloquent pleas, in whispers and screams, in every imaginable setting, anytime day or night, from people who—by God's grace—recognize their need for a Savior, who recognize that Jesus is the Savior sent by God.

Not every synagogue leader in Jesus' day recognized who this rabbi was, but Jairus did. And when his daughter was near death, he went to Jesus—and he trusted Jesus' ability to heal her. The request began humbly: "Please come." Then hear Jairus's confidence: "Put your hands on her so that she will be healed and live." She *will* be healed!

But then word came that she had died. Jesus encouraged the father to continue to believe, and Jesus honored that faith—perhaps only the size of a mustard seed. He walked into the girl's room, spoke, "Little girl . . . get up!"; and "immediately the girl stood up" (vv. 41–42).

CRY OUT TO YOUR SAVIOR
AND WATCH HIM WORK.

LEFTOVER BLESSINGS

Taking the five loaves and the two fish and looking up to heaven,
he gave thanks and broke the loaves. Then he gave them to his
disciples to distribute to the people. He also divided the two fish
among them all. They all ate and were satisfied, and the disciples
picked up twelve basketfuls of broken pieces of bread and fish.

MARK 6:41–43

Imagine being in the middle of nowhere. Five thousand men plus women and children have gathered. It's the dinner hour, but you can't possibly feed them all. You just don't have the resources! Five loaves of bread and two fish just won't do it.

But you give Jesus those five loaves of bread and two fish. He thanks God for this provision and then hands you some food so you can start feeding the crowd.

So you start walking, wondering just how far you'll get before you run out of food. But as you keep putting one foot in front of the other, you don't seem to be running out of food. You keep walking— and Jesus keeps providing!

Maybe, in your current situation, resources seem meager or even nonexistent. Keep walking and, just as those twelve disciples did, watch Jesus provide what you need—and then some. There were leftovers at that impromptu picnic!

KEEP WALKING—AND WATCH GOD PROVIDE.

FOCUS MATTERS

"Lord, if it's you," Peter replied, "tell me to come to you on the water."

"Come," he said.

Then Peter got down out of the boat, walked on the water and came toward Jesus. But when he saw the wind, he was afraid and, beginning to sink, cried out, "Lord, save me!"

MATTHEW 14:28–30

Is your default, "I can hardly wait to see what God does here," or thoughts of the worst-case scenario? Some of us, by nature, are more pessimistic than others. But if you default to the worst possible outcome, maybe a change of focus will help.

Peter's experience shows us the value of keeping our eyes focused on Jesus rather than on life's circumstances. With his eyes on Jesus, who was walking on the water toward the boat, Peter boldly stepped out and took some steps toward Jesus. "But when he saw the wind"—when Peter took his eyes off Jesus—his courage disappeared. Fear took over and, with it, gravity's normal pull.

There is nothing like fear to make us doubt. As he "reached out his hand and caught him," Jesus offered that diagnosis to Peter: "You of little faith," he said, "why did you doubt?" (Matthew 14:31).

We doubt when we focus on circumstances instead of our Savior.

HELP ME KEEP MY EYES ON YOU, JESUS.

THE HEART'S MOTIVE

"You are looking for me, not because you saw the signs I performed but because you ate the loaves and had your fill. Do not work for food that spoils, but for food that endures to eternal life."

JOHN 6:26–27

Think about the one or two people who know you best. Maybe they can finish your sentences for you. Or they are able to read you and know your mood even before you speak.

As close as you are to those dear people, realize that Jesus knows you even better—and, in fact, knows you even better than you know yourself. After all, Jesus knows your heart before you put any spin on what you're thinking or feeling. Jesus also knew the hearts of the crowd that had gone to Capernaum to find him. Specifically, Jesus knew—and knew why—their first stop had been "near the place where the people had eaten the bread after the Lord had given thanks" (John 6:23).

Jesus knows why people go to him. This crowd wanted food; they weren't interested in what that sign pointed to. They were preoccupied by life in this world. "Food that endures to eternal life" was a secondary concern at best.

What are you, metaphorically speaking now, more concerned about—tangible bread or bread that leads to eternal life?

WHY ARE YOU GOING TO JESUS— OR WHY AREN'T YOU?

THE BREAD OF LIFE

Jesus said . . . "It is not Moses who has given you the bread from heaven, but it is my Father who gives you the true bread from heaven. . . . I am the bread of life. Whoever comes to me will never go hungry, and whoever believes in me will never be thirsty."

JOHN 6:32, 35

How are you?" "Fine." A clichéd question; a clichéd answer. Two can play the game.

A question that does more to build relationship is, "How are you and the Lord doing?" or "What's the Lord doing in your life or your heart?" We are both spiritual and physical beings, yet the physical too easily takes precedence over the spiritual. It certainly did for this crowd.

They touched on the spiritual just a bit: "What must we do to do the works God requires?" (John 6:28). Jesus answered straightforwardly: "The work of God is this: to believe in the one he has sent" (v. 29). But the crowd quickly returned to the issue of bread, reminding Jesus of manna that Moses provided (Jesus corrected them, saying, "It was God!") and at one point boldly saying, "Sir . . . always give us this bread" (v. 34).

Ironically, Jesus does "always give us this bread" because he—Emmanuel, "God with us"—is "the bread of life."

LORD, PLEASE GIVE ME AN APPETITE FOR
SPIRITUAL BREAD, A HUNGER FOR YOU.

"MY FLESH, MY BLOOD"

"I am the bread of life. Your ancestors ate the manna in the wilderness, yet they died. . . . I am the living bread that came down from heaven. Whoever eats this bread will live forever. This bread is my flesh, which I will give for the life of the world."

JOHN 6:48–49, 51

So how do you do with blood?

People can be very sensitive to blood, and maybe that's one reason why Jesus chose this metaphor: he got people's attention—and then he ran with the imagery: "Whoever eats my flesh and drinks my blood has eternal life. . . . My flesh is real food and my blood is real drink. Whoever eats my flesh and drinks my blood remains in me, and I in them. . . . The one who feeds on me will live because of me. . . . Whoever feeds on this bread will live forever" (John 6:54–58).

In his Bible commentary (written 1708 to 1710), Matthew Henry explained Jesus' metaphor this way: "Eating this flesh and drinking this blood mean believing in Christ. We partake of Christ and his benefits by faith. . . . We live by him, as our bodies live by our food."[9]

I RARELY MISS A MEAL. MAKE ME AS CONSISTENT IN MAKING TIME TO FEAST ON YOU, LORD JESUS.

A HARD TEACHING

"You do not want to leave too, do you?" Jesus asked the Twelve.
Simon Peter answered him, "Lord, to whom shall we go? You
have the words of eternal life. We have come to believe and to
know that you are the Holy One of God."

JOHN 6:67–69

Postmodernism holds that all viewpoints—all religions—are equally valid. Morals are a matter of opinion: you define right and wrong one way, and I define it another way. What is wrong for you is, relative to me, perfectly acceptable. Don't like a teaching? Tweak it. Personalize it. It's all relative.

Jesus was aware that his teaching was hard to hear and even harder to live out. He knew that saying, "My flesh is real food and my blood is real drink" (John 6:55) would cost him some followers—and it did. John reported, "From this time many of his disciples turned back and no longer followed him" (v. 66). (Don't like a teaching? Turn away!)

Following Jesus involves more than listening to his teaching and admiring his character. Following Jesus means walking so closely to him that he changes our hearts and our lives.

HELP ME FOLLOW YOU MORE FAITHFULLY.

"WHO DO PEOPLE SAY THAT I AM?"

[Jesus asked his disciples,] "Who do people say I am?"
  They replied, "Some say John the Baptist; others say
Elijah; and still others, one of the prophets."
  "But what about you?" he asked. "Who do you say I am?"
  Peter answered, "You are the Messiah."

MARK 8:27–29

The world is round, not flat," and "The sun, not the earth, is the center of the universe." These basic facts were not always accepted as such. And the basic fact that Jesus is the Messiah still isn't. One day everyone "in heaven and on earth and under the earth" (Philippians 2:10) will accept it as truth, but in the meantime the statement brings mockery and persecution.

Peter didn't fully understand the exact nature of the kingdom that Jesus would usher in, but he was willing to stand up for what was not the majority opinion: "You are the Messiah." Yes, a very human Peter denied knowing Jesus the night he was arrested, but he stayed closer than the other disciples did as this strange turn of events unfolded.

May we, like Peter, be willing to both proclaim our belief about who Jesus is and stand alone in that belief.

JESUS' QUESTION IS THE MOST
IMPORTANT ONE YOU WILL EVER ANSWER:
"WHO DO YOU SAY THAT I AM?"

FROM CONFIDENCE TO CONFUSION

[Then Jesus] began to teach them that the Son of Man must suffer many things and . . . be killed and after three days rise again. He spoke plainly about this, and Peter took him aside and began to rebuke him. . . .

Jesus turned and . . . rebuked Peter. "Get behind me, Satan!"

MARK 8:31–33

The skier is in the lead when his tip catches the flag, and he's down! Just one more semester before she'll have a degree—and she's dropping out? Now? Why?

Like sporting events, people's behavior can take unexpected turns. We go from cheering for Peter when he confidently proclaims, "You are the Messiah" (Mark 8:29) to moaning, "Peter! Don't you get it?" Of course we have the distinct advantage of looking back from this side of the cross.

At this point, Peter did not get it. Jesus' rebuke sounded harsh, but Jesus understood the intense spiritual dimension of his crucifixion and death. Of course Satan would be doing his all to discourage the Son of Man from doing what he came to do.

TEACH ME TO LIVE WITH A LASER
FOCUS ON YOUR CONCERNS,
ALMIGHTY AND HOLY GOD!

TAKE UP THE CROSS

[Jesus] called the crowd to him along with his disciples and said: "Whoever wants to be my disciple must deny themselves and take up their cross and follow me."

MARK 8:34

None of us signed up for these tougher-than-we-ever-expected situations, for these things we would have avoided if we could have. We didn't sign up—and we certainly wouldn't have volunteered for it! Who volunteers to suffer?

Jesus. He came to die (Mark 10:45).

Dying on that cross was what Jesus had signed up for, exactly what he had volunteered for. The sinless Lamb of God, sacrificed for the sin of all mankind, would endure not only excruciating physical pain on the cross but also the excruciating spiritual pain of the never-before-experienced separation from his Father. Jesus asked in Gethsemane if the plan could change—but he qualified his request: "Yet not as I will, but as you will" (Matthew 26:39).

TAKING UP YOUR CROSS AND FOLLOWING JESUS MEANS LIVING THAT PRAYER: "YET NOT AS I WILL, BUT AS YOU WILL."

TRANSFIGURED

[Jesus] was transfigured before them. His face shone like the sun, and his clothes became as white as the light. Just then there appeared before them Moses and Elijah, talking with Jesus. . . . A bright cloud covered them, and a voice from the cloud said, "This is my Son, whom I love; with him I am well pleased. Listen to him!"

MATTHEW 17:2–3, 5

S ometimes seeing helps believing. A pregnancy is more real after that first ultrasound. The job offer in writing helps you believe the too-good-to-be-true verbal offer.

Peter, James, and John were blessed with the opportunity to see Jesus in a way that helped their belief that he was God's Son. At the top of a high mountain, Jesus "was transfigured before them. His face shone like the sun, and his clothes became as white as the light."

As if that weren't spectacular enough, then Moses and Elijah, representatives of Old Testament law and the prophets, joined him. And then the voice of God confirmed Jesus' identity and told the disciples, "Listen to him!" What a picture of the fact that Jesus was the fulfillment of the Law and the One whom the prophets had pointed to.

THINK ABOUT WHAT YOU HAVE
SEEN—PERHAPS LIVED OUT BY GOD'S
PEOPLE—THAT HAS HELPED YOU BELIEVE.

A DIFFERENT KIND OF KING

[Jesus] was teaching his disciples. He said to them, "The Son of Man is going to be delivered into the hands of men. They will kill him, and after three days he will rise." But they did not understand what he meant and were afraid to ask him about it.

MARK 9:31–32

When you were in school, were you an I-never-raise-my-hand student? You never raised your hand—not in kindergarten, high school, or college—because you didn't want to look stupid. Yes, plenty of teachers told you through the years, "If you have a question, other people have that same question. Don't be afraid to ask it"—but you weren't convinced. What if you asked what had just been said? Apparently the disciples weren't willing to raise their hands either.

The disciples didn't need to ask questions. Jesus knew they needed more information, so he explained that people would soon "kill him, and after three days he will rise." What kind of talk was that for this new King? It definitely didn't fit expectations. All the great kings of ancient Israel—King David, King Solomon—had been warriors, builders, and diplomats. Wouldn't the new King be the greatest warrior of all? But rather than talking about a regime change, rather than gathering a cache of weapons or training soldiers to topple Rome, Jesus spread the message, "Open your heart to God!"

WHAT DO YOU DO TO KEEP YOUR HEART OPEN TO GOD?

NOT YET

> *Jesus, still teaching in the temple courts, cried out . . . "I am not here on my own authority, but he who sent me is true. You do not know him, but I know him because I am from him and he sent me."*
>
> *At this they tried to seize him, but no one laid a hand on him, because his hour had not yet come.*

JOHN 7:28–30

Timing is key. Grooms-to-be wait for the perfect time to pop the question. Parents wait for the perfect time to talk to their high schoolers about grades.

Jesus also knew the importance of timing, specifically of God's timing for the events to unfold as he approached the cross. (It is, of course, no coincidence that the Lamb of God was to be sacrificed for our sins at Passover: Jesus' blood saved us from eternal death just as the lamb's blood on the doorways in Egypt saved the firstborn son in each Hebrew family from physical death.)

But as the sovereign Author of history oversaw this chapter—and it's true for every chapter—even nonbelievers could not undermine God's timetable. The Author of history oversees the actions of nonbelievers and believers alike, guaranteeing that his plan for all history—including his plan for your life—will unfold in his perfect time.

THE TRUTH OF GOD'S ABSOLUTE SOVEREIGNTY IS AN UNFAILING SOURCE OF HOPE AND PEACE.

THE LIGHT OF THE WORLD

When Jesus spoke again to the people, he said, "I am the light of the world. Whoever follows me will never walk in darkness, but will have the light of life."

JOHN 8:12

Speak French fluently in a month! This is the greatest financial investment you can make! These abs can be yours! Perfect kids in five easy steps!"

Maybe you are a bit skeptical about these claims and similar ones—and rightfully so. Some claims simply are too good to be true. Other claims, however, sound too good to be true, but actually are true. The claims of Jesus fall into this category of "too good to be true—but 100 percent true!" Jesus, for instance, claimed to have authority to forgive sins (Mark 2:10), he taught that he has overcome the world (John 16:33), and he promised to be with us always (Matthew 28:20).

Of course people took issue with some of the claims Jesus made. In John 8:12, Jesus said he was the light—but only God himself is the source of light! In John 8:23, Jesus said he was "from above"—but only God claims residence in heaven! Jesus was setting out the clear, fateful, and eternal choice.

WALK IN GOD'S LIGHT OF LIFE AND
GROWTH, GUIDANCE AND LOVE.

SAY WHAT?

"Whoever obeys my word will never see death." . . .

"Abraham died. . . . Are you greater than our father Abraham?" . . .

"Your father Abraham rejoiced at the thought of seeing my day; he saw it and was glad. . . . Before Abraham was born, I am!"

JOHN 8:51–53, 56, 58

Jesus was not surprised that when he said people who obey "my word will never see death," the Jews reacted. They knew Abraham had obeyed God—and he died!

And that's when Jesus spoke, alarmingly, as if he had personal knowledge of Abraham: Jesus claimed to know that Abraham "was glad" when he thought about the coming of Jesus to the earth. In essence, Jesus told the crowd that he existed before Abraham was even born, that his life was without beginning, that he was God— and the crowd turned into a lynch mob. The people "picked up stones to stone him, but Jesus hid himself, slipping away from the temple grounds" (John 8:59).

The time for Jesus to be arrested had not yet come. The sovereign Author of history was in total control, protecting Jesus even as he allowed the religious leaders to work themselves into a rage.

TRY TO HEAR WITH THE EARS OF HIS
CONTEMPORARIES THE TRULY OUTRAGEOUS
STATEMENTS THAT JESUS MADE.

LAZARUS'S DEATH, GOD'S GLORY

*[Jesus] went on to tell [his disciples], "Our friend Lazarus has
fallen asleep."* . . .

*His disciples replied, "Lord, if he sleeps, he will get better."
Jesus had been speaking of his death. . . . So then he told them
plainly, "Lazarus is dead, and for your sake I am glad I was not
there, so that you may believe. But let us go to him."*

JOHN 11:11–15

We can be quick to judge the disciples even though our
thoughts and our words in that same conversation with Jesus
would have been no different.

Lazarus's sisters sent word to Jesus that their brother—his
beloved friend—was sick. Then came the juxtaposition of "Jesus
loved . . . Lazarus" and "he stayed where he was two more days"
(John 11:5–6). As if that weren't puzzling enough to the disciples,
then came Jesus' statement that Lazarus was asleep—which, to the
disciples, meant that Lazarus was asleep. So why were they going back
to where the Jews just tried to kill Jesus? Jesus explained—"he told
them plainly"—"Lazarus is dead."

Jesus was driven by a passion to show people the glory of God.
And waking the sleeping Lazarus—literally, raising the dead Lazarus
to life—would indeed give God great glory!

LIVE YOUR LIFE DRIVEN BY A PASSION TO
SHOW PEOPLE THE GLORY OF GOD.

WORDS OF TRUTH AND HOPE

Jesus said to her, "Your brother will rise again."

Martha answered, "I know he will rise again in the resurrection at the last day."

Jesus said to her, "I am the resurrection and the life. The one who believes in me will live, even though they die."

JOHN 11:23–25

Words can ring hollow. After all, they can't change either past circumstances or present-day pain. The death, the disease, the divorce, the disappointment—words won't change any of that. Unless they're Jesus' words.

Jesus told Martha that Lazarus "will rise again" (John 11:23)— which Martha already knew. She had heard enough of Jesus' teaching to know that, yes, "in the resurrection at the last day" Lazarus would again live (v. 24). Her theology was rock solid.

In this conversation, though, Jesus made a statement that has been a lifeline of hope to generations: "I am the resurrection and the life" (v. 25). Standing graveside or attending a celebration of life is a very different experience when we stand in the truth that Jesus *is* "the resurrection and the life." These heaven-sent words never fail to bring blessings of comfort and hope to aching hearts.

WITH WHOM DO YOU NEED TO SHARE THE TRUTH THAT JESUS IS THE RESURRECTION AND THE LIFE?

"IF YOU HAD BEEN HERE . . ."

"Lord," Martha said to Jesus, "if you had been here, my brother would not have died. But I know that even now God will give you whatever you ask."

JOHN 11:21–22

Friends let us down. They disappoint us—like when they aren't with us physically when we need them most—and those disappointments sting.

Martha and Mary knew such disappointment: their friend Jesus wasn't there for them when they most needed him. He hadn't hurried to Lazarus's bedside when he learned that this dear friend of his was ill. And Jesus apparently hadn't made an effort to be at Lazarus's side—and with his sisters—as he breathed his last. In fact, Lazarus had been in the tomb for four days when Jesus finally showed up (John 11:17). The sisters' disappointment is certainly understandable—and they didn't keep their thoughts and feelings a secret.

In two separate interactions, each one-on-one with Jesus, both Martha and Mary made the same statement: "If you had been here, my brother would not have died" (vv. 21, 32). Jesus didn't respond with anger, he didn't dismiss their feelings, and he said nothing in his defense.

JESUS CAN HANDLE HEARING OUR DISAPPOINTMENT: HE WHO KNOWS OUR HEARTS ALREADY KNOWS IT ANYWAY.

"LAZARUS, COME OUT!"

"Take away the stone," [Jesus] said. . . .

So they took away the stone. . . .

Jesus called in a loud voice, "Lazarus, come out!" The dead
man came out, his hands and feet wrapped with strips of linen,
and a cloth around his face.

JOHN 11:39, 41, 43–44

Imagine the emotional roller coaster that Martha and Mary had been riding during Lazarus's illness and since his death four days earlier. Their questions, their disappointment, their grief, and perhaps even some anger would make for a heavy load.

And so would the mixture of myrrh and aloes, plus the linen that Lazarus was wrapped with before he was placed in the tomb. Nicodemus and Joseph of Arimathea took between seventy-five and one hundred pounds for Jesus' body, and there's no reason to think that the ointment and cloths for Lazarus weighed any less.

The stone was rolled away, Jesus cried, "Come out!" and the dead man did. And we have to smile at the fact that Jesus needed to nudge the stunned crowd to help the poor man, the walking mummy: "Take off the grave clothes and let him go" (John 11:44).

God was indeed glorified in Lazarus's resurrection!

GOD MAY ALLOW PAIN IN YOUR
LIFE SO THAT YOU WILL BE BLESSED
WITH GREATER FAITH IN HIM.

"LIKE A LITTLE CHILD"

[Jesus] said to [his disciples], "Let the little children come to me, and do not hinder them, for the kingdom of God belongs to such as these. Truly I tell you, anyone who will not receive the kingdom of God like a little child will never enter it."

MARK 10:14–15

It's not just semantics. *Childlike* and *childish* have very different meanings. One is a precious trait in God's kingdom; the other, not so much. The first speaks of wonder; the second, of immaturity. The first can be endearing; the second, annoying.

And, as Jesus taught, we are to have faith "like a little child"— or childlike faith. Belief comes easily to children. They are learning all the time, but they are also ready to believe what they don't fully understand. Trust comes easily to children. It may be that distrust is taught, while trust is more natural and closer to God's design. And receiving comes easily to children. They don't play the "I'm not worth it" or "How can I repay?" tapes in their minds. Hear in your mind their giggles of joy!

Picture it: Jesus welcomed the children, took them in his arms, and blessed them.

MAY I HAVE FAITH LIKE A CHILD!

HARD BUT GOOD, PART 1

"One thing you lack," [Jesus] said. "Go, sell everything you have and give to the poor. . . . Then come, follow me." . . .

[The man] went away sad, because he had great wealth.

[Jesus said], "How hard it is for the rich to enter the kingdom of God!"

MARK 10:21–23

What is the hardest thing you have ever asked a loved one to do for his or her own good? Taking away an older parent's car keys may come to mind. A family intervention would definitely qualify. The words you had to speak may have felt and even sounded harsh, but you spoke those words because you love the person.

Jesus' words to the wealthy man may sound harsh, but notice the context: "Jesus looked at him and loved him" (Mark 10:21). Jesus knows that what he asks us, his followers, to do is hard—but anything he would ever ask us to do is for our good.

And asking the rich man to get rid of his wealth was asking him to remove from his life the idol that was competing most with God. The fact that Jews believed wealth to be a sign of God's blessing made Jesus' assignment more puzzling and perhaps more difficult. But Jesus had his reason, and that reason was love.

EVERY SINGLE COMMANDMENT IN GOD'S WORD IS GIVEN FOR OUR GOOD.

HARD BUT GOOD, PART 2

"No one who has left home or brothers or sisters or mother or father or children or fields for me and the gospel will fail to receive a hundred times as much in this present age . . . along with persecutions—and in the age to come eternal life."

MARK 10:29–30

What is the hardest thing God has ever asked you to do? Reflect on how his request reveals now (even if it wasn't too clear then) his love for you.

And then there's Peter, still scratching his head a bit over Jesus' comment to the wealthy believer—"Go, sell everything you have" (Mark 10:21). Peter spoke up: "We have left everything to follow you!" (v. 28).

Jesus made it clear that following him will cost us. But Jesus promised that the blessings of doing so will be worth the cost in this life—and, soon, in the glory of life eternal with him.

So, yes, Jesus asks you, his follower, to let go of anything that keeps you from following him wholeheartedly. He knows that doing so is hard—and yet he asks anyway. Why? For your good. Because he loves you.

EVERY SINGLE COMMANDMENT IN GOD'S WORD IS GIVEN FOR YOUR GOOD.

WHAT DON'T YOU UNDERSTAND?

"We are going up to Jerusalem," [Jesus said to the Twelve],
"and the Son of Man will be delivered over to the chief
priests. . . . They will condemn him to death and will hand him
over to the Gentiles, who will mock him and spit on him, flog
him and kill him. Three days later he will rise."

MARK 10:33–34

Few people legitimately understand rocket science, and few are qualified to perform brain surgery. The Russian language is notoriously difficult—and then there's calculus. We don't feel too bad when we don't understand these esoteric topics. But sometimes—like the disciples—we can miss the straightforward, even when it's spelled out to us.

Early in his ministry, Jesus was cryptic when he needed to be for his own protection. But as he got closer to Calvary, his descriptions of what awaited him got very clear. The words were simple and stark: *condemn . . . death . . . mock . . . spit . . . flog . . . kill.* Which of these did the disciples not understand?

Jesus was—as clearly as he could—letting the disciples know that what was about to unfold—as horrific as it would be—was God's plan. It was, in fact, the very reason that Jesus came to this earth.

GOD'S WAYS AREN'T OUR WAYS, BUT HIS
WAYS ARE ALWAYS PURPOSEFUL AND GOOD.

"HOSANNA!"

When [the two disciples] brought the colt to Jesus and threw
their cloaks over it, he sat on it. Many people spread their cloaks
on the road, while others spread branches they had cut in the
fields. Those who went ahead and those who followed shouted,
"Hosanna!"

MARK 11:7–9

I t wasn't big like Macy's Thanksgiving Day Parade or the Rose Parade, but the parade of Jesus and his disciples as they entered Jerusalem was huge in terms of significance. Eternal significance.

As prophesied in Zechariah 9:9, Jesus was on a donkey, an animal of peace.[10] His choice of animal communicated that Jesus was not entering Jerusalem to lead a rebellion against Rome. Jesus was coming in peace: by means of the cross Jesus would make peace between holy God and sinful people.

Yet as Jesus rode along, cheering people waved palm branches, a symbol of freedom. In contrast to Jesus' donkey of peace, these branches were the people's way of saying they wanted freedom from Rome—and the means to that end would not necessarily be peaceful.

JESUS CAME TO SAVE PEOPLE FROM
A FAR GREATER TYRANNY THAN
THAT OF ROME. HE CAME TO BRING
FREEDOM FROM SIN! HOSANNA!

WHERE'S THE MEEK AND MILD JESUS?

Jesus entered the temple courts and drove out all who were buying and selling there. . . . "It is written," he said to them, "'My house will be called a house of prayer,' but you are making it 'a den of robbers.'"

MATTHEW 21:12–13

We can write a check, but in Jesus' day offerings were much more complicated, and the dishonest people involved in the system increased both the complications and the expense. For starters, offerings could only be presented to God at the temple. Worshipers traveling any significant distance would wait to buy a lamb—or, if they were poor, a dove—when they arrived.

Not only did merchants corner the market and charge high prices, but they didn't accept foreign coins. So money changers offered their services, for a fee, of course.

And Jesus was livid! The loud, noisy, smelly courtyard was hardly a place of worship! Jesus overturned the first table. As the birdcages fell off, the doors flew open and the doves flew free. Jesus upended the money changers' tables too, and coins clattered as tables crashed.

JESUS DOESN'T PASSIVELY WITNESS UNRIGHTEOUSNESS!

A STEP TOWARD ETERNAL GOOD

"Now my soul is troubled, and what shall I say? 'Father, save me from this hour'? No, it was for this very reason I came to this hour. Father, glorify your name!"

JOHN 12:27–28

Even when we are confident that the step must be taken, even when we are confident that it leads to good, we can still feel unsettled and troubled as we anticipate actually taking that step.

Jesus knew all too well what awaited him in Jerusalem. He had known before he came to live on this broken planet. He hadn't thought much about the physical pain because he knew that, as excruciating as that would be, it would be nothing compared to the pain of being totally separated from his Father.

So of course Jesus' "soul is troubled" (John 12:27). And even as he tried yet again to help the crowd understand that he had come to die, he reminded himself that, by being "lifted up from the earth" on a cross, he would "draw all people to [himself]" (v. 32). That step had to be taken, and it led to eternal good.

"AMAZING LOVE! HOW CAN IT BE THAT THOU, MY GOD, WOULDST DIE FOR ME!" CHARLES WESLEY (1739)

THE TRAITOR STEPS FORWARD

Satan entered Judas. . . . And Judas went to the chief priests
and the officers of the temple guard and discussed with them how
he might betray Jesus. They were delighted and agreed to give
him money. He consented, and watched for an opportunity to
hand Jesus over to them when no crowd was present.

LUKE 22:3–6

Maybe you know someone who seemed to have all the advantages growing up—but is still wandering aimlessly through life in his forties. . . . And talk about advantages! This man spent almost three years with the Rabbi from Jerusalem. He was one of the small band of disciples who heard teachings the crowds didn't, who saw Jesus live what he preached, who saw him live in intimate relationship with his heavenly Father—and there he was agreeing to hand Jesus over to the chief priests for a handful of coins. Judas had had all the advantages when it came to realizing who Jesus was, and he was either very blind or very confused.

Yet are we that different from Judas? Of course we know what God says is right and wrong, but sometimes in the moment, whatever we're doing—however disobedient, wrong, and sinful it is—somehow seems okay. We are doing exactly what we would never have expected ourselves to do, and somehow we just keep going down that path.

FATHER, I'M NOT THAT DIFFERENT FROM
JUDAS. HELP ME BE MORE LIKE JESUS.

THE ULTIMATE PASSOVER

Jesus' disciples asked him, "Where do you want us to go and make preparations for you to eat the Passover?" . . .

The disciples left, went into the city and found things just as Jesus had told them. So they prepared the Passover.

MARK 14:12, 16

Yes, it's a pop quiz about Passover parallels!

What was the final plague that convinced the Pharaoh to let the people of Israel leave Egypt? *The angel of death took the lives of the firstborn in every family in Egypt.*

What sign told the angel to pass over the home of faithful Jews? *The spilled blood of the sacrificed lamb on the doorway.*

Fast forward . . .

Which firstborn died on Calvary? *Jesus. But his life was not taken; it was given.*

What lamb was killed at this Passover? *The pure and perfect Lamb of God.*

Since before time the Almighty planned the parallels: unblemished sacrificial lambs shed their blood to protect God's people from the angel of death.

THE SINLESS LAMB OF GOD SHED
HIS BLOOD TO PROTECT GOD'S
PEOPLE FROM ETERNAL DEATH.

THE MASTER'S EXAMPLE

Jesus knew that the Father had put all things under his power,
and that he had come from God and was returning to God; so
he got up from the meal . . . and began to wash his disciples'
feet, drying them with the towel that was wrapped around him.

JOHN 13:3–5

The basins and towels sat waiting. The foot-washing would be a remarkable experience.

Of course, for the disciples in the the Upper Room, the scene must have been considerably more unsettling in other ways, but this was plenty uncomfortable. It was one thing to wash someone's feet. It was pretty awkward to have a friend wash your feet. But when the pastor—also a friend, but still the pastor—washed your feet! And imagine having Jesus wash your feet . . .

Jesus washed the feet of the Twelve to give them—and us—an example to follow: "Now that I, your Lord and Teacher, have washed your feet, you also should wash one another's feet" (John 13:14).

We will be able to follow Jesus' example—we can volunteer more willingly for the lowliest job—when, as Jesus himself did, we keep in mind whose we are.

AS CHILDREN OF THE KING, WE FIND
OUR VALUE IN HIS LOVE, NOT IN
WHAT WE DO ON THIS EARTH.

"SURELY YOU DON'T MEAN ME?"

Jesus was troubled in spirit and testified, "Very truly I tell you, one of you is going to betray me. . . . It is the one to whom I will give this piece of bread when I have dipped it in the dish." Then, dipping the piece of bread, he gave it to Judas. . . . As soon as Judas took the bread, Satan entered into him.

JOHN 13:21, 26–27

What recent conversation or interaction comes to mind when you hear the word *awkward*?

Whatever came to mind could not have been anywhere as awkward, as tense, as strained as this moment around the Passover table. Jesus, "troubled in spirit," said simply, "One of you is going to betray me." And he must have said that loudly enough for everyone to hear, because John reports that "his disciples stared at one another, at a loss to know which of them he meant" (John 13:22).

When John asked him who it was, Jesus answered by handing Judas a piece of bread and soon thereafter saying to Judas, "What you are about to do, do quickly" (v. 27).

Before Judas left, however, the disciples asked Jesus a question that helps us realize that we ourselves are entirely capably of betraying our Lord: "Surely you don't mean me?" (Mark 14:19).

MAY I NEVER BETRAY YOU IN THOUGHT, WORD, OR DEED, MY SAVIOR AND MY LORD.

THE BODY AND THE BLOOD

Jesus took bread, and when he had given thanks, he broke it and gave it to his disciples, saying, "Take and eat; this is my body."

Then he took a cup, and when he had given thanks, he gave it to them, saying, "Drink from it, all of you. This is my blood of the covenant."

MATTHEW 26:26–28

Foreshadowing may remind you of a high school English teacher who saw way too much in every novel the class read. Yet foreshadowing happens not only in a fictional literary world; it happens in day-to-day life as well. At the Passover meal, after Judas left, Jesus also offered his disciples a sense of what was to come.

At this Passover meal, Jesus used actions and words to foreshadow the fact that he was to be broken and poured out. Taking on the punishment for humanity's sin—for your sin—would literally cost him his life. His body would be broken and his blood "poured out for many for the forgiveness of sins" (Matthew 26:28).

The Passover location had been prearranged. Jesus had washed his disciples' feet. He had talked about one of them betraying him. And now he was saying strange things. What was going on?

MAY I NEVER GET NUMB TO THE
AMAZING GRACE THE BREAD
AND THE WINE REPRESENT.

A COMMAND, A PROMISE, AND A HELPER

"If you love me, keep my commands. And I will ask the Father, and he will give you another advocate to help you and be with you forever—the Spirit of truth. . . . When he, the Spirit of truth, comes, he will guide you into all the truth."

JOHN 14:15–17; 16:13

What makes you feel loved? Whatever came to mind was probably an action. Being ignored or not spoken to can't make anyone feel loved!

According to Jesus himself, one way we show our love for him is to obey his commandments, that we primarily love God and love others. Knowing we will fail at this, our gracious and kind God told us about an invaluable blessing he has for us: a Helper, an "advocate to help you and be with you forever."

Jesus' Holy Spirit, also known as the Spirit of truth, helps us to discern Jesus' truth as well as to obey his commands. The Spirit is also with us forever as our Comforter when the troubles of the world come—something else Jesus promised (John 16:33).

The Spirit of truth comforts us, guides us, and helps us keep our eyes on Jesus' ultimate victory over sin and death.

THANK YOU, SPIRIT, FOR BEING WITH US AS WE TRAVEL THROUGH THIS TEMPORARY BUT TROUBLE-FILLED EXISTENCE ON THIS EARTH.

THE AGONY OF GETHSEMANE

[Jesus] fell with his face to the ground and prayed, "My Father,
if it is possible, may this cup be taken from me. Yet not as I will,
but as you will." . . .

He went away a second time and prayed, "My Father, if it is
not possible for this cup to be taken away unless I drink it, may
your will be done."

MATTHEW 26:39, 42

After Jesus and the Eleven finished the Passover meal, they walked to the Mount of Olives. They had probably gone there many times before for prayer and conversation, but the disciples were well aware that this night was not like any other. And they were probably aware even before Jesus spoke these words: "My soul is overwhelmed with sorrow to the point of death" (Matthew 26:38).

Of course, it was as he anticipated what the next twelve or fifteen hours held. He knew of the torturous physical pain of the cross; he knew of the even more crushing pain of separation from his heavenly Father, as he, one member of the Triune God, was cut off from the others. Yet Jesus submitted to the Almighty's will.

The time of prayer ended. Judas the betrayer arrived. Jesus was arrested.

NOTHING IN GOD'S WILL FOR YOU WILL EVER
REQUIRE WHAT HIS WILL FOR JESUS DID.

Jesus answered, "This very night, before the rooster crows, you will disown me three times." But Peter declared, "Even if I have to die with you, I will never disown you."

MATTHEW 26:34–35

In the moment we can make bold promises. In other moments, we may come to the defense of someone we love without thinking through the ramifications. We're not that different from good-intentioned Peter.

First, Jesus' prediction: Peter confidently declared that he would never desert Jesus—to which Jesus told him that he would deny even knowing his Lord three times before the rooster crowed.

Now, Peter's reaction: Jesus stepped toward Judas and the mob when they arrived in Gethsemane. When they said they were looking for Jesus of Nazareth, Jesus said, "I am he" (John 18:8). Realizing what the mob's next move would be—and hardly the timid type—Peter came to his Lord's defense. Brandishing his sword, he cut off the servant's ear (which Jesus later reattached, as told in Luke 22:51). Clearly, Peter didn't fully understand Jesus' mission or method, so Jesus spoke up: "Put your sword away! Shall I not drink the cup the Father has given me?" (John 18:11).

JESUS, TEACH ME TO COME TO
YOUR DEFENSE IN WAYS THAT
REPRESENT YOU WELL.

"I DON'T KNOW THE MAN!"

*When some there had kindled a fire in the middle of the
courtyard . . . Peter sat down. . . . A servant girl saw him seated
there . . . and said, "This man was with him." But he denied it.
"Woman, I don't know him," he said. . . .*

The Lord turned and looked straight at Peter.

LUKE 22:55–57, 61

Did I really say that? We can try for decades to train ourselves to
think before we speak—and still not always succeed. In fact,
we can fail in the worst of circumstances. Ask Peter.

Peter normally reacted to trouble by wrestling it to the ground,
not running from it or avoiding it. So quite naturally, Peter was the
disciple to follow Jesus and the soldiers who had arrested him back
to the high priest's house.

Joining those gathered around the fire in the courtyard, Peter was
recognized by three people. And how did Peter respond? "Woman,
I don't know him" (v. 57). "Man, I am not!" (v. 58). "Man, I don't
know what you're talking about!" (v. 60). And that's when the rooster
crowed. Then his Lord made eye contact.

And Peter went outside the courtyard "and wept bitterly" (v. 62).

GOD GROWS OUR CHARACTER WHEN
WE RECOGNIZE OUR WEAKNESSES,
FAILINGS, AND NEED FOR HIM.

PILATE'S NO-WIN SITUATION

[Pilate] went out again to the Jews gathered there and said, "I find no basis for a charge against him. . . . Do you want me to release 'the king of the Jews'?" . . .

The chief priests and their officials . . . shouted, "Crucify! Crucify!"

JOHN 18:38–39; 19:6

What no-win situation have you found yourself in at some point? For four years Pilate had governed the region of Judea. Historical records reveal that he was no friend of the Jews. Yet when the Jewish leaders asked him to judge Jesus as a subversive threat, Pilate was caught. If he refused to condemn Jesus, Jewish accusers would portray him as no friend of Caesar. If Pilate agreed to crucify Jesus, he'd be acting against his own judicial instincts and, perhaps worse, caving in to those he despised. He needed to question this prisoner himself.

And when Pilate did, he found no reason to crucify this rabbi (John 19:4). But Pilate did have Jesus flogged. Roman soldiers placed a crown of thorns on his head. And the crowd shouted, "Crucify him! Crucify him!"

JESUS' APPEARANCE BEFORE PILATE PUT THE RULER IN A NO-WIN SITUATION; JESUS' MARCH TO THE CROSS PUT HIS FOLLOWERS IN AN ETERNAL-WIN SITUATION.

SHOWING MERCY UNTIL THE END

"Don't you fear God[?]" he said. . . . "We are punished justly. . . . But this man has done nothing wrong. . . . Jesus, remember me when you come into your kingdom."

Jesus answered him, "Truly I tell you, today you will be with me in paradise."

LUKE 23:40–43

Despite the indescribable physical pain of the excruciating and slow death of the cross, Jesus continued to be merciful and gracious.

The mockery was loud and persistent: "He saved others . . . but he can't save himself!" (Mark 15:31); and, from one of the criminals being crucified with him, "Aren't you the Messiah? Save yourself and us!" (Luke 23:39).

Yet Jesus spoke words of grace. He asked his Father to forgive the Roman soldiers "for they do not know what they are doing" (v. 34). He also forgave the criminal who wasn't mocking him, who actually came to Jesus' defense. This criminal then asked for Jesus' mercy— "Remember me when you come into your kingdom"—and Jesus assured him, "Today you will be with me in paradise."

JESUS CHOSE TO NOT SAVE HIMSELF,
CHOOSING INSTEAD TO SHOW MERCY
TO HIS TORMENTORS AS WELL AS TO
ONE OF HIS PARTNERS IN DEATH.

"IT IS FINISHED"

About three in the afternoon Jesus cried out in a loud voice, "Eli, Eli, lema sabachthani?" (which means "My God, my God, why have you forsaken me?"). . . .

When he had received the drink, Jesus said, "It is finished." With that, he bowed his head and gave up his spirit.

MATTHEW 27:46; JOHN 19:30

Consider how reliable you are, how well you do with follow-through, and how consistently you fulfill responsibilities you take on. Know that Jesus has set that bar high! Even from the cross, Jesus responsibly and compassionately provided for his mother, assigning his disciple John with her care (John 19:26–27).

Then, from noon until three in the afternoon, "darkness came over the whole land" (Luke 23:44). According to John, at about that time Jesus cried out those heartbreaking words—"My God, my God, why have you forsaken me?"

The perfect Lamb of God "bowed his head and gave up his spirit." Jesus had done what he had come to the earth to do: he had died on behalf of sinful human beings so that we could once again be in relationship with our holy God.

"WE HAVE BEEN MADE HOLY THROUGH THE SACRIFICE OF THE BODY OF JESUS CHRIST ONCE FOR ALL." (HEBREWS 10:10)

DIRECT ACCESS TO OUR HOLY GOD

At that moment the curtain of the temple was torn in two from top to bottom. The earth shook, the rocks split. . . . When the centurion and those with him who were guarding Jesus saw the earthquake . . . they were terrified, and exclaimed, "Surely he was the Son of God!"

MATTHEW 27:51, 54

God made his presence very clearly known on the afternoon that Christ died. No one could miss the earthquake, and later it was noticed that the curtain in the temple had been "torn in two from top to bottom." And that was no insignificant event.

This curtain hung at the doorway to this room, known as the Holiest of Holies. At fifteen feet, the curtain hung from about twice the height of most ceilings today. It was also very heavy, requiring several men to lift it.

When Jesus died—at that moment when he gave up his spirit—the curtain tore from top to bottom. Even if the curtain had been lighter, the idea that some human being had torn it from the top to the bottom was beyond credibility. This divine tearing of the temple curtain symbolized what God had done through his Son's sacrificial death on the cross:

SINFUL-BUT-FORGIVEN HUMAN BEINGS NOW HAVE DIRECT ACCESS TO THEIR HOLY GOD.

> "Sir," [the chief priests said to Pilate], "we remember that while
> he was still alive that deceiver said, 'After three days I will rise
> again.' So give the order for the tomb to be made secure until the
> third day. Otherwise, his disciples may . . . steal the body and
> tell the people that he has been raised from the dead."

MATTHEW 27:63–64

The grave is terrifying for people who don't know the resurrected
Lord. Christians, however, can celebrate the gospel truth that
the one they love is now truly alive and with Jesus, the Victor over
sin and death. But that's getting ahead of the story.

Jesus had been buried by Joseph of Arimathea and Nicodemus
in Joseph's new tomb. And that's exactly where the chief priests and
Pharisees wanted Roman soldiers to stand guard until the three days
Jesus had spoken of had passed.

NOW THAT YOU HAVE SOME BACKSTORY,
IMAGINE THE DIFFICULTY OF STEALING
JESUS' BODY. YET "THIS STORY HAS BEEN
WIDELY CIRCULATED AMONG THE JEWS
TO THIS VERY DAY" (MATTHEW 28:15).

"AFRAID YET FILLED WITH JOY"

The angel said to the women, "Do not be afraid, for I know that
you are looking for Jesus, who was crucified. He is not here; he has
risen, just as he said. Come and see the place where he lay." . . .

So the women hurried away from the tomb, afraid yet filled
with joy.

MATTHEW 28:5–6, 8

Contronyms are those words that have two contradictory meanings. *Dust*, for instance, can mean to remove dust or to cover with dust. *Sanction* can mean to approve of something or to boycott something. And *fear* may qualify as well: it can mean terrified and wanting to run, or it can mean awed by and intrigued enough to draw near.

The women who went to the tomb to anoint Jesus' body wondered who would move the stone for them—and they needn't have worried. An angel of the Lord had arrived before them and rolled back the heavy stone. He was, in fact, sitting on it. Of course the angel's first words were "Do not be afraid." Not be afraid? But the women's terror was tempered by the good news that Jesus "has risen, just as he said." So "afraid yet filled with joy," the women ran to tell the disciples that Jesus had risen from the dead.

WHO WILL YOU JOYFULLY TELL THAT JESUS HAS RISEN FROM THE DEAD?

SOLID EVIDENCE

*Peter and the other disciple started for the tomb. Both were
running. . . . [Peter] saw the strips of linen lying there, as well as
the cloth that had been wrapped around Jesus' head. The cloth
was still lying in its place, separate from the linen.*

JOHN 20:3–4, 6–7

Throughout the centuries, skeptics have wanted believers to
prove that the resurrection really happened. Much proof exists,
and here are a few points:[11]

- The seal was broken—an act punishable by death—and
  the Roman government would have sought the guilty party.
- The Roman guards had fled their duty station, aware that
  immediate execution would be the consequence.
- The tomb was empty. Jesus' body simply had to be found
  and displayed. That never happened.
- The stone at the tomb's entrance weighed between two
  thousand and four thousand pounds—and it had been
  rolled aside.
- Over five hundred witnesses and even hostile witnesses
  saw the resurrected Jesus.

JESUS IS RISEN! HE IS RISEN INDEED!

"I HAVE SEEN THE LORD!"

[Mary] did not realize that it was Jesus. He asked her, "Woman, why are you crying? Who is it you are looking for?"

Thinking he was the gardener, she said, "Sir, if you have carried him away, tell me where you have put him, and I will get him."

JOHN 20:14–15

We hear it whether we're listening for it or not. We human beings seem to have extra sensitive radar when it comes to hearing our name.

Now imagine the grief-stricken Mary in the quiet of the garden that Sunday morning. The angels who had been sitting in the very tomb where Jesus had been placed hadn't helped her find the body of her Lord. Even the gardener had been no help. That's when Mary unexpectedly heard her name, gently spoken, said with love, in a voice she recognized. "Rabboni!" she exclaimed (John 20:16).

The Jesus she had been looking for had spoken her name. The one she had thought was the gardener was actually her risen Savior!

Doing as he instructed, Mary hurried to the disciples: "I have seen the Lord!" (v. 18).

THOSE WHO, LIKE MARY, SEEK THE
LORD WILL FIND HIM. AND HE, YOUR
GOOD SHEPHERD, KNOWS HIS SHEEP
BY NAME. LISTEN FOR YOURS.

OH! NOW I GET IT!

When [Jesus] was at the table with them, he took bread, gave
thanks, broke it and began to give it to them. Then their eyes
were opened and they recognized him. . . . They asked each
other, "Were not our hearts burning within us while he talked
with us on the road and opened the Scriptures to us?"

LUKE 24:30–32

Arrest . . . Middle-of-the-night trials . . . Flogging . . . Calvary . . .
Darkness at noon . . . The events of the past few days gave these
two travelers much to talk about. And that's when the resurrected
Christ appeared and started walking with them.

These downcast friends told Jesus, the One they thought "was
going to redeem Israel" (Luke 24:21), about the reportedly empty
tomb. And then began the travelers' glorious tutorial. As Luke put
it, "beginning with Moses and all the Prophets, [Jesus] explained to
them what was said in all the Scriptures concerning himself" (v. 27).

It's hard to know the tone of voice Jesus used when he said,
"How foolish you are, and how slow to believe all that the prophets
have spoken!" (v. 25), but the conversation that followed cemented
their faith.

JUST AS JESUS HELPED THESE TWO
DISCIPLES BETTER UNDERSTAND
HIS WORD, HIS VERY SPIRIT WILL
HELP YOU DO THE SAME.

AMAZEMENT AND JOY

Jesus himself stood among [his disciples]. . . . They were startled and frightened, thinking they saw a ghost. He said to them . . . "Look at my hands and my feet. It is I myself! Touch me and see; a ghost does not have flesh and bones, as you see I have."

LUKE 24:36–39

Sometimes we hear something again and again before we get it. And sometimes we need to hear it told from someone else, with slightly different words. And maybe that new voice is what helped the disciples finally understand.

That new voice was the voice of the *resurrected* Jesus reviewing for them why he came to earth, whom he delivered the Jewish people from, and what the crucifixion and resurrection were all about.

Jesus had suddenly appeared in the room with them. He had invited them to touch his flesh-and-bones body, and he had eaten some of the broiled fish they had. Then, once again but perhaps with a more open and attentive audience, Jesus had helped them better understand what his ministry was all about. The disciples' fear had given way to amazement and joy.

And much of all they had experienced—all that they had seen and heard—in the past three years was suddenly making sense.

RESPOND TO THE RESURRECTED JESUS WITH AMAZEMENT AND JOY!

A BAD RAP!

[Jesus] said to Thomas, "Put your finger here; see my hands. Reach out your hand and put it into my side. Stop doubting and believe."

Thomas said to him, "My Lord and my God!"

Then Jesus told him . . . "Blessed are those who have not seen and yet have believed."

JOHN 20:27–29

Are we really so different from Thomas? After all, what human being has ever been the paragon of unwavering faith and absolute 24/7 confidence in Jesus? (That's honesty, not blasphemy.)

God is "other": often we don't understand his ways. God is intangible: we tend to define *real* according to what we can see, touch, and measure. And God has defeated sin, death, and the devil: although he is leashed, Satan whispers in our ear, "Did God really say . . . ?"

So are we really very different from Thomas? Can't we imagine wanting to see for ourselves the risen Lord?

Thomas had that opportunity, and then, believing, he proclaimed, "My Lord and my God!" And it is thought that the believing Thomas went on to evangelize India: he who had seen the risen Jesus preached powerfully to those who had not—and many believed.

I HAVE NOT SEEN WITH MY EYES, LORD, BUT I BELIEVE. STRENGTHEN MY BELIEF.

BREAKFAST AT THE BEACH

Jesus said to them, "Bring some of the fish you have just caught." . . .
Jesus . . . took the bread and gave it to them, and did the same with
the fish. This was now the third time Jesus appeared to his disciples
after he was raised from the dead.

JOHN 21:10, 13 14

What is your default activity when you're feeling unsettled, when you're waiting for something to happen, or when you need to process recent events? Maybe you take a walk, go for a bike ride, call a friend, or grab a fishing pole.

That last option was Peter's choice during this period of waiting for the resurrected Jesus' next instructions. Some of the other disciples joined him for the fishing trip—and no one caught a single fish. That's when the stranger on the shore called to them to cast in their nets on the right side of the boat. When they did, they were unable to haul the net in because of the large number of fish: 153 to be exact (John 21:11).

That's when John exclaimed, "It is the Lord!" (v. 7). As impulsive as ever—and despite the still-throbbing pain of having denied knowing his Lord—Peter jumped into the water and made his way toward Jesus and breakfast, and more.

HELP ME, LIKE PETER, NEVER
HESITATE TO RUN TO YOU.

"Simon son of John, do you love me?"

Peter was hurt because Jesus asked him the third time, "Do you love me?" He said, "Lord, you know all things; you know that I love you." . . .

[Then Jesus said to him,] "Follow me!"

JOHN 21:17, 19

Have you noticed how annoying some journalists can be with their insensitive questions? The house has just burned down: "How are you feeling right now?" The game was just lost, and this player's mistake made the difference: "How are you feeling right now?" *Really?*

And maybe Peter felt a little bit like that when he and Jesus talked after breakfast. Three times Jesus asked him the same question: "Do you love me?" *Yes, of course. Yes, you know I do. Yes, and it hurts to have you not believe me.*

Jesus asked not because he doubted Peter's love as much as to give his disciple closure on a dark moment in his life. It had been in the courtyard of the high priest, in the dark of night, after a long and emotional and puzzling day. Three times Peter had denied even knowing "the man" arrested in Gethsemane and dragged before the high priest. Now three times Jesus gave Peter the opportunity to declare his love. Closure.

DO YOU LOVE JESUS? FOLLOW HIM.

JESUS' GREAT COMMISSION

"All authority in heaven and on earth has been given to me. Therefore go and make disciples of all nations, baptizing them in the name of the Father and of the Son and of the Holy Spirit, and teaching them to obey everything I have commanded you."

MATTHEW 28:18–20

B ecause I said so!" When the person making that statement has the proper authority over the one being addressed, those four words just might prove reason enough for obedience and cooperation.

Jesus had the same starting point when he issued the Great Commission. He stated, "All authority in heaven and on earth has been given to me." The instructions to come were divine in origin, eternal in purpose. Simply put, they were not to be ignored.

Then—as the last words of Jesus that Matthew recorded in his gospel—came the assignment: "Make disciples . . . baptize . . . teach . . ."—and do this in "all nations," an impossible task except for Jesus' promise that immediately follows his instructions: "Surely I am with you always" (Matthew 28:20).

And may our response to Jesus' Great Commission reflect the apostle John's purpose in writing his account of Jesus' ministry:

". . . JESUS IS THE MESSIAH, THE SON OF GOD, AND THAT BY BELIEVING YOU MAY HAVE LIFE IN HIS NAME." (JOHN 20:30–31)

NOW WHAT?

After his suffering, [Jesus] presented himself to [his disciples] and gave many convincing proofs that he was alive. He . . . gave them this command: "Do not leave Jerusalem, but wait for the gift my Father promised. . . . For John baptized with water, but in a few days you will be baptized with the Holy Spirit."

ACTS 1:3–5

Now what? Maybe you've asked yourself that question after reaching a goal, moving to a new city, or facing a situation you never expected to find yourself in. *Now what?*

Jesus' disciples may have wondered that same thing. What would following Jesus look like now? He reminded his disciples of the gift that God had promised them—the Holy Spirit—as well as their assignment—being his witnesses in the city, the nation, and the world. Then Jesus "was taken up before their very eyes, and a cloud hid him from their sight" (Acts 1:9).

Now what? The waiting would continue, and then the next chapter of God's story would begin.

LORD, WHEN I'M WONDERING, *NOW WHAT?*
MAY I FIND HOPE AS WELL AS DIRECTION,
PEACE AS WELL AS STRENGTH, IN YOU.

TONGUES OF FIRE

When the day of Pentecost came, [the apostles] were all together in one place. Suddenly a sound like the blowing of a violent wind came from heaven. . . . They saw what seemed to be tongues of fire that . . . came to rest on each of them. All of them were filled with the Holy Spirit and began to speak in other tongues as the Spirit enabled them.

ACTS 2:1–4

S ome people have the gift of being able to learn languages—and not just the similar French, Spanish, and Italian. They've also learned Russian and Swahili.

Such linguistic accomplishments are quite remarkable and impressive—and that was pretty much the reaction of the God-fearing Jews from around the world when they heard their own languages being spoken in Jerusalem. They were "utterly amazed" as they heard the Galileans "declaring the wonders of God in our own tongues!" (Acts 2:7, 11). Of course the skeptics blamed alcohol, but the apostles themselves knew that wasn't the case.

Peter spoke up and explained that this was a fulfillment of Joel's prophecy: "'God says, I will pour out my Spirit on all people'" (v. 17).

The followers of Jesus now had greater power with which to serve the Lord.

AND THE SPIRIT'S POWER IS
AVAILABLE TO YOU AS WELL.

BEFORE AND AFTER

[Peter] addressed the crowd . . . "Jesus of Nazareth . . . was handed over to you by God's deliberate plan and foreknowledge; and you, with the help of wicked men, put him to death by nailing him to the cross. But God raised him from the dead. . . . God has made this Jesus, whom you crucified, both Lord and Messiah."

ACTS 2:14, 22–24, 36

They're a marketer's coup! The *before* pictures show bellied, wrinkled, out-of-breath couch potatoes. And in the remarkable *after* pictures, they are twenty-five pounds lighter, wrinkle-free, fine physical specimens. But those transformations are nothing compared to the ones we find in the Bible.

The *before*: Peter vowed never to betray the Lord, yet in a matter of hours a servant girl recognized him as being with Jesus—and Peter denied it (Luke 22:57). And the *after*: Now Peter was proclaiming truths like, "God has made this Jesus, whom you crucified, both Lord and Messiah."

How did the intimidated-by-a-slave-girl Peter become the bold and intimidated-by-no-one preacher? The people of Jerusalem figured it out: They "realized that [Peter and John] . . . had been with Jesus" (Acts 4:13).

BEING WITH JESUS WILL MAKE YOU BOLD FOR HIM!

A COMMUNITY OF LOVE

They devoted themselves to the apostles' teaching and to
fellowship, to the breaking of bread and to prayer. They sold . . .
possessions to give to anyone who had need. . . . They broke
bread in their homes and ate together with glad and sincere
hearts, praising God and enjoying the favor of all the people.

ACTS 2:42, 45–47

Maybe you've heard the Groucho Marx line that runs something like this: "I don't want to belong to any club that would accept me as one of its members."

When outsiders look at a group of God's people, however, they should want nothing more than to be part of that community of love. The Acts 2 fellowship of believers clearly reflected the warm and selfless love of Jesus: his followers genuinely cared for and about one another. Like their Lord, these Christians didn't merely talk about love; they loved with their actions, they loved sacrificially, and they loved with servants' hearts.

No wonder "the Lord added to their number daily those who were being saved" (Acts 2:47). The Spirit was working in people's hearts, prompting them to want to join a community of love.

MAY YOUR FELLOWSHIP OF BELIEVERS
BE A GREAT ADVERTISEMENT
FOR THE LORD'S LOVE!

"THESE MEN HAD BEEN WITH JESUS"

When [the rulers, the elders and the teachers of the law] saw
the courage of Peter and John and realized that they were
unschooled, ordinary men, they were astonished and they took
note that these men had been with Jesus.

ACTS 4:13

One day as he and John were going to the temple, Peter healed a man lame from birth. Not only did the man praise God, but so did all the people who recognized him. Peter gave God full credit for the miracle and then boldly confronted his listeners: "You handed [Jesus] over to be killed. . . . You disowned the Holy and Righteous One and asked that a murderer be released to you. You killed the author of life, but God raised him from the dead" (Acts 3:13–15).

The temple authorities commanded the two disciples to stop teaching about Jesus. Not intimidated, Peter and John chose to obey God, not the religious authorities (Acts 4:19). They added, "We cannot help speaking about what we have seen and heard" (v. 20).

WOULD SOMEONE WATCHING YOU BE ABLE
TO TELL THAT YOU HAVE BEEN WITH JESUS?
PROVIDE EVIDENCE FOR YOUR ANSWER.

MARTYRED FOR HIS FAITH

While they were stoning him, Stephen prayed, "Lord Jesus, receive my spirit." Then he fell on his knees and cried out, "Lord, do not hold this sin against them." When he had said this, he fell asleep.

ACTS 7:59–60

Nodding along with a given truth is very different from living out that truth (Matthew 5:11). Stephen had the opportunity to live out the truth that Jesus' followers will be persecuted, falsely accused, and even killed because of their loyalty to Jesus.

Stephen was framed by enemies of the gospel. When the high priest confronted him about the false charges brought against him, Stephen answered with a recap of God's great story of redemption, its climax beginning with the arrival of his Son to this earth. Then, at one point, Stephen said, "You have betrayed and murdered [the Righteous One]" (Acts 7:52).

These words angered the Sanhedrin, and their anger grew as Stephen continued to speak. They dragged Stephen outside the city to stone him. There, facing the martyr's death, Stephen said the faith-filled words—"Lord Jesus, receive my spirit"—and the grace-filled words—"Lord, do not hold this sin against them"—that his Savior himself had spoken.

MAY YOU, LORD GOD, ENABLE US TO LIVE
WITH SUCH FAITH AND SUCH GRACE.

FROM PERSECUTOR TO PREACHER

As [Saul] neared Damascus on his journey, suddenly a light from
heaven flashed around him. He fell to the ground and heard a
voice say to him, "Saul, Saul, why do you persecute me?"
"Who are you, Lord?" Saul asked.
"I am Jesus, whom you are persecuting," he replied.

ACTS 9:3–5

In today's culture of entitlement, a hard-working, motivated, goal-oriented individual can be a source of inspiration.

Saul was definitely hard-working, but his goal was to rid his world of the followers of the Way. Saul was heading to Damascus to "destroy the church" (Acts 8:3). But God had other plans.

On that road, God initiated a conversation with Saul—and then struck him blind. God sent Ananias to Saul. By God's power working through him, Ananias healed Paul's blindness. Then Paul "got up and was baptized, and after taking some food, he regained his strength" (Acts 9:18–19).

Imagine the people's surprise when Paul began to preach that Jesus is the Son of God. In fact, Luke reported, "Saul grew more and more powerful and baffled the Jews living in Damascus by proving that Jesus is the Messiah" (v. 22).

SHOW ME, LORD, THE TRUTH ABOUT JESUS.

WIDENING THE CIRCLE

[Peter] saw heaven opened and something like a large sheet being let down to earth by its four corners. It contained all kinds of four-footed animals, as well as reptiles and birds. . . . "Get up, Peter. Kill and eat."

"Surely not, Lord!" Peter replied. "I have never eaten anything . . . unclean." . . .

"Do not call anything impure that God has made clean."

ACTS 10:11–15

What is the most radical shift in thinking you've had to undergo in your life? Was it tantamount to learning that what you've always called red was actually blue? That was the case for God's chosen people when he called them to welcome the Gentiles.

The Gentile centurion named Cornelius was told in a vision to send his men after Peter. And Peter himself saw a vision of foods that the Jews had long called unclean. And God was saying, "It's all good!"

When God brought Peter and Cornelius together, a shift in the age-old paradigm began. Peter learned that God invites people from every ethnic group and nation to accept the gospel of Jesus. As this Gentile audience responded with faith and repentance, they were filled with the Holy Spirit just as the Jewish believers had been at Pentecost. This was indeed a new beginning!

SHARE THE GOSPEL WITH THE WORLD.

"BUT THE CHURCH WAS EARNESTLY PRAYING"

Suddenly an angel of the Lord appeared and a light shone in the cell. He struck Peter on the side and woke him up. "Quick, get up!" he said, and the chains fell off Peter's wrists. . . . Peter followed him out of the prison. . . . They passed the . . . guards. [The iron gate] opened for them by itself, and . . . suddenly the angel left.

ACTS 12:7, 9–10

When have you been surprised by an answer to your prayers? When the answer came, you were thrown off a bit. Like Rhoda below.

Rome was persecuting the church, and Peter had been thrown into prison. The night before his trial, "Peter was sleeping between two soldiers, bound with two chains, and sentries stood guard at the entrance" (Acts 12:6). And apparently Peter was sleeping well: the angel who came to rescue him had to strike him to wake him up!

Peter went straight to where people had been praying for him and knocked on the door. When the servant Rhoda went to the door, "she was so overjoyed she ran back without opening it and exclaimed, 'Peter is at the door!'" (v. 14).

Peter knocked until the door was opened. After explaining how the Lord had freed him from prison, Peter fled to safety.

DON'T MISS GOD'S ANSWERS TO YOUR PRAYERS!

SPREADING THE WORD

Standing up, Paul motioned with his hand and said: "Fellow
Israelites and you Gentiles who worship God, listen to me! . . .
We tell you the good news: What God promised our ancestors he
has fulfilled for us, their children, by raising up Jesus."

ACTS 13:16, 32–33

Doing what God wants you to do, where he wants you to do it, is empowering and fulfilling, a blessing to you that honors your God.

An itinerant preacher with a past that might have haunted him, the one-time persecutor of Christians—now called Paul instead of Saul—faithfully proclaimed the good news of God's grace and forgiveness through Christ: "Through Jesus the forgiveness of sins is proclaimed to you. Through him everyone who believes is set free from every sin, a justification you were not able to obtain under the law of Moses" (Acts 13:38–39).

But little did Paul know what his blessed calling would cost him, what he would endure for the good news that he so boldly and effectively proclaimed.

LIKE PAUL, SHARE THE GOSPEL—
PREACH THE RESURRECTED JESUS—TO
ANYONE WHO WILL LISTEN.

THE COST OF PREACHING

On the next Sabbath almost the whole city gathered to hear the word of the Lord. When the Jews saw the crowds, they were filled with jealousy. They began to contradict what Paul was saying and heaped abuse on him.

ACTS 13:44–45

Sometimes it's a backhanded compliment, having people interfere with what you know the Lord has called you to do. After all, the truth can threaten and offend before it frees and transforms.

The abuse the jealous Jews heaped on Paul and Barnabas was part of God's big-picture plan for the expansion of his kingdom: "We had to speak the word of God to you first. Since you reject it . . . we now turn to the Gentiles" (Acts 13:46).

This was a radical departure from God's millennia-long focus on his chosen people Israel, yet this was very much the Lord's plan (Habakkuk 1:5). The Gentiles' reaction—"They were glad and honored the word of the Lord; and all who were appointed for eternal life believed" (Acts 13:48)—was very different from that of the Jewish leaders who incited opposition and persecution. God's kingdom was advancing, and "the disciples were filled with joy and with the Holy Spirit" (v. 52).

LIKE PAUL, AND BY GOD'S GRACE, ENDURE WHATEVER SHARING HIS GOOD NEWS MAY COST YOU.

GODS OR *THE* GOD?

[The crowd shouted,] "The gods have come down to us in human form!" Barnabas they called Zeus, and Paul they called Hermes because he was the chief speaker. The priest of Zeus . . . brought bulls and wreaths to the city gates . . . to offer sacrifices to them.

ACTS 14:11–13

People have said it different ways through the years, but the fact is this: human beings were made to worship, and each of us will worship something.

In Lystra, Paul healed a man lame since birth, and in doing so he unleashed a crowd longing to worship not God, but Paul and Barnabas!

Horrified, the two disciples tore their clothes, a sign of deep grief. Paul and Barnabas were grieved to be mistaken for gods, grieved that the miraculous healing of the lame man didn't point people to the one true God.

So Paul and Barnabas added these words: "We too are only human, like you. We are . . . telling you to turn from these worthless things to the living God, who made the heavens and the earth and the sea and everything in them" (Acts 14:15).

ASK GOD TO HELP YOU RECOGNIZE
AND THEN TURN AWAY FROM
"WORTHLESS THINGS" YOU MAY BE
WORSHIPING INSTEAD OF HIM.

PRAISE IN THE DARKNESS

About midnight Paul and Silas were praying and singing hymns to God, and the other prisoners were listening to them. Suddenly there was such a violent earthquake that the foundations of the prison were shaken. At once all the prison doors flew open, and everyone's chains came loose.

ACTS 16:25–26

Resistance to the gospel came for a variety of reasons—personal, political, economic. Paul was no stranger to resistance to the gospel, and in this instance, economics fueled that resistance.

After days of being followed around and hearing the fortune teller shout, "These men are servants of the Most High God, who are telling you the way to be saved" (Acts 16:17), Paul had had enough. He cast out of her the spirit that enabled her to predict the future— and that earned her owner a lot of money. Realizing their cash cow was ruined, her owners dragged Paul and Silas before the authorities.

Paul and Silas were stripped, beaten, flogged, and imprisoned. At midnight they were "praying and singing hymns to God" and then preaching salvation to the jailer. He heard the message, and after the earthquake, "he and all his household were baptized" (v. 33).

MAY MY JOY IN HARD TIMES ATTRACT PEOPLE TO THE GOD OF GRACE.

TROUBLE: AN OPPORTUNITY TO TRUST GOD

One night the Lord spoke to Paul in a vision: "Do not be afraid; keep on speaking, do not be silent. For I am with you, and no one is going to attack and harm you, because I have many people in this city."

ACTS 18:9–10

You've undoubtedly noticed that the roller coasters of life can be much harder on your nerves than any you'll find in an amusement park. Paul and Silas knew that.

After freeing the demon-possessed slave—and costing her owners their livelihood—Paul and Silas had been imprisoned. Thessalonica was another rough stop. Some Jews and Greeks believed, but "other Jews were jealous; so they rounded up some bad characters from the marketplace, formed a mob and started a riot" (Acts 17:5).

In Berea, Paul found a receptive audience, although Jewish opponents stirred up the crowds against Paul again. In Athens, the philosophical Greeks were not receptive to the gospel. In Corinth, Paul testified to Jews and Greeks alike that Jesus was the Messiah.

The Lord appeared to Paul in a vision and said, "Do not be afraid; keep on speaking, do not be silent. For I am with you, and no one is going to attack and harm you."

MAY I WELCOME TROUBLE AS AN OPPORTUNITY TO TRUST GOD.

THANK GOD FOR YOU

We always thank God for all of you and continually mention you in our prayers. We remember before our God and Father your work produced by faith, your labor prompted by love, and your endurance inspired by hope in our Lord Jesus Christ.

1 THESSALONIANS 1:2–3

Imagine not having the New Testament love letters Paul wrote to early believers. They offer truth and encouragement, correction and hope for today. We'll begin with 1 Thessalonians.

- You . . . welcomed the message in the midst of severe suffering with the joy given by the Holy Spirit. . . . Your faith in God has become known everywhere. . . . They tell how you turned to God from idols to serve the living and true God. (1:6, 8–9)
- We speak as those approved by God to be entrusted with the gospel. We are not trying to please people but God, who tests our hearts. We were not looking for praise from people. . . . Just as a nursing mother cares for her children, so we cared for you. Because we loved you so much, we were delighted to share with you not only the gospel of God but our lives as well. (2:4, 6–8)

FOCUS ON PLEASING GOD.

"MAY GOD HIMSELF SANCTIFY YOU"

May God himself, the God of peace, sanctify you through and through. May your whole spirit, soul and body be kept blameless at the coming of our Lord Jesus Christ. The one who calls you is faithful, and he will do it.

1 THESSALONIANS 5:23–24

The Bible helps us see that human nature hasn't changed much through the ages. Consider, for instance, the circumstances of your life in which the words below from 1 Thessalonians—probably written around AD 51—are relevant and life-giving today.

- May the Lord make your love increase and overflow for each other and for everyone else, just as ours does for you. May he strengthen your hearts so that you will be blameless and holy in the presence of our God and Father when our Lord Jesus comes with all his holy ones. (3:11–13)
- Rejoice always, pray continually, give thanks in all circumstances; for this is God's will for you in Christ Jesus. (5:16–18)
- The grace of our Lord Jesus Christ be with you. (5:28)

CHOOSE ONE OF THE 1 THESSALONIANS PASSAGES TO MEMORIZE AND/ OR SHARE WITH SOMEONE.

TRUTH OR TREASURE?

"Paul has convinced . . . large numbers of people . . . that gods made by human hands are no gods at all. There is danger not only that our trade will lose its good name, but also that the temple of the great goddess Artemis will be discredited; and the goddess herself . . . will be robbed of her divine majesty."

ACTS 19:26–27

The more things change, the more they stay the same." Such was the observation of French writer Alphonse Karr.

The city of Corinth was devoted to paganism and hostile to Christianity. And Paul clearly stated that the best minds in Greece couldn't solve all the problems or answer all of humanity's questions, and that the Jesus who died and rose again is the key to peace—and peace with God.

After leaving Corinth, Paul went to Ephesus, where he stayed for two years. When many sorcerers burned their scrolls, "the word of the Lord spread widely and grew in power" (Acts 19:20). And then came the riot, when a resident spoke up about the potential economic impact of Greeks turning away from their worship of Artemis.

Twenty centuries later, God's truth is still challenged by paganism and greed. The more things change, the more they stay the same.

THE LORD CAN HELP YOU SEE WHAT
THREATENS HIS TRUTH IN YOUR LIFE.

BY THIS GOSPEL YOU ARE SAVED

*By this gospel you are saved . . . that Christ died for our sins
according to the Scriptures, that he was buried, that he was
raised on the third day according to the Scriptures.*

1 CORINTHIANS 15:2–4

A key component of unity is focus: Paul provided the Corinthian
believers with a clear statement of the gospel as their focal
point.

The gospel facts of Jesus' death and resurrection were confirmed by eyewitnesses to the resurrected Jesus:

- He appeared to Cephas, and then to the Twelve. After that,
  he appeared to more than five hundred of the brothers and
  sisters at the same time, most of whom are still living. . . .
  Then he appeared to James, then to all the apostles, and
  last of all he appeared to Paul. (15:5–8)
- If I speak in the tongues of men or of angels, but do not have
  love, I am only a resounding gong or a clanging cymbal. . . .
  If I have a faith that can move mountains, but do not have
  love, I am nothing. If I give all I possess to the poor, but do
  not have love, I gain nothing. (1 Corinthians 13:1–3)

MAY YOUR LOVE FOR OTHERS TESTIFY
TO YOUR FAITH IN THE GOSPEL.

WHO HAS BEWITCHED YOU?

I am astonished that you are so quickly deserting the one who called you to live in the grace of Christ and are turning to a different gospel—which is really no gospel at all. Evidently some people are throwing you into confusion and are trying to pervert the gospel of Christ.

GALATIANS 1:6–7

Jewish Christians believed that certain practices of Judaism remained obligatory for followers of Jesus. Paul said, "Not so!" He proclaimed that people cannot be saved by performing good works in general or by adhering to the Law of Moses in particular.

- In Christ Jesus you are all children of God through faith, for all of you who were baptized into Christ have clothed yourselves with Christ. There is neither Jew nor Gentile, neither slave nor free, nor is there male and female, for you are all one in Christ Jesus. (3:26–28)
- It is for freedom that Christ has set us free. Stand firm, then, and do not let yourselves be burdened again by a yoke of slavery. (5:1)

BE BLESSED BY THE FREEDOM
OF WALKING IN THE SPIRIT.

MINISTERING WITH LOVE AND COURAGE

> When Paul had finished speaking, he knelt down with all of [the
> elders of the church in Ephesus] and prayed. They all wept as
> they embraced him and kissed him. What grieved them most was
> his statement that they would never see his face again.

ACTS 20:36–38

Some good-byes are easier than others. Some actually offer relief; others offer pain. Sometimes the reason is joyous and exciting; at other times the reason is sad or even hopeless. The distance in terms of geography and time can also make a good-bye either harder or easier.

Paul's farewell to the Ephesian elders was sad and painful, darkened by the apostle's statement that "they would never see his face again." The Ephesians loved Paul, indicating that he must have served with the kind of love he described in his letter to the Corinthians. Paul practiced what he preached: "If I . . . do not have love, I am nothing" (1 Corinthians 13:2).

Practicing what we preach—living out with integrity what we say we believe—honors the Lord, and our genuineness attracts people to the gospel.

EVERY BELIEVER IS A MINISTER! WHAT GIVES YOU THE OPPORTUNITY TO SHARE GOD'S LOVE?

Seizing Paul, [the people] dragged him from the temple, and immediately the gates were shut. . . . They were trying to kill him. . . . When the rioters saw the commander and his soldiers, they stopped beating Paul.

ACTS 21:30–32

Ben Franklin's wisdom often brings a smile. Consider this observation: "Guests, like fish, begin to smell after three days."

Paul's visit to Jerusalem started off well. His companion Luke reported, "The brothers and sisters received us warmly" (Acts 21:17). He made it past day three, but on day seven, things got ugly. Jews from Asia stirred up the Jerusalem Jews by shouting that Paul was against their people. That's all it took for the crowd to seize Paul and try to kill him.

When the rioters calmed down at the sight of the Roman soldiers, Paul asked to speak to the crowd. Permission was granted, and Paul began to speak. "I am a Jew, born in Tarsus of Cilicia, but brought up in this city. I studied under Gamaliel and was thoroughly trained in the law of our ancestors. I was just as zealous for God as any of you are today. I persecuted the followers of this Way to their death" (22:2–4). And Paul was just getting warmed up!

TAKE ADVANTAGE OF EVERY OPPORTUNITY
TO SHARE THE TRUTH ABOUT JESUS.

THE PIVOTAL MOMENT

"About noon as I came near Damascus, suddenly a bright light from heaven flashed around me. I fell to the ground and heard a voice say to me, 'Saul! Saul! Why do you persecute me?'

"'Who are you, Lord?' I asked."

ACTS 22:6–8

When you think of moments that changed your life, what comes to mind? The day you got married? The day a child was born? Or, like Paul, the day you recognized that Jesus is the Messiah?

That was the life-changing event that Paul talked about when he had the crowd's attention. According to his conversion experience, Paul went to Damascus where Ananias had been told to go specifically to meet Paul. Ananias said simply, "Brother Saul, receive your sight!" (v. 13). And Paul was able to see again.

Then Ananias shared this message from the Lord: "The God of our ancestors has chosen you to know his will and to see the Righteous One and to hear words from his mouth. You will be his witness. . . . Get up, be baptized and wash your sins away, calling on his name" (vv. 14–16).

Saul the persecutor was now Paul the believer and the preacher God would send to the Gentiles.

YOUR CONVERSION EXPERIENCE IS AN
EXAMPLE OF GOD'S AMAZING GRACE.

THE PECKING ORDER

The commander ordered that Paul be . . . flogged and
interrogated. . . . As [the soldiers] stretched him out to flog him,
Paul said to the centurion standing there, "Is it legal for you to
flog a Roman citizen who hasn't even been found guilty?"

ACTS 22:24–25

The pecking order is usually clear in high school. Students know where they fall on the scale ranging from "nerd" to "cool." And the "cool" kids are treated in a very different way from those at the other end of the social spectrum.

The rankings in Roman society were even more rigid. Roman citizens were at the top of the pile. And this arrest and the flogging without a trial was hardly standard procedure for a citizen by birth of Rome: "Those who were about to interrogate him withdrew immediately. The commander himself was alarmed when he realized that he had put Paul, a Roman citizen, in chains" (v. 29).

Roman citizens deserved much better treatment than what Paul had received. Similarly, we should treat people whose "citizenship is in heaven" (Philippians 3:20) with the respect and honor due the Almighty's followers.

EVERY PERSON WAS CREATED BY GOD
AND IS LOVED BY GOD—MAY THAT TRUTH
GUIDE OUR INTERACTIONS WITH THEM.

DIVINE ENCOURAGEMENT

Some Jews formed a conspiracy and bound themselves with an oath not to eat or drink until they had killed Paul. . . . They went to the chief priests and the elders and said, "We have taken a solemn oath not to eat anything until we have killed Paul. . . . Petition the commander to bring him before you."

ACTS 23:12–15

Sometimes encouragement is clearly spoken in words, and sometimes it comes in the form of actions. Maybe you've been blessed to be an encourager—as well as to be encouraged by those who care about you.

After the people of Jerusalem treated him so badly, Paul was a great candidate for encouragement, and the Lord spoke up with this promise: "Take courage! As you have testified about me in Jerusalem, so you must also testify in Rome" (Acts 23:11).

Those words of encouragement came to Paul none too soon. The next morning Paul learned from his nephew that some Jews were conspiring to kill him. When the Roman commander heard of the plot, he didn't hesitate to act. He called two centurions and commanded them to take Paul to Governor Felix. Paul would now be someone else's concern.

ASK GOD TO GUIDE YOUR ACTIONS.

NOT AN EASY VOYAGE

*"Last night an angel of the God to whom I belong and whom
I serve stood beside me and said, 'Do not be afraid, Paul. You
must stand trial before Caesar; and God has graciously given
you the lives of all who sail with you.' . . . Nevertheless, we must
run aground on some island."*

ACTS 27:23–26

We who have named Jesus our Savior and Lord know the end
of the story: we will live in heaven for eternity where "there
will be no more death or mourning or crying or pain" (Revelation
21:4). And that is good news to know, especially when, like Paul on
his voyage to Rome, "we must run aground on some island." Or, as
Jesus put it, "In this world you will have trouble" (John 16:33).

Paul knew trouble. He had been attacked, arrested, and wrongly
held against his will. He had appeared before Felix, Festus, and King
Agrippa. Now he was on his way to a trial before Caesar. As Paul
had warned, though, the timing of this voyage to Rome was wrong.
For a total of fourteen days the boat continued to be driven across
the Adriatic Sea. All the ship's crew could cling to was the word
from Paul's God, the promise that no life would be lost. Paul made it
to Rome; you'll arrive in heaven.

WHEN YOUR WORLD IS STORMY,
GOD WILL PROTECT YOU.

BE STRONG IN THE GRACE
THAT IS IN CHRIST JESUS

Do not be ashamed of the testimony about our Lord or of me his prisoner. Rather, join with me in suffering for the gospel, by the power of God.

2 TIMOTHY 1:8

Paul was martyred during the reign of Nero in AD 67 or 68. During his final days, he wrote one last letter, a personal letter to Timothy. Paul poured out his heart in words that reflect loneliness, tenacious faith, and concern for believers during Nero's persecution.

Be strong in the grace that is in Christ Jesus. Remember Jesus Christ, raised from the dead, descended from David. This is my gospel, for which I am suffering even to the point of being chained like a criminal. But God's word is not chained. (2:1, 8–9)

STANDING STRONG IN GOD'S GRACE, WE CAN SUFFER FOR THE GOSPEL, LIVE A GODLY LIFE DESPITE PERSECUTION, CONTINUE TO DO GOOD WORKS, AND FIGHT THE GOOD FIGHT.

JESUS WINS

The revelation from Jesus Christ, which God gave him to show his servants what must soon take place. He made it known by sending his angel to his servant John. . . . Blessed is the one who reads aloud the words of this prophecy, and blessed are those who hear it and take to heart what is written in it.

REVELATION 1:1, 3–4

Be honest! When someone mentions the book of Revelation, what is your immediate reaction? Now try to figure out why that's your response.

Every book in God's Word offers words that encourage, teach, guide, provide hope, increase understanding, and bless us. Yet Revelation is the only book that, in its opening passage, promises to bless the readers of what comes as well as "those who hear it and take to heart what is written in it." Maybe we students of Scripture need to see in black and white the promise of blessing, because this book can be a little intimidating! But we needn't be intimidated.

The custodian opened the gym for some seminary students. As they played basketball, he read his Bible. One of the students asked him what he was reading—"Revelation"—and then asked, "Do you understand it?" And the custodian confidently said, "Yes. Jesus wins."

WE CAN HAVE AS OUR TAKEAWAY ABSOLUTE CONFIDENCE IN THE FACT THAT JESUS WINS!

"Very truly I tell you, whoever hears my word and believes him who sent me has eternal life and will not be judged but has crossed over from death to life."

JOHN 5:24

APPENDIX: THE STORY CONTINUES

To go deeper in *The Story*, use this chart to reference the complete text that is excerpted in this book. Each devotion is listed by the chapter in which it appears in *The Story*, and the page numbers listed in **bold italic** refer to the page numbers used in *The Story*.

Creation: The Beginning of Life As We Know It

God Builds a Nation

Joseph: From Slave to Deputy Pharaoh

Deliverance

The Battle Begins

A Few Good Men . . . And Women

The Faith of a Foreign Woman

Standing Tall, Falling Hard

From Shepherd to King

The Trials of a King

The King Who Had It All

The Beginning of the End (of the Kingdom of Israel)

The Kingdoms' Fall

The Queen of Beauty and Courage

Rebuilding the Walls

The Birth of the King

Jesus' Ministry Begins

No Ordinary Man

Jesus, the Son of God

The Hour of Darkness

The Resurrection

Paul's Final Days

The End of Time

NOTES

1. "An Overview of the Solar System," Nineplanets.org, http://nineplanets .org/overview.html.
2. Seth Miller, "If the earth were the size of a golf ball," Seth Miller's Site, June 30, 2013, http://sethdavidmiller.com/2013/06/30/if-the-earth-were -the-size-of-a-golf-ball.
3. Jacob Gebhard, "How many came out of the exodus of Egypt?" Hebrew Research Center, http://www.ancient-hebrew.org/39_exodus.html.
4. Ibid.
5. "Discoveries of archaeology verified the reliability of the Bible," Manavai.com, http://www.manavai.com/articles/art1.htm.
6. Hank Hannegraaff, "The Canaanites: How Could a Just God Command His People to Destroy an Entire Nation," Christian Research Institute, Equip.org, March 17, 2009, http://www.equip.org /perspectives/the-canaanites-how-could-a-just-god-command-his-people -to-destroy-an-entire-nation.
7. "The Beatles," The Ed Sullivan Show, http://www.edsullivan.com/artists /the-beatles.
8. These dictionary topics are from the *Holman Bible Dictionary*, published by Broadman & Holman, 1991. All rights reserved. Used by permission of Broadman & Holman. Bibliography Information: Butler, Trent C. Editor. Entry for 'Hope'. *Holman Bible Dictionary*. http://www.studylight .org/dic/hbd/view.cgi?n=2841. 1991.
9. "Step 1," 12Step.org, http://12step.org/the-12-steps/step-1.html.
10. "Matthew Henry's Concise Commentary," Christ Notes, http://www .christnotes.org/commentary.php?com=mhc.
11. Helen Haidle, *Journey to the Cross: The Complete Easter Story for Young Readers* (Grand Rapids, MI: Zondervan, 2001), 22.
12. James Allan Francis, "One Solitary Life," egodbless.com, http://reading .takecaregodbless.com/2011/09/18/one-solitary-life.aspx.

THE STORY

POWERED BY **ZONDERVAN**

READE THE STORY. EXPERIENCE THE BIBLE.

> Here I am, 50 years old. I have been to college, seminary, engaged in ministry my whole life, my dad is in ministry, my grandfather was in ministry, and **The Story has been one of the most unique experiences of my life**. The Bible has been made fresh for me. It has made God's redemptive plan come alive for me once again.
>
> —Seth Buckley, Youth Pastor,
> Spartanburg Baptist Church, Spartanburg, SC

> As my family and I went through *The Story* together, the more I began to believe and the more real [the Bible] became to me, and **it rubbed off on my children and helped them with their walk with the Lord**. *The Story* inspired conversations we might not normally have had.
>
> —Kelly Leonard, Parent, Shepherd of the Hills Christian Church, Porter Ranch, CA

> **We have people reading *The Story*—some devour it and can't wait for the next week**. Some have never really read the Bible much, so it's exciting to see a lot of adults reading the Word of God for the first time. I've heard wonderful things from people who are long-time readers of Scripture. They're excited about how it's all being tied together for them. It just seems to make more sense.
>
> —Lynnette Schulz,
> Director of Worship
> Peace Lutheran Church,
> Eau Claire, WI

FOR ADULTS

9780310950974

FOR TEENS

9780310722809

FOR KIDS

9780310719250